back on the market

A Realtor's Guide to Love and Life

HOLLY PARKER

with Laura Morton

Forefront
BOOKS

Back on the Market
A Realtor's Guide to Love and Life

Published by Forefront Books.

Cover Design by Bruce Gore, Gore Studio Inc.
Interior Design by Bill Kersey, KerseyGraphics

ISBN: 978-1-948677-46-2
ISBN: 978-1-948677-47-9 (eBook)

Dedication

To my wonderful husband, Marc, who still loves me, even after reading this book. And to our sons Parker and Mason: we waited a long time for you. You turned our house into a home.

Contents

Introduction

Dating is like real estate; the longer you're on the market, the more people are going to wonder what's wrong with you.

WHEN I WAS A LITTLE GIRL, MY FATHER, ARTIE, SAT ME DOWN one day and said it was time to have a talk.

No, not that talk. Artie wanted to share his feelings about men.

"Holly, men are basically shit. Women need to stand on their own two feet. If you want something in life, you have to build it—that way a man can't take it all away. Men hide, cheat, and steal. While not all men are bad, it sure is a lot harder to find a good man than it is to find a good woman. So never think a man is going to give you a life. You need to create your own life. And if, by chance, a man *has* given you a life, don't rely on it. He can destroy it in the blink of an eye. Men are dogs. I'm ashamed to be one."

I was five years old when my father shared this ... advice ... insight ... scary thought. But I've never forgotten it. It's as if he said it to me yesterday. And he would remind me of this viewpoint several times a year so I wouldn't forget to always stand my ground emotionally and financially.

I've never been someone who believed that marriage could save me. I always thought I'd be the last of my friends to bite the bullet. I wasn't a damsel in distress who needed to be rescued by a man on a white horse. I was a free spirit. I wanted to travel the world, get my master's degree, and say "I do" to Asia, South America, and India before saying it to a partner.

I was okay on my own—at least, that's what I told myself and God.

As the saying goes, "We make plans, and God laughs."

Well, He must have been laughing His ass off when He heard my plan.

Clearly, there was another design in motion—one I didn't see coming.

Although it wasn't my intention to be saved—nor did I make an effort of any kind—I fell head over heels in love.

For a while.

In New York, a city full of princesses, I'm one of the lucky few who can say I really lived the fairy-tale dream. But then, at age thirty-two, I suddenly found myself divorced after seven years of marriage. It felt as though my enchanted life had come crashing down on me.

Looking back, I can't say the split was totally unexpected. Even though I was the one to file, the harsh reality of becoming a divorcée hit me hard. Somehow that was more unexpected than the breakup of my marriage. Whenever I've read stories about people jumping in front of moving trains, I've wondered what it takes to throw yourself onto the tracks. How much pain do you have to be in to make yourself do something like that? And now, after everything I've been through, I think I understand how they must have felt.

Divorce is the kind of blow that takes you down with singular force. Nothing hits as hard as life. It isn't about how badly you get thwacked, it's about how much you can take and keep moving forward. You must be willing to endure the pain without placing blame on anyone else. Only cowards do that, and though I was deeply hurt, I'm not a coward.

Even so, the sting can remain long after the impact—and mine would linger for some time.

My prince and I grew up together in a small Rhode Island town. Our families were friends, so he and I were too. It was a congenial town where everyone knew one another, a quintessential white-picket-fence community right on the water. We learned to sail in the local harbor, played soccer in the fall, and went sledding on the nearby golf course in the winter, sipping our hot cocoa from thermoses while watching other kids attempt the suicide run, where there was about a 90 percent chance of a wipeout because of the pitch. Though we don't always know it at the time, it's amazing how much our families, community, and neighbors shape and program us for our futures.

My prince was witty, funny, and—I'll be frank—hot. Like, *super hot.* He was the kind of guy Connie, my mother, thought would never go for a girl like me. Not that there's anything wrong with me; my mother just thought he'd pick a different kind of girl.

Did she really say that?

She did. Yet I learned to laugh when she said things like this. My mother didn't offer commentary all the time, but when she did, her "Connie zingers" were beyond blunt observations; they were so brutal that they were actually funny. Hilarious, even. Or at least I learned to think they were, because if I didn't laugh, I would certainly cry. Her remarks only made me stronger and helped prepare me for a world where rejection was part of the game and nobody gave a shit about your feelings—or so I told my therapist. So when you meet somebody who actually *does* care about your feelings, it can throw you—especially when you come from a family like mine, where zingers were tossed around as casually as Frisbees. And not those soft Nerf Frisbees they have nowadays; no, I'm talking about one of those hard, 1970s Wham-O Frisbees that could level you with one hit.

My prince was everything any girl could ever want. Handsome, from a good home, super smart, an amazing athlete . . . did I mention handsome? I hate admitting I'm shallow that way, but looks have always mattered to me. Good hygiene matters too—but it's still second to looks. Without chemistry and attraction, there's zero chance we'd hit it off on a date. Either he needed to be smokin' hot or ridiculously funny, and preferably an equal blend of the two. Look, I'm all for women's rights and equality, but everyone, and I mean *everyone*, wants to be wooed from time to time.

When you're young, you buy into that fairy tale. As they grow up, girls are sold on the fantasy that someday their prince will come. I was no exception. And even though my family would agree that I'm unconventional in many ways, always going against the grain or away from the pack, I also wanted that kind of fabled love. I don't think my mind could even grasp any idea other than the full mythical package. All I ever expected (and deeply wanted) was to meet my Prince Charming, have children, and live happily ever after, like Snow White, Sleeping Beauty, or Cinderella. It never dawned on me that the first of these women lived with seven little men she didn't know, basically as their maid, the second was in a coma in the woods when her prince found her, and the last had vermin for friends and got so wasted on her first big night out that she lost an irreplaceable shoe. Point is, these princesses weren't really pictures of stability. *They* actually did need rescuing.

As a little girl, I daydreamed about where I would be when I met *him*. I spent hours imagining all the places we would travel together and fantasized about our wedding and what a fabulous party it would be. I don't think I was alone in this. That's what little girls did in the '70s. That's what all the stories I read back then were about—an amazing, handsome, exquisitely dressed, accomplished, dashing young man who rescues a damsel in distress. Oh, and don't forget about his royal lineage.

Okay, so my life wasn't distressed, and I never really thought of myself as a damsel—ever—but I loved everything about those stories, and knew that even if I were alone in an attic dressed in rags with three little mice as my only friends, the ending would be the same: I would be scooped up and liberated from that dark reality and would live happily forevermore with my prince.

Even Snow White was magically brought back from the dead by a kiss from a well-dressed man who wore his hair slicked back. Not only were his locks perfect but this guy was perpetually ready for his close-up even after galloping through the dark forest on horseback. I never doubted that this man existed. Not then, anyway.

Why?

My whole childhood supported the theory that it was truly a girl's destiny to find her greatest love and then live in a gorgeous castle nearby. Love and real estate—they have always been undeniably connected for me.

In this story, I reunited with my gorgeous prince and his cute cousin when they showed up at my family home in Rhode Island the day after Christmas one year to take my sister and me to a fabulous holiday party. I'd always had a thing for my prince's cousin. You see, my prince was much shorter than I was when we were growing up. He was also a bit of a bookworm and skipped all the way to second grade because he was smart. He did what he was told and was a big rule follower, a short toad of a boy—while I was the type to raise my hand to go to the lavatory at exactly half past the hour in order to meet my friends and play tag in the hallway. (Yeah, that was a thing.) My prince had his head in a book in the classroom, not even knowing the fun he was missing, so our paths didn't cross too much.

And now, twelve years since I last saw him, here he was in my kitchen, standing six foot two and absolutely gorgeous. He also didn't look like he followed the rules anymore. He definitely had my attention.

The party was held at an opulent restaurant that had once been a bank in downtown Providence. It was spectacularly festive, with so many friends from the past and present. My prince made me laugh the entire night; I adore a man with a good sense of humor. It's one thing to be attractive, but to be attractive *and* funny? Well, in my eyes, that's a perfect combination.

We made plans to get together again on New Year's Eve, and that's when we shared our first kiss. It was magical—the kind of magic that turns a toad into a prince. Dark magic. (Just kidding.) I went from smitten to falling head over heels in love, all before the stroke of midnight. I couldn't eat or sleep. I had it bad. And he must've felt the same way, because sixty-two days later we were engaged. It felt right. That's how it's done in fairy tales: the prince shows up, gives you a true-love kiss, and then wedding announcements are sent throughout the kingdom. Ours was a New England fairy tale.

Eight months after that, we had our dream wedding, with all our friends and family in attendance to help us celebrate. It was exactly as I'd imagined it when I was a little girl. Tiny bluebirds made my wedding dress. Well, they *could* have; I don't know what happens after you leave Bergdorf's bridal salon. There was revelry for days leading up to the big event—lobster bakes, boat rides, brunches, and beach parties all preceded my dream wedding to my dream man.

There we stood in front of the crowd in a church built in the 1800s. The 1800s—how romantic. How many brides had stood there before me? Only now it was even better because we didn't have to worry no one was suffering from yellow fever. I held my breath as the priest asked, "If anyone knows any reason why these two should not be united in holy matrimony, speak now or forever hold your peace." I thought, *Please, Connie, not now.*

There was an awkward silence.

Luckily, no one spoke up.

When you think about it, does anyone ever stand and say, "Father, forgive me, but these two idiots are doomed"?

Looking back, I imagine most of the attendees must have been thinking that, but everyone still smiled and congratulated us as if falling in love and getting engaged after sixty-two days is completely normal. Please. It's an act of insanity. Kind of like eating a poisonous apple you got from some strange old lady in the woods…hmm. Seems clear now that damsels don't always make the best choices, but no one ever focuses on that.

I should have known there would be problems ahead when we chose "Can't Help Falling in Love" as our wedding song. You know the one; *"Wise men say / only fools rush in / but I can't help / falling in love with you . . ."* We should have chosen "Young Dumb & Broke."

Were we crazy?

Maybe, but his parents got engaged after only three weeks, and his grandparents after only seven days. They made it work, so why couldn't we? This speed of love was more than a tradition in his family—it was a rite of passage. It seemed like a natural evolution. Surely we wouldn't be the couple that didn't make it. His family's toast to us on our wedding night was "What took you so long?"

The nuptials were perfect, and even better than what I'd dreamed of. I was floating on air most of the time. Okay, only some of the time—until seven years later when I fell out of the sky, dropping what felt like thousands of feet and landing on my head. That was the moment I found myself checking that dreadful box we all fear so much (what the hell is it about that box? Why must every formal document have one? Don't the powers that be know that they're terrifying millions of people all over the world with that box?): the one marked DIVORCED. Well, there I was, at age thirty-two, an official box-checker. *DIVORCED.* Don't believe me? Look at the box.

Hardest check I ever wrote.

The fateful day came in 2003. My hands started shaking when I saw the number on my phone. There was nothing I could say or do that would change the news I was about to receive.

Trembling, I answered, "Hello ...?"

I heard his voice first. My husband. My friend. My lover. My ex.

Tears began to well, and the lump in my throat made it difficult to speak.

The court-appointed mediator had called to give us what she thought would be good news—as if, somehow, I'd be happy to hear those four words: "Your divorce is final."

She was clearly mistaken. I wasn't happy. Not at all. If anything, I felt incredibly sad. And sick. My entire body felt heavy from the thought of no longer being married. My parents had been married for forty years. All their friends were still married. My siblings had amazing marriages. Their friends and my friends were happily married. There was no predecessor to make me feel okay about this. How could I have failed at something I wanted so much?

As a luxury real estate broker in Manhattan, I think of just about everything in real estate terms. Maybe it's because I eat, sleep, and dream about real estate. I've had to deliver powerful and sometimes "not the ending we'd hoped for" news many times throughout my career, so I knew how hard it was to make that call, no matter how cheery a spin the mediator put on it. Hearing the declaration of divorce felt as if I'd suddenly fallen out of contract, as if both the buyer and the seller of the ultimate dream home had decided to back out. In many ways, it was exactly like that.

Nothing about my divorce felt ... *good*. It sucked. I didn't realize how hard it would be. It was like I'd been leasing a place with plans to buy and renovate, and now the pending sale had gone bad.

I had no secret wish to be back on the market. To be certain, I was nowhere close to being ready to relist either. I felt like a ramshackle fixer-upper—a home with good bones but in need of a gut renovation.

I stood quietly in my apartment—the one I'd shared with *him*— alone, with only my thoughts to keep me company, tears streaming down my already raw cheeks. I was on the other side of the fairy tale. What was meant to be a castle now felt like a dungeon.

There's a saying that redheads are a little crazy—and while that may be true, there's another side to that: redheads feel more pain—or at least a different kind of pain. For instance, one study found that people with red hair are more sensitive to thermal pain, while another showed that they're less sensitive to electrically induced pain. They bleed and swell more than others too, so it's not as simple as saying that redheads are more or less tolerant of pain—we just tend to feel pain differently. Overall, I'd say we're tougher than pretty much all the other hair colors. Most of the time, anyway.

In that moment, I wasn't feeling so tough. In fact, I'm not sure I'd ever felt lower.

For the first time in years, I wasn't certain of what to do. Maybe dye my hair blonde I'd heard that they have fun, and I could have used a bit of that right then. I was usually so confident and secure, but I knew only one thing could make me feel better: I needed to talk to my best friend. So I did what came naturally.

I called my newly ex-husband. (Yes, that was strange to think, let alone say.) My voice was noticeably shaky, my tone just above a whisper.

We both cried. We could barely utter any cohesive words in between our sniffling and sobs.

"Want to meet at the Odeon for dinner?" I asked.

"Sure," he said.

It was so ... *normal.*

Not my *old* normal, of course, because everything was different.

I had no more say. I wasn't his best friend, partner, or wife anymore. Not only were my opinions not needed, they had to be stifled for this departure of hearts to take place. It was an agonizing and seemingly unnatural occurrence. Every step away from each other felt like a jagged rip in my fragile heart. It was like driving by the house you used to live in and seeing the lights on. I knew that, soon enough, someone else would be living there.

In a way, divorce felt as though I'd made a deal with the devil. Walls were built, armor was worn, and hurt was pushed aside, at least for the moment.

This was my new normal.

"Was it wrong to call?" I asked myself afterward.

Maybe. But it was just . . . a reflex. A habit. One I'd have to learn how to break. But I wasn't ready. Not that day.

It felt as if everything would be okay if we could just meet at a restaurant that we'd been to so many times before. A place full of happy memories. I kept telling myself to focus on the positives, to remember all the good times—and there were many we shared.

Perhaps that was my way of putting one final, perfectly mono- grammed wax seal on the proverbial envelope so we could have closure. I wasn't sure, but it didn't really matter. I wanted to see him.

My ex and I were just two people who fell in love and tried to make it work. Like, *really* tried. But we failed. And I wasn't used to failing— not in real estate, and certainly not in my relationships. I went into my marriage like a first-time buyer goes into their starter home: not totally understanding what's missing or what I really expected before committing with my whole mind, body, and soul. I fell in love with the exterior without giving much thought to the potential fractures inside the home. Over time, lots of layers ended up getting peeled away, revealing those cracks and slowly leading to this unexpected place. No one can live with leaky pipes forever. You'll end up with black mold, which makes it hard to breathe.

I didn't know about these fractures; certainly not then.

I'd always thought of myself as so unconventional, but as it turned out—and much to my surprise—I really wished for a more traditional life. I wanted kids, and I wasn't necessarily looking for a big career. When I met my ex, I was making $14,000 a year. I had just started my first year selling real estate during the day and waitressing at a high-end bar and restaurant near Lewis Wharf in Boston at night. By the time we got married, I was working seven days a week. Slowly, I transitioned to real estate full-time, increasing my income with every passing year until it became clear I could make a living at it. Relationships survive on the strength of their foundation, and our foundation was constantly shifting.

When it came to my marriage, there were things I could ultimately tolerate and things I couldn't. Marriage doesn't have to be one thing or another to work, but it does need to have a set of clear rules, a complete understanding of expectations, and mutual respect. If those things are missing, the relationship is destined to fail. They're like running water and electricity; without those in a home, living there is very difficult.

I arrived at the restaurant first. I wanted to sit facing the door like a Mafia don so I could see him when he arrived. I ordered a vodka soda with a splash of cranberry. It's amazing how fast a cocktail can go down, especially when you're nervous. At that moment the vodka was like a best friend gently squeezing my hand.

I definitely needed my server to be on her A game that night, and she was. I was obviously tense, and the alternative to getting me good and drunk was to watch me fall to pieces. She chose correctly.

"Can I get you another drink?"

"Sure. Keep 'em coming, especially after my friend arrives." I said.

Friend.

Were we destined to just be friends?

"Holly," I heard him say. And then, as though we were strangers, "Mind if I sit down?"

There he was. Once my Prince Charming, my best friend; now someone who needed permission to sit.

I didn't say yes—at least I don't think I did. I just smiled while vowing to hold back my tears. I didn't want that night to be sad. I wasn't sure what I wanted it to be, but I was glad we were there.

As we ate, or, in my case, pretended to eat because my stomach was in knots and my heart so very heavy, I kept staring at him, thinking, *We were so in love.*

And we were. So how did we end up here?

We were in love, yes, but it was a surface love. We were smitten at first with who we thought we were. I was raised to look for a castle, and would certainly have been happy with a classic colonial (which I thought I'd found), but I married a fifth-floor walk-up. Which, when you think about it, is what most castles are, because anything built in medieval times didn't have an elevator. If that sounds unkind, it's not meant to be; it's just that we struggled throughout those years more than we lived large. It wasn't all his fault. What happened was a clash between what I wanted and expected from a marriage and what was missing from ours. Does marriage bring you instant happiness and security? For some it does, and for others it's more about the wedding—the ring, the dress, and the party. There are those who believe marriage will provide financial security, or at least someone with whom to evolve into that state. I was in love with someone I believed wanted a big life, someone who had goals and aspirations. And he did have those things, but after enduring one too many disappointments in business, his desire to achieve them waned. His foundation was fine, until a few big storms hit. It wasn't anyone's fault; it was force majeure. As hard as I tried, I just couldn't help him find the motivation to chase those goals again. In retrospect, it wasn't really my responsibility, though at the time I thought it was. Only he could get himself there.

The only reason I could bring myself to say goodbye to this beautiful and amazing creature I loved so dearly was because, somehow, in the midst of this magnificent love, he seemed to have lost himself— and no matter how much I tried to guide him home, this gorgeous, funny, crazy-smart man could not find his compass with me in his life. If I loved him, I had to set him free. It was no one's fault. There was just sadness, sadness, and more sadness. I never stopped loving my ex. Even now, I can't say there isn't love there. And I never stopped wanting to help him, never stopped wishing him well. I became the great seasoned Realtor I am now partly because of the inexperienced life partner I was then. I never went to the basement or checked the attic. All I knew of him was what I saw from the front porch—what I could glimpse through the windows. Years later, when I was invited inside, I was blown away by the décor, the charm, and the morning light. It was beautiful and cozy, elegant but likeable. Handsome and funny too. It was my dream house, and it had always been right next door. So eager was I to take it off the market that I bought it without venturing beyond the first two floors. I never went into the attic to see the warped boards, the buckets placed to catch the rainwater, or all the boxes marked Private. I had never seen the cold basement or the aged boiler. The bones weren't what I had assumed they were.

CHAPTER ONE

———

Falling Out of Contract

*There are three rings in marriage: the engage-
ment ring, the wedding ring, and the suffering.*
—Anonymous

*F*ALLING OUT OF CONTRACT IS JUST NOT SEXY.
Any way you slice it, the reason is that something didn't work
or it turned out to be a mistake. Maybe it was the financing, the
inspection, flaws in the foundation, or a board turndown. It doesn't
really matter if it was the buyer or the seller who caused the deal to
fall apart. For most brokers, it's seen as the unknown variable that
wasn't planned for—a wrong turn, a mishap, a mysterious problem.
And when it does happen, brokers will always give you a polished
and well-rehearsed response. But regardless, you can't help thinking,
What's the real story here?

So—why do things fall out of contract?

Apartments and homes mostly fall out because something wasn't what it appeared to be. Maybe the home was on the bank's "Do Not Lend" list because the building hadn't properly managed its budget. Maybe the buyer had an unsavory secret that came out during the co-op board interview. (A co-op is a cooperative of residents who jointly own the building. When you buy into one, you don't own your apartment outright; rather, you become a member of a corporation and own shares based on myriad factors. If one person leaves, the overall mortgage is still due. If one person falls behind, their deficit is picked up by their neighbors. For this reason, prospective buyers are intensely scrutinized.)

One of my first board turndowns was of an elderly couple whom I absolutely adored. The wife must have gotten up at three o'clock in the morning each day to complete her hair and makeup by eight a.m. Blending in her foundation was a concept as foreign to her as skinny-dipping in Central Park. Nevertheless, she was lovely. We got the dreaded phone call from the managing agent letting us know that the board had conducted my clients' personal interviews but had turned them down, denying them ownership of their new apartment. They had been jumping through hoops for ten weeks, not to mention the thousands of dollars they'd spent on attorneys, applications, and appraisals, and the six months of pavement pounding to find the right home.

Sometimes you never know the reason a board rejects a buyer. There could have been jealousy issues over the favorable deal the buyer was getting, or maybe someone had a friend or relative who wanted to buy the unit instead. Maybe it's an elevator vendetta between board members sparked by the seller's poodle snubbing another owner's schnauzer, and it's payback time. Or maybe it was the nosy neighbor in 3A; she hates everyone. Whatever the cause, putting a property back on the market after it's been under contract makes it a lot harder to sell because everyone knows *something* went down, and any future client is likely to get only a sliver of the real story.

To better understand what went wrong with that elderly couple, I scheduled an emergency meeting with them. When I asked them to recall the events of their interview, they couldn't remember exactly what they'd said, so I decided to role-play to see if I could figure it out. I sent the couple out the door and had them knock just as they had the night they met with the board. I invited them in and went through several routine questions. I didn't hear anything out of the ordinary. When I asked what they liked to do in their spare time, the wife bubbled over with energy and enthusiasm, declaring, "My husband and I love to gamble. We go to Atlantic City and have a wonderful time."

And there it was.

"Is that what you said at the meeting?" I asked, knowing, of course, that it was.

"Yes, it's our favorite pastime," she said.

"Well, I think we found the answer to why you were turned down. And it's going to have to be our little secret going forward, because co-op boards on the Upper East Side of Manhattan definitely do not like to hear that you routinely take part of your financial security and throw it on the blackjack table."

They were dumbfounded. What was a joyous activity for my clients was a deterrent to their prospective neighbors.

In life, just as in real estate, people also fall out of contract. They move on, break up, leave, die, or, in my case, outgrow each other. And sometimes people just change their minds. Real estate isn't about speed, it's about stamina. And I have a boatload of that.

Big decisions such as marriage, divorce, and real estate are often based on emotion, yet science tells us that the soundest decisions are typically those made without emotion. Doesn't that fact negate some of the biggest decisions we make in life? Is that why we keep getting so much wrong?

Maybe an arranged marriage is the one that lasts. It's entered into with practicality and purpose. Our wise ancestors led the way on this one. I once heard a story about an arranged marriage that lasted seventy-three years. The wife died, and one year later, to the day, the husband did too. He simply couldn't live without her. And still, throughout the marriage, he often said, "Divorce? Never! Murder? Maybe . . ."

So many people hope for love at first sight. They say things such as, "I'll know it when I meet him." And when it comes to homes, they say, "I'll know it when I see it." The fantasy of attachment is really no different in these two scenarios. Yet when we fall in love and our endorphins start working overtime, we are anything but ourselves—so how can we really know when the real deal comes along? At the very moment we fall in love, we begin to see the world through a different lens. Some even say colors are brighter, food tastes better, and the world is just a happier place. I call this "heroin love," because you're high on those endorphins, and at the peak of that high, life is never better. It's usually in this altered state that we make some of the biggest decisions of our life. The problem is, like heroin, once that initial high wears off, you're constantly chasing that feeling, usually to no avail. Not that I would know about the heroin part—I'm just equating love at first sight to a dangerous substance I'd never want to try. My larger point is that love is a drug, one we all stand in line hoping to get a prescription for. Heck, who am I kidding? It's a drug we would steal and lie for, and one we desperately crave as soon as we've tried it.

When my prince and I reconnected, he was living and working in a suburb just north of New York City, and I was living in Boston. When we married, I gave up my job at Coldwell Banker on the Boston waterfront and moved in with him. We lived in a house owned by a Portuguese couple. It was a three-family home in a neighborhood where every holiday was celebrated with gusto. Halloween, Thanksgiving, Christmas, and Easter gave each of the neighbors a chance to show off their decorating skills. I loved it.

The walls in the home were paper-thin, though. We could hear our landlords arguing all the time, screaming things like, "You know that I know you're an idiot!" For whatever reason, that always made my prince and I laugh.

I spent my first few months of married life furnishing the house and sporadically working odd jobs. Downtime has never been my forte, so once the house was decorated, the rooms were spotless, and there was nothing left to bake, I signed up with a temp agency to explore different businesses in the area. During that time my husband and I were like two ships passing in the night. He would work all day and then head out to play baseball with his friends in the evening. Several days a week he'd be gone from 8:00 a.m. to midnight. I didn't know a soul in town, as it was his territory first. I was dying a slow death, starving for stimulation and interaction with other people. Three months after we got married, I knew we had to move to the city. This was not the place for us.

As we looked for a new home, everyone told us not to buy because the market was so high. But I didn't like the alternative; I couldn't understand laying out all of that money in rent and fees and never seeing it again. At that time in New York City, there were finder's fees involved when you rented an apartment. Those fees were on top of the usual first and last month's rent and security deposit, and the broker's fee could be as high as 15 percent of the annual rent. When you tallied the numbers, it was close to a small down payment. Why would anyone do that? Throwing away that money on rent just didn't feel right to me. Since my prince would be commuting to Westchester for work, we needed to be located near Grand Central Terminal. One Sunday during our apartment search we came across the most peculiar staircase off East 42nd Street. We followed the mysterious steps to the top and found ourselves in the middle of what looked like a medieval fortress. There were thirteen buildings around two adorable parks. We immediately fell in love with this strange hamlet and walked into one of the buildings to inquire about any vacancies. Before we opened our mouths the doorman said, "You two here for the open house? You can head right up that elevator on your right."

The apartment was perfect. We bid on it right then and there, and our offer was accepted by the time we left the building. We would be in contract five days later. It was meant to be.

So many people told me that real estate agents in New York were ruthless sharks. They said the market was too competitive in the city and that it would be nearly impossible to make it as a broker. I didn't see it that way. I was born and raised in New England. I had a certain amount of grit and a work ethic handed down to me by my parents. I had lived in France and the UK and went to college in the Pacific Northwest. Starting over in a new locale never bothered me. On the contrary, it motivated me. Even though I knew only a handful of people in New York City aside from my husband, I had worked in real estate in Boston and felt like I could sell anything. While it's true that I didn't have a dynamic circle of friends and contacts to help give me a leg up in the New York market, the idea of taking an entry-level position in ad sales that paid $22,500 a year really didn't appeal to me. That's when I thought, *I'll take my chances and become a broker.* What was the worst that could happen?

I started my first real estate job at Citi Habitats in Manhattan in December 1997. It was primarily a rental agency. I knew from the start that if I was going to make a name for myself in this business, it wouldn't be from showing rental apartments, but I needed work immediately. I had just bought my first apartment, so income mattered—a lot. I closed my first sale within four weeks of starting. That felt amazing, and completely reassured me that I could do this. Six months later I moved on to Corcoran, where I was determined to light the world on fire. During my interview, the manager, Chris, questioned whether selling real estate was a hobby or a career for me. He looked me up and down and said, "*Look at you, with your Tiffany earrings and your beautiful wedding ring. This is obviously just a plaything for you.*" I assured him that this was a real career choice. Still, he squinted his eyes in doubt. Clearly, he had been burned one too many times by salespeople who didn't really want to work.

"What kind of car do you drive?" he asked.

"A Saturn," I responded.

"Oh, God. You do need to work!" he gasped. And with that, he gave me my own desk, and the rest, as they say, is history. My real estate career took off just as my marriage began falling apart.

When my husband and I ultimately fell out of contract, I saw only one thing: failure.

And that hurt.

It was failure on my part to get into contract in the first place, and failure because I didn't have the ability to make it work.

I was looking for inspiration anywhere I could find it. Books such as *He's Just Not That into You* and *Skinny Bitch* were bestsellers at the time. I read them, searching for a silver lining or anything that could help me find my way. What I wanted were messages that empowered women—messages demonstrating that *she* might not be that into *him*, and that that was okay.

I remember reading about J. K. Rowling's early years. She was a research writer when her mother passed away from multiple sclerosis. Rowling described her mother as the "love of my life" and was deeply affected by her death. After her mother's demise, Rowling moved to

Portugal and began teaching English. She soon met her husband. The two married and had a daughter. The couple eventually separated due to domestic abuse, leading Rowling to move to Edinburgh, where she could be closer to family. When she divorced, she considered herself a failure. She was an unemployed single mother on welfare benefits, living a very difficult life. As a result of her loss, she was diagnosed with clinical depression. Desperate, she started teaching to help make ends meet and writing in cafés during the evening.

After years of living in poverty, Rowling, inspired to write a novel about a mother's love, finally finished her first book, *Harry Potter and the Philosopher's Stone*, which was rejected by twelve publishing houses before being published in the United States and released as the *Harry Potter and the Sorcerer's Stone*. Her editor encouraged her not to quit her day job. A couple of years later, Rowling was winning awards for her novel and had published a sequel. The books continued, as did the prizes, royalties, and movie deals. Of course, Harry Potter is now a $15 billion global brand. J. K. Rowling is the first person to become a billionaire from writing a novel.

Her story inspired me to see that greatness can and often does come from darkness. She persevered through much harder circumstances than I was facing. And if she could find her way out, so could I. One thing I'm certain of is that we each have the ability to change ourselves. No matter how hard we try to change someone else, it's usually futile. They must want to change too, or any shift will be temporary. When you fall out of contract, you can only change how you answer the board's questions. You can't change the board.

I spent a lot of time walking around New York City during this period, feeling as if I couldn't be the only one experiencing this failure. If 50 percent of marriages don't work, then there must be countless people passing me on the sidewalks every day who were going through the same pain, hardship, and humiliation that I was. They were likely also putting on a smile to hide their pain. Apartments are empty because someone left for any number of reasons. And those reasons are usually the same when it comes to relationships. Either way, someone outgrew it, felt stifled or confined, got bored, or needed change. Then I began thinking about all the other kinds of struggles people go through in addition to heartache, loss, and financial woes, such as illness, chronic pain, hunger, and loneliness. So many of us suffer in silence. Looking into crowds of people wherever I went, I wondered, *How many of these expressions are just masks?*

It shook me to think about how sad so many people must be.

I knew how I felt, and the pain changed me forever. It affected everything from the way I addressed a frustrating cabdriver going the wrong way to how I dealt with a waitress who messed up my order. I lost my edge and found my empathy. It wasn't that hard, because empathy was needed almost everywhere I looked. This practice became a real difference-maker in the way I saw and understood emotional struggles. I never gave it a lot of thought before my divorce, but afterward, it was impossible for me to ignore.

So even though I fell out of contract, all was not lost. My life was not over. But it was changed forever. In some ways, the change was for the better, even if it would take me some time, trials, and tribulations to reclaim my life again—or maybe even to claim it for the first time.

Funny how the Universe does that.

It takes away something so dear to you, and though you might not know it at the time, it leaves you a new gift. It's like the fables we read as kids in which some cosmic deal takes place that turns out to be nothing like what was expected.

People didn't know what to say, so the common battle cry from the balcony seemed to be, "That which does not kill you makes you stronger."

I hated hearing that. I mean, I *really* hated it.

It's easy to say while you're eating hot dogs and popcorn on the sidelines. It's something else entirely when you're in the arena, pumping yourself up for the charge of the bull. Yet there it was: suffering. The unexpected twist that can change everything for the better.

How many of us rise to the top because we've been reduced to ashes? It's almost a rite of passage. Seeing the world from the bottom seems to give many of us the clarity we need to get to the top.

Now, I'm not saying it was easy, nor was it fast—but maybe life was telling me I could be my own prince and rescue myself from this dark place. Or maybe I should just eat a box of Krispy Kremes and cry a lot.

It was definitely a process, and one I needed to go through to get to the other side.

CHAPTER TWO

Making a House a Home

"Home is not a place. It's a feeling"
—ANONYMOUS

WHAT MAKES A HOME?
Is it a person or a place?
For some, it's both.

Home is a protective shell. It's supposed to be a safe space.

When you think about it, we're the only species with a shell we leave and return to on a daily basis. A snail might leave its shell, but once it's out, it never goes back inside. Oh yeah, smother that baby in butter and garlic and now we're talking. When I was growing up, my mom would use snail shells decoratively at dinner parties. As a little girl, I loved to glue things onto driftwood I found at the beach, but the only things I could never use were those shells.

We come out of our shells—these structures we call homes—to explore the world. Even when we're out of them, they're a part of us and who we are. But what happens when that shell no longer feels like home?

After my divorce, I knew I could no longer live in the apartment I once shared with my ex. Two years before we separated, we'd saved up enough money to buy a big loft in a prewar condo a block from Gramercy Park. We committed to this apartment in 2002, during its conversion phase. We basically bought it based on architectural plans a solid two years before it would be ready to move into. And wow, did those two years wear on us. At the time, we were living in Midtown Manhattan in a beautiful apartment with spectacular views of the Chrysler Building. It was a great apartment, but it was in a C location. In order for us to make a better investment, we needed to get to the very best location we could afford. The new apartment we bought was in the city's sweet spot at the time—a solid A location.

We had finally bought that "perfect" place, or at least I thought we did. It was coveted space. Back then, there were few, if any, apartments like it on the market. While it didn't have everything on my dream list, it checked enough boxes for us, back when box checking was fun. The reality is, most homes will never check every box, so we tend to choose the features we want the most and sacrifice those we can live without. Our apartment was a condo, not a co-op, which gave us the freedom to do whatever we wanted. By that I mean if our life plans changed, we could rent it for as long as we needed or wished. And if we decided to sell it, we could sell to whomever we wanted without the formal and sometimes torturous board approval process. What we were buying was freedom, and that was worth every penny in my book.

The building was called the Bullmoose, named for Teddy Roosevelt's short-lived political party. Teddy himself was born just a few doors down. His house has been restored and is open to the public as a museum today. The area is called "Ladies' Mile," because it was a prime shopping district for well-to-do women in Manhattan in the late 1800s—and now it would be our home too. Ours was a turn-of-the-century building with a lavish decorative facade, and our loft was breathtaking. It had soaring twelve-foot ceilings and large, dramatically arched windows that suggested the opulence of years gone by, when a woman in a leg-of-mutton-sleeved blouse would have gently waived down to Mrs. Roosevelt, out for an afternoon stroll. The developers were able to buy the entire building and fully restore and renovate it. That meant that everything was new. A huge, fabulous kitchen with stunning marble countertops, top-of-the-line stainless-steel appliances, and tons of storage for all those beautiful wedding presents still packed in their boxes because we previously had no place to put them. It also had a rich, prewar history and was located right above Gramercy Tavern, one of my favorite Manhattan restaurants, and consistently ranked as one of the most popular in Zagat's as well. I knew it would be a good investment and easy to flip if we ever wanted to. It was the perfect combination of old and new.

When we bought the apartment, my ex was unemployed. Of course, neither of us had seen that coming. When we married, he was the vice president of marketing and sales for a virtual-reality start-up. They created simulation games for different sports, including baseball, soccer, and football. He loved his work, but all start-ups can be volatile, especially in his field, because of the rapidly changing nature of technology. As the company encountered one challenge after another, my prince just couldn't let go. He was a perfectionist determined to make everything right. He became practically obsessed with turning things around. I dubbed his condition AFD: Attention Fixation Disorder. I, on the other hand, suffered from ADD: Attention Deficit Disorder. We were definitely on opposite ends of the spectrum.

When the company started to fold, my ex wanted to buy it. I had some serious reservations. Putting his own money into it seemed very risky to me. I thought that seeking investors would be a good idea.

Go in search of OPM—Other People's Money. If they were willing to inject capital into the company, then maybe there was something worthwhile there. It was a good barometer to see if it had potential for the future. In the end, though, my ex proceeded to buy the business himself without telling me. I was both hurt and humiliated. As his wife, I thought we had a real partnership. Perhaps my prince was living in a virtual reality where my avatar had no say. Costly decisions that have long-term ramifications should be agreed upon and made together in the real world. I had strong reservations about the company, which I voiced, yet my opinion wasn't valued. When you're in a relationship, I believe you have the responsibility and the right to speak your mind whenever you see something your partner can't, won't, or doesn't want to admit. I mean, it's not the 1950s. Your husband can't write off your opinions as if they're just hysterical outbursts.

After the ultimate demise of the business, my ex was crushed. It took some time, but he finally decided to go back to school to pursue his MBA. Although our wounds were fresh, and trust had certainly been broken, I still held some optimism that we could move beyond these events. Although I was working seven days a week to pay the mortgage and our other bills, it was gratifying to see him happier and more fulfilled than he had been in years. In those days we hosted a dinner at our apartment every week, filling our table with friends old and new. I wanted us both to meet as many people as we could. And for a while, we were meeting very interesting people—Vicky and Esteban from Argentina among them. Esteban was in my prince's class at school. After one semester in New York, he returned to Argentina to propose to Vicky. She was just twenty-one at the time, and had never lived outside of Buenos Aires. The two were married, and Vicky came to New York with Esteban when the following term began. The first time they came to our home for dinner, Vicky told me she wanted to be a fashion designer. I liked that she was ambitious, even though I thought to myself, *You and every other girl in New York*

City. Good luck with that. Fashion is undoubtedly a tough business, but the wonderful thing about our guests was that they were actively pursuing their dreams. I caught up with Vicky years later, and wouldn't you know it: she had built a thriving design business in Buenos Aires after all.

About a year into his MBA program, my ex got involved with another sports-related venture. I was thrilled for him at first, but again there were several significant occasions when my input was ignored, much to our financial and emotional detriment. I could no longer be a silent partner in our marriage. The strain of not being heard was wearing on me. And while I was at odds with some of his choices, I was also pained to see this person I loved come home so bruised by the battle to succeed.

I had issues of my own to deal with too. I'd been in therapy since I was in middle school. My mom was ahead of her time and had leaned heavily on psychologists to do a little co-parenting with her, so I was cognitively aware that there was something off about my marriage. My therapist was telling me that I had a fear of intimacy. Sometimes things felt great, and other times they were completely overwhelming. I was trying to figure out what journey I wanted to be on. I knew I wanted children, and yet, at times, I felt as if I already had one. There were moments when my ex's vulnerabilities were all I could see. I didn't know whether I should love him or burp him.

And that broke my heart.

Shortly after moving into our new apartment, we separated. On the day my prince left, he grabbed just a few of his things, turned to me, and said, "You can figure out what to do with the rest."

While some women would have gladly tossed it all, I wasn't one of them. I wasn't bitter or angry. I was sad. I realized he wasn't capable at that moment of moving more than he took. I had to sort through his belongings and decide what he should keep and where it should be sent. To his parents' house? To his new home? And, of course, I had to determine what to throw away as well—things like the silver cup we drank from at our wedding. I mean, what do you do with that? Dog bowl, maybe? But I had no dog. And the countless photo albums we had: Did I really want to keep those pictures? Did he? Were we destined to have our happy wedding memories bought by a savvy gay couple at an estate sale because they wanted the sideboard that housed the albums? When my ex moved out, he handed me his wedding ring and said, "Keep it. I hope someday you'll give it back to me." I had saved mementos in a beautiful box my mom, a talented artist, had painted for us when we got married. The box was meant to store all our special keepsakes, from the wedding invitation to the silver cup, and more. I never thought I would be filling it with our wedding rings and pictures. I couldn't bring myself to throw them away. The box became like something out of *Raiders of the Lost Ark*. It now sits on a dark shelf somewhere in one of my three storage units, unopened and undesired. I wonder how many people also have hidden boxes that haunt them from storage units across town.

It took me some time to work up the courage to dive in and start sorting among his, mine, and what used to be ours. I spent weeks in our beautiful loft, listening to Linkin Park on my iPod, poring through what I thought my *why* was, only to realize I had never been more unhappy or miserable than I was then. Money doesn't buy happiness, and neither does your dream home. It felt so ironic to me. There I was, sitting in this gorgeous loft in one of the best neighborhoods in Manhattan, listening to my sad rap rock. I finally had the thing I'd wanted and worked so hard for over the course of seven years—a beautiful life in a beautiful home—yet I had never been more miserable. The place felt hollow, empty, and cold. I couldn't stand being there. It felt as though the walls were almost laughing at my loneliness. The high ceilings only amplified the emptiness. To be completely transparent, I hated it there.

It had never felt like a home.

Never.

Both my sister Heather and sister-in-law Marcela were incred ibly supportive. They came to visit whenever they could. One day Marcela took my iPod and went for a run. When she came back, she said, "Holy suicide set. What in the hell do you listen to? Your music is so depressing!" And she was right. I was so melancholy that I only wanted to listen to music that matched my mood. Anything that was sad or gloomy or considered a breakup song was on my playlist. I especially enjoyed songs with vocalists who screamed. They helped me feel as though I wasn't the only person in the world whose rage needed release. Somewhere my sadness had turned into anger, though it wasn't directed toward him so much as toward the cards I'd been dealt. I was in my "Why me?" phase. I often wondered what I'd done in some past life to merit all this torture. Was I a bank robber? A murderer? Did I kill small bunnies? Whatever it was, it must have been really bad, because I was surely paying the piper now. I had been a princess for a short period of time, and now it was as though I were locked in a tower of my own design. I wasn't going to be rescued this time, and I knew it.

Sometimes I'd put on my headphones and just cry. I cried all the time. There were nights when I wept so much that I'd weigh myself afterward, because I thought it must be physically impossible not to lose weight after shedding such a waterfall of tears. It felt as though I dropped two pounds with every good cry. By the end of the night, my face was swollen and irritated from the salt in my tears. That's when I swore to cut back on my sodium intake. Whenever I thought it was safe to pull myself out of bed and move about the loft, I'd take a shower. I always hoped it would relieve the pain, but as I breathed in the steam, I would only break down and cry some more.

Funny thing about divorce: many of us end up looking better than we have in years. The divorce diet is a real thing. We dye our hair and try new lipstick colors, and when we do eat, we burn it off immediately.

Nothing boosts the metabolism like secret sadness. You'll drop weight you didn't even know you had. People will tell you how fabulous you look. The thing is, it's hard to enjoy any of the compliments when you feel worse than you ever have.

This process of purging our possessions and crying went on for weeks. I was miserable. Plain and simply *miserable*. It was clear that I needed to change just about everything in my life if I was going to be happy again someday. But let's be real: change takes optimism and energy. When you're crying your eyes out all night long, you're definitely not greeting the morning with a bright and cheery attitude. And when you're popping over-the-counter sleep aids like they're Skittles, waking up in the morning at all is a reach. Dark and ugly thoughts prey on the weak and sleepy, and I was no stranger to them. I was physically and psychologically exhausted, and so tired of being sad. Until the divorce, I had been someone who was generally happy and upbeat, full of vitality and joy. Where had that spirit gone?

Maybe it was in a box on a shelf in one of my storage units.

I felt so lifeless, like a hydrangea left out in the sun without water. I was unable to bloom. The only things I felt were failure, shame, and sadness—sadness for me, and sadness for him. I was feeling the pain for both of us. He seemed too numb to feel pain in the moment, but what protection did I have while carrying out the dreadful task of packing up his things?

It was certainly a challenge, but my ever-present TV friend Ina Garten helped. As the Food Network played softly in the background, I could hear her making her delicious double chocolate brownies and not sparing the butter in any way. Everything is better with butter, isn't it? And sometimes a little Pinot Grigio to wash it down.

I'm a bit OCD, so organization is everything to me. It's my equivalent to porn. It's addictive. It's freeing. Is there anything better than a beautifully ordered closet? Not to me. So when the going gets tough, the tough get tidy! When life is out of your control, you can always take charge of your closet. Goodbye shoes that hurt my feet. I'm done with hurt! Uggs became my Pied Piper, leading the pain away. Oh, and look at this minidress that the prince hated. I will not only keep this dress but wear it to finish organizing.

To me, arranging and organizing is something you do before anything else so that whatever you do, it's not all mixed up. Everything is in its place, and there's a place for everything. No secret fantasy football roster can ambush you when you're having a good day if it's been dispatched to a box marked "HIS." I made a plan and then stuck to it. Monday night I attacked the front hall closet. Tuesday I hit the bedroom closets. Wednesday I went through our kitchen cabinets, and Thursday I got rid of the old magazines, newspapers, and other items that seemed to mysteriously pile up. Friday was reserved for the junk drawers—all of them—and Saturday was for the bathrooms and linen closet. Sunday? Even God rested on the seventh day! And He had less to do, or at least wasn't as emotionally taxed as I was.

When it comes to organizing, I'm a bit obsessed. I use the Twelve-Month Rule. If I haven't worn something in twelve months or more, it goes to relatives, a consignment shop, or a donation center. When in doubt, throw it out. And by throw it out, I mean find someone who needs it. I actually have a really hard time throwing anything out, especially clothes, because one person's trash is always someone else's treasure. It's a matter of where you're at in that cycle.

A properly organized closet takes some planning. The hangers should face the same direction (preferably with the hook facing inward). The clothes should be neatly categorized into sections for dresses, blazers, shirts, and pants, and, of course, they should be color coordinated. When someone looks in that closet, it should appear as if Julia Roberts's stalker in *Sleeping with the Enemy* had been there ... or that the owner attends OCD Anonymous meetings. Not that I would know. Or, not that I'll admit. (Okay, it's me.)

I'm talking scary systemization.

Why?

No prospective buyer wants to see overstuffed closets or bookshelves crammed with personal memorabilia that has value only to you. And under no circumstances should it ever appear that the sellers are moving because they're bursting at the seams and need more space. Besides, it's always gross to look at the bulges of other people's belongings.

Once a seller has finished ridding their home of all these personal "collectibles," they often feel what we're hoping every buyer will feel: a sense of peace, of belonging, and that there's more than enough space to keep growing.

In sales, people are attracted to the bright and the shiny. But there's also a psychology to reaching a buyer. When the windows are sparkling in the sunlight, the walls are gleaming with new paint, and the enticing scent of fragrant candles fills the air, you can't help but feel a sense of comfort and connection. All of these elements create a subliminal message set by design.

In dating, we see this all the time. Take, for instance, the guy who wears his dad jeans and worn-out sneakers from the late '90s, or the woman who doesn't wear any makeup and looks as if her neighbor's son, who's studying to be a mortician, cut her hair in his basement. These singles are announcing, "If they don't like me the way I am, then they're not the right person for me." If you're wearing a sweatshirt with a mustard stain on it and can't remember the last time you ate mustard, you are *not* being folksy. Yes, you do look "lived in," but it's like a hotel room with dirty underwear on the floor; no new guest says, "Look, someone really enjoyed staying a night here."

It's just naive to believe that anyone wants to live in someone else's clutter, or that they can see past it. In the same way that sellers must cross off every item on the to-do list I give them, singles undoubtedly need to cross off every item on similar to-do lists in order to get back on the market. There are no shortcuts or exceptions.

For a home to truly feel alive, I always recommend including fresh flowers and plants. I can't say enough about life in the home—plant life, that is. Plants never fail to wake up a room, bringing energy, movement, and sophistication to the space. They also show the world that you love your home and yourself. Who wouldn't want something that someone else has loved so much? Nobody is looking for a place that's dead and stale inside.

When we were selling our apartment in Midtown, I hired a feng shui expert to come and work on the space. Feng shui is the ancient Chinese practice of harmonizing a space with the spiritual forces that reside in it. While I love fresh flowers, back then I also loved dried flowers, especially hydrangeas. The first thing this expert told me was to lose the dead (dried) flowers. He said, "You want live plants in your space, because they activate the room. They bring oxygen and energy into the home." That was the best advice I'd ever gotten when it came to livening up a household. Look—under the best of circumstances, moving is stressful, and breakups are stressful too. Anything that invites more vibrancy into a home is a good thing, right? Not only does plant life make a big difference aesthetically but it also makes a big difference spiritually. It keeps the air flowin' and the juju goin'! Casinos pump extra oxygen onto their gambling floors to keep people awake and motivated. Why not do the same for ourselves, in a healthier way? Now my home is never without fresh flowers and plants. I love a white orchid in the bathroom, a simple fern in the living room, and a pot of beautiful herbs in the kitchen. It's okay if you don't have a green thumb. Believe me, I used to be the Hannibal Lecter of the plant world—as in, "One must put the water in the pot." Admittedly, I've come a long way. Now I just have the occasional casualty. And when I do kill a plant—about one every three months—I thank it for its service and simply buy another one, knowing, of course, its days will be numbered too.

In a challenging market where buyers are few and price reductions are significant, getting a home into perfect condition is absolutely critical to the competitive process of selling. The buyers in a tough market are purchasing property because it's a good deal, but also for instant gratification. They don't want to do a lot of work. Many times, they want something as close to turnkey as possible.

Is that feasible?

Of course it is, if you prep the property perfectly in advance. Say that three times fast!

The reason for all of this preparation and hard work is that buyers are looking for that instant emotional connection. "I'll know when I see it..."

They want a fresh start, which always begins with a fresh scent.

I've long been a fan of aromatic candles in the home. I think they bring a sense of warmth and comfort to any room. Smell is linked to the parts of the brain that process emotion and memory. Unpleasant odors actually send pain signals to the brain. The sense of smell integrates with our other senses too. It's an important part of attraction.

What if your Prince Charming had horrible body odor or halitosis? Would you still have a crush? Or would the odor turn you off for good? And the same goes for the princess: Would Prince Charming ever have combed the kingdom looking for Cinderella if that glass slipper had a funky foot odor?

It's the same when you walk into a home. The sense of smell can easily sway a homebuyer's decision. It can raise the attraction level, or it can squash it in an instant. If we take anywhere from seven to thirty seconds to judge a person based on first impressions, you'd better believe that your sniffer is working overtime to assess how happy it's going to be in its new environment. Can you get past the smell of dirty sneakers wafting from the hall closet, or the whiff of wet dog coming from the mudroom? How about last night's fish dinner?

Is that attractive?

Do those scents make you want to move right in? Or to pack light? Maybe bring just your toothbrush?

I don't think so.

Why?

They're gross, and gross is never attractive—and if you think it is, you need help. Or, at the very least, you need your own closed Facebook group to share these thoughts, because no one else wants to hear about them. Certainly not those afflicted with OCD.

It took me some time, but after several months, I successfully cleaned out the apartment. The air was definitely lighter. There were boxes stacked by the door, neatly categorized by where they were headed. Interestingly, the moment I finished packing up my ex's closet, I was able to dry my tears and spot a silver lining: I had just doubled my closet space! I could spread out. I had lots of room to grow. I could live every day the way I coach my clients to live during a sale: with a feeling of space and simplification. There was a light flutter in my heart that night as I moved my shirts over to the newly emptied walk-in—not of sadness but rather excitement. The crying had stopped, and my puffy eyes were beginning to heal. Maybe, just maybe, there was optimism on the other side of this.

But what do you do with feelings of great love?

Can someone please tell me where they go?

Does they just go into a box marked "Loving Memories"?

Can you really compartmentalize your heart just like your closet, leaving room for someone new?

Because I never stopped loving this man. I may have stopped being *in love* with him, but I never stopped loving him.

How does a heart recover?

Does a heart ever recover?

Would I be able to forgive him?

Would I be able to forgive myself?

Would I ever experience a good night's sleep again?

These were all questions I had ahead of me—none of which I could answer for a very long time.

This was unexpected change. And it was a *big* change.

Its full impact was still unknown. For someone like me, the unknown is a scary and painful place to live. It made me terribly uncomfortable. But there I was, in the abyss of the unknown, and there wasn't anything I could do but accept it.

My life was in massive transition, and it was evident that I would be in this state of suffering for quite some time. You never get used to that awful piercing feeling in your heart, the one that makes you think you're having a heart attack. Until my divorce, I never realized how absolutely physical heartbreak is. There was excruciating pressure and pain all around, and especially *in*, my fragile, broken heart. All those descriptions in sad breakup songs suddenly rang true. Heartbreak in real time.

CHAPTER THREE

Fixing the Foundation

"Rock bottom became the solid foundation on which I rebuilt my life."
—J.K. Rowling

I N REAL ESTATE, AS IN ANYTHING, A HOUSE IS ONLY AS STRONG AS the foundation on which it stands. If there's a good structural foundation, the house can stand for a lifetime—or several. If there are any cracks or weaknesses, the house is bound to fall. Not many deals can be saved if there's a real problem in the foundation. That's why buyers hire structural engineers to perform inspections to make sure the foundation is indeed intact. Even the most gorgeous townhouse can have a beautiful facade, exquisite landscaping, picturesque window boxes full of cascading flowers, and an interior design worthy of a spread in *Architectural Digest*, yet still have foundation issues. If the engineer comes back and says there's a problem, chances are this deal is dead.

I always have sellers fix their problem areas before putting their houses on the market. A fresh paint job can make a property look like new, while cracked caulk in the bathroom is inexcusable, and sagging floorboards are never charming. You will always get more money for a property when you can show that the sellers took great care of it and that they loved living there. It's important to create that emotional connection with buyers. Sure, a buyer knows that they can hire someone to come and fix the caulking. You can even do it yourself overnight. But as with everything, it's the first impression that matters most. True pride of ownership is the secret sauce. Caulk the cracks, people! It will be well worth it.

It's actually easy to find structural issues in a building. It's much harder to look inward to find them in ourselves. While there is no structural engineer you can call for yourself, there is a go-to person every New Yorker has on speed dial: their therapist. Which is why August in Manhattan is a horrible time to date anyone new. It's hot and smelly (putting everyone in a bad mood), and all therapists go on vacation.

When my ex moved out, my father saw how much pain I was in. He handed me a check and said, "I don't care how much it costs. Go see someone. You're going to need help getting through this." My dad can be one of the most frugal men I know, so when he's generous, it always makes me emotional. This was an incredible gesture on his part. I wasn't expecting him to understand how I felt, but somehow, he did.

I'd gone to therapy many times before my divorce. My ex and I had been in couples therapy for years, but clearly those sessions didn't get a rave review from me on Yelp. Although I knew my dad's assessment was correct, it was important for me to find the right doctor this time around. I bumped into someone who had just come back from Sierra Tucson (an addiction and mental health treatment center in Arizona). She was recovering from post-traumatic stress syndrome after surviving 9/11; she had been in the towers that dreadful day. I don't remember her name now, but she was so kind to me when we spoke. She could see that I was suffering and suggested that I reach out to a woman who could help me find the right person. That's how I met Jane.

Jane is wonderfully maternal. Although she's a bit too young to actually be my mom, she represented everything I dreamed a mom could be. She is softer, more urbane, and more encouraging. Not that I don't love my mother—I most certainly do—but she was never a doting, super-affectionate parent. It wasn't her fault. That's just the way the women were in her family. My mom is nurturing in her own way, but different from Jane. I love my mom—she's smart, brave, and elegant—but she's one tough cookie. She doesn't believe in coddling or sugarcoating *anything*. She always speaks her mind, often with a side of witty sarcasm. She's still one of the funniest women I know, and I definitely got my sense of humor from her. Had she been a mother who babied me, I would be a completely different human being. She pushed me and, within reason, tried not to shield me from the harsh things in life. While there are things that she lacked, my mom can be summed up succinctly by the Brené Brown quote, "The person that challenges you and holds you accountable loves you more than the person that watches you stay the same and settle for mediocrity." I prefer to celebrate her best traits. Seeing the cup as half full—focusing on what we have and not on what's missing—isn't a bad way to view the world.

I felt immediately connected to Jane. She was wise, empathetic, and no stranger to pain. Twenty-five years into a fantastic marriage that gave her three children, her husband was killed in a terrible car accident. As tragic as that was, I found it comforting to know that she herself had experienced extreme grief and loneliness and had somehow survived the terrifying abyss of the unknown. She was kind enough to share some of those moments at appropriate times to let me know that I wasn't alone—that other people's lives had taken sharp left turns along the road, taking them, as I had been taken, to a place none of us could ever have imagined.

Visiting her office was like going to your best friend's house and having their mom invite you into her room to give you advice. Although I had never met a mom—or any other person, for that matter—like Jane, she felt like home to me. Everything about her was safe and comfortable.

She always had the most magnificent bouquets of flowers in her office, and there were big arrangements of tree branches in each corner that she rotated depending on which blooms were in season. One week they would be irresistible cherry blossoms; the next week, apple blossoms. Sometimes the arrangements were six feet tall. The fresh-cut flowers and trees made the whole office smell like spring. Eternal optimism oozed from every leaf and petal. If you could bottle optimism, this is surely what it would smell like. She was a home, not a house.

I felt secure with Jane, as if she would protect me and guide me through the changes necessary to survive this horrific period of my life. I had been to several therapists in the past. They would ask questions and listen to my answers, often nodding and writing down notes. When I asked them what they thought, they would usually turn the question around to me: "Well, let's think about how *you* feel about this."

Annoying!

I mean, like, *really* annoying.

Jane didn't do that. She would clap her hands and say, "You know what, we need to change this all around." She gave her opinions. She had emotions. And she would always give it to me straight. Jane wasn't afraid of rolling up her sleeves and sorting through the clutter in my mind. She pointed out cobwebs that needed to be cleared and handed me tissues while I sorted through long-forgotten keepsakes.

It's crucial to find *that* person. For many people, just saying the word *therapist* is scary; they can't even imagine seeing one. You don't necessarily need a psychologist to help you heal. There are many kinds of healers, from your priest or rabbi to your Reiki practitioner or yogi. Healing is about the process of really studying yourself, and it helps to have someone who will push you to be honest about your strengths and especially honest about your weaknesses. If you don't know what triggers cause you to fall, you'll never learn to navigate around them. Jane showed me how to find the arsonist instead of simply putting out the fires that seemed to constantly burn all around me.

Jane is a lot of wonderful things, and, as I quickly discovered, we shared a lot of beliefs in common. One of them was living with intentionality. So many people wake up each day with good intentions, and most fail to follow through with them. There's a big distinction between good intentions and living with intentionality. *Wanting* to do good isn't the same as actually *doing* it. Right? I mean, if your guy said he was going to buy you flowers but couldn't remember what kind you like, all his good intentions don't really mean much. Now, if he shows up with an armful of dyed carnations . . . I think you get the point.

Jane also encouraged me to let go. She taught me that letting go was really about acceptance—accepting things as they are, not as we want them to be. She challenged me to give up control by releasing all the pressure to figure things out. You can white-knuckle things for only so long before you eventually go numb. Sometimes you have to disconnect to connect. And when you do connect, you need to tune in to what your inner voice is telling you to do. Our intuition is rarely wrong. Learning to dial in and listen to it is critically important. You have to be very quiet to hear it—not literally, but the noise in your head needs to be turned all the way down. (I had to switch my "head noise" from blaring grunge rock to soft Mozart.) When we push for an answer before we're ready to receive it, sometimes we create anxiety—and that anxiety tends to cause anxiety about our anxiety. Jane taught me to detach and throw the question out into the Universe, and eventually, the answer will surface. As I've always said, the Universe unfolds exactly as it should.

In the beginning, I saw Jane three times a week. I know that sounds like a lot—and it was—but I just had so much on my plate. She calmed me and gave me the confidence and comfort I needed to keep going. It wasn't easy; the "what if" questions were getting the best of me. Every day I wondered, *What if I never manage to pull my life together? What if I'm never attracted to anyone again?*

That was a big one for me. It forced me to look at my commitment issues, especially when it came to love. (When it came to big mortgages, though, I had no problem committing. Why? They keep me motivated. In love, commitment has to do with your head, heart, and soul. In real estate, commitment has to do with your head, heart, and wallet.)

Jane gave me homework and was insistent that I do it. There were many weeks when she'd send me out the door with books to read. I took her assignments very seriously. One of the books she gave me was *When Things Fall Apart* by Pema Chödrön, a well-known American Buddhist nun. For obvious reasons, several people had already given me this book. I kept a copy on either side of my bed and one on the bookshelf in the living room. Whenever someone toured my apartment, they'd laugh and say, "Wow. Three copies? Your life really must have sucked!"

The book's message is about leaning into our pain. Chödrön encourages us to feel it, to give in to it, and then to release it, just like we would in yoga. It helped me understand that I couldn't run away from my pain or distract myself into health. My foundation was cracked, and I needed to give it some attention if I was going to build a stronger home. I couldn't just slap some spackle on it. I needed a serious repair—possibly a new foundation altogether.

When I opened the book for the first time and began to read it, I was struck by the epigraph at the beginning of chapter one: "Fear is a natural reaction to moving closer to the truth." Reading this stopped me cold. It helped me to realize that living in a fantasy is sometimes easier than living in reality. To move forward and really grow, you must step into the here and now. You can't live up in the clouds if you want to progress. We all do it; we avoid what's hard, but we have to face our fears if we truly want to work through them.

And I did.

I didn't want to live in fear any more than I wanted to live alone.

If I was ever going to move past these roadblocks, I would first have to learn how to love myself. And in order to love myself, I would have to forgive myself. Now, *that* was something I would need to walk through.

The thing about a weakened foundation is that it's rarely beyond repair. Sometimes it needs a teardown, but mostly you can fix it. You won't arrive at divorce without having a cracked foundation—and there's no emerging from it whole again without doing a proper renovation.

Like any massive undertaking, fixing your foundation takes time, patience, and a lot of self-love. You have to give yourself the room to make choices, some of which will work and some of which will fail. But always hold on to the belief that you're getting stronger, things are getting better, and you're moving in the right direction.

And while therapy is a wonderful tool to help you see the big picture and to lay the plan for repairing those cracks we all have, when it comes to fixing your foundation for good, there are lots of other things you can do as well.

For instance, I had to figure out how to sleep at night. The later it got, especially during the wee hours of the morning, the more fears invaded my head. I would toss and turn and turn and toss. I'd count sheep, meditate, read something dreadfully boring, or, if all else failed, take a long, hot shower. Sometimes I'd take two, three, four, or even five showers. Really. It was always the last-ditch effort to help me calm down. By morning, every towel I owned would be on the floor, making my bathroom look like the aftermath of a wild toga party.

Jane was my home base, and all I needed to do was return to her in order to wrestle these fears back under control. After seeing her, I always felt as though she had cleared my negative thoughts, especially the ones that crept in during those sleepless nights. I'd leave her office breathing deeply again, if only for the day. My mind felt cleaned up, like everything had its place and all was orderly. My goal was to figure out how to hold on to that peacefulness for as long as I could. It was difficult for me if I didn't get to see Jane. Jane was my contractor, so to speak—one to whom I was apprenticing.

There were days when I woke after only thirty minutes of sleep. My head was cloudy, my body exhausted, and my nerves shot. These were not exactly the makings of a champion. I would drag myself to the office where the distractions of the real estate market were very welcome. I was extremely lucky in that I got to work with some of my closest friends, and the love and support from them and from my incredible family were overwhelming, in a good way. But pain is isolating, and no matter how many people reached out, I still felt utterly and totally alone. One day, my assistant, Morgan, who took the very best care of me, drove me to an appointment at 15 Central Park West. It was an amazing new building, and some of the biggest sales in the city were being made there. I was meeting new clients that morning, but I was feeling particularly low. When Morgan asked, "Holly, are you going to be okay on this showing?" I immediately began to cry. Why is it that when you think you're managing to keep it together but someone recognizes the discomfort and grief you're feeling underneath your mask of stoicism, the protective wall that was holding all of that back just crumbles and falls? As I began to sob into my hands, almost on cue, it started to rain, as if even the sky were commiserating with me. Morgan and I sat there for several minutes listening to the windshield wipers go back and forth as I tried to stifle more tears. It was like when a foundation has just been laid and the new owners go in to celebrate their new beginning, but then they step on the concrete and find that it's still wet. My foundation looked stable from afar, but if you touched it the way Morgan did, you would find that it just wasn't set yet.

"Holly, I think that's your client; you gotta go," Morgan said in his gentle southern drawl.

I looked up to see the doorman greeting them.

"Yes, that's them," I whispered. "They're five minutes early."

I whipped out my makeup bag and did whatever damage control I could on my poor sleep-deprived and now tear-stained eyes and cheeks. When I was done, I turned to Morgan and asked, "How do I look?" knowing full well he'd have to lie through his perfect white teeth to get me through this day.

"You look fine, Holly! Now, go get 'em! You got this."

I took a deep breath and opened the door, fanning my blotchy face to try to get the red out as I walked to the entrance.

For me, the great thing about being an empath, a caretaker, and being in sales is that I can flick a switch and almost go into autopilot. The energy of meeting new people and the responsibility of representing the agency transport me to another time and space. It's almost as if I'm playing a part in a movie. On that day, it was a role without pain. Playing this character entailed getting excited about these buyers' lives and their possible adventures in their new home; luckily, it didn't entail my thinking about my own life. Work allowed me a mental escape, and it was a welcome break indeed.

I said hello to my clients and chatted with them as we rode the elevator up to the sixteenth floor to look at the home. Upon entering the apartment, we headed into the grand living room, which was flanked by stunning views of Central Park. Seeing even a part of the more than eight hundred acres of lush greenery from this vantage point is a coveted experience, one that's enjoyed by very few. To live in New York City and overlook such a beautiful oasis of trees and plant life, as well as the zoo and ball fields, is very rare and special.

My buyers seemed to like it right away. They clasped each other's hands as we continued to tour the apartment. I thought they might be in their late fifties and suspected that this was a second marriage for each of them. The curiosity was killing me. "How many years have you been married?" I asked.

"We'll be married for twenty-seven years this September," they responded. "We met in college." And just like that, I was triggered. The floodgates opened.

"How nice for you," I said, before scrambling to the farthest reaches of the apartment where I could hide my efforts to fight back tears. I needed someone to ask me if everything was okay like I needed hole in my head, so into the closet I went to try to regain my composure.

"Bathrooms sure are pretty," I called out when I thought I had it under control.

"Perfect location for your whole family to be right on the park," I shouted from the abyss.

It would be like this for the next several months. Some days, I thought the pain and anxiety were behind me. I even had a little spring in my step. Other days, it seemed to suck me under. Those were the days when I would simply pull the plug at work and head home. If I was going to lean into pain, it couldn't be while I hid from clients in a huge walk-in closet. I would turn off all forms of outside communication and stare blankly at the television as Ina made a savory soufflé for her book group. Talk about comfort food: some people eat it when they're depressed, but I like to watch it being made. Another time Ina whipped up margaritas from scratch. It was so calming. Her sweet and loving face; it seemed to me that all she wanted to do was cook for her loved ones and make them happy. My immersion into the Barefoot Contessa's cozy, flawless world would continue for hours, episode after episode, well into the night. Of course, my sleep cycle was off. Every evening I was determined to turn in early and get a good night's rest, yet the Universe seemed determined to keep me awake. I couldn't find rest mentally, so I decided to find it physically.

Every day, I would show up at the gym and make myself run until I collapsed. I'm not a big runner and really never have been, but one particular morning I suddenly ran just shy of four and a half miles. I was indeed exhausted. I noticed that for the remainder of the day, I was relatively calm and relaxed. When I returned to my apartment, I felt so much better. I was proud of myself for running so far and, while I was beyond tired, I was a little amazed that I had done it. As I sat alone in my big, empty living room, I actually felt a little bit hopeful. *Maybe I* do *have what it's going to take to get my life back together*, I thought. But first I had to concentrate on beating the pain and anxiety, which meant fixing my foundation once and for all. How would I do that? I would have to create a plan and be more disciplined. No more all-night sobbing sessions, no more last-resort showers, and no more psycho-serial watching Ina. From now on there would be a twelve-stick-of-butter limit: I would keep count through each recipe, and when Ina dumped her twelfth stick of butter—whether into bread or brownies—that marked the last episode for the night. The insanity needed to stop.

CHAPTER FOUR

The Homelessness Problem

Chaos is merely order waiting to be deciphered.
—José Saramago

W HEN I WAS IN HIGH SCHOOL, I REMEMBER READING A FABLE about two prisoners who had committed a crime. Each was brought in front of the king and offered a choice of punishment. The king said they could pick what was behind a closed door, or they could pick death by hanging. (Like the worst episode of *Let's Make a Deal* ever!) "The choice is yours," he said.

Both prisoners chose death by hanging.

Seemingly perplexed, the king remarked, "There hasn't been a prisoner yet who has chosen the door. Behind that door is freedom.

Instead, they would rather face certain death than encounter the unknown."

What would you have done?

Does the fear of the unknown hold you back?

Of course it does. Our imagination is somehow always creepier than the reality. Maybe there were four million killer ants waiting to sting and slowly eat the prisoners, thereby making the first choice, death by hanging, sound like a day at the spa!

There was no doubt my heart was broken, and my task was to put the million little pieces back in place. I couldn't even think about starting a new relationship, let alone dating. Who was I, now that I had lost my best friend and had no one to care for? When our mediator announced to us that we were no longer married, a shock ran through my whole body. We had been together for eight years as a couple, a pair, a family. I had signed so many contracts of sale in my career that when we signed the divorce papers, it was as if I had just signed another one. But oddly, after penning my name on that agreement, I had no idea where or how I was going to live. We had married as children, but I certainly wasn't a child anymore. And though I had a big, beautiful apartment, I felt homeless and lonelier than ever. Somehow being in that fabulous space seemed ironic, as if the walls were laughing at me for thinking that happiness could ever come from drywall and paint. Happiness and the feeling of home were far more complex, and definitely out of my reach at that moment.

It's amazing how fear rushes through our bodies when we don't know what's ahead of us. The mystery of what lies around the corner can be literally paralyzing. I was in no condition to search for and build a new home. It was as if I were sitting in a field of smoldering ashes that stretched on for miles. The land was scorched clean of every living creature. But that's what fear can do to you; it can put a dark and foreboding twist on everything you see. In the same way that everything seems to be more brightly colored when you're in love, everything seems grayer when fear gets its grip on you.

What I ultimately discovered, though, is that when you're about to start building your life again, it's only natural for fear to be your first visitor. I had been a serial monogamist for my whole life, and here I was at thirty-two, totally alone. I had been such a caretaker, and now I didn't have anyone to take care of. To be certain, caretakers thrive on attending to others while putting themselves last on the list. But now, the person I most needed to take care of was me; I had moved up to first place. The concept was so foreign to me that it took me a while to comprehend. At that point, you would have had better luck getting me to rebuild the engine of your car than getting me to understand what the term *self-care* meant.

Even so, I needed to get it together if I was going to make it on my own. This was my time to show myself that I could live by myself and be truly independent.

That didn't last long.

JAAAANE!

During one of my endless treks around Manhattan, I heard a familiar voice. It was my friend Carrie, with whom I'd fallen out of touch. Carrie and I had met in Spain years before when we were both studying abroad. We lived with a crazy woman named Carmen in a big, beautiful house in Seville. Carmen had two adorable little children and no man in sight, but she had thousands—and I mean *thousands*—of stories about her suitors. Mentioning almost anything would bring on a tale about how her lovesick beau had taken her to Paris, praising her enchanting beauty the entire time, or about how another had proposed to her on the Eiffel Tower, but alas, cruel Carmen turned him down. She would go on to tell how her famous good looks had beguiled and bewitched men from all around the globe. If you mentioned the weather, a book, a lamp, even a pizza, a story about her enchanted love life was sure to follow.

Every night in Seville there would be a knock at the door from some poor soul attempting to woo the gorgeous Carmen. In Carmen's head, she needed to beat them back with a stick. Confidence is king; we live in the reality we make. I needed to channel the aura of Carmen, with her boundless confidence and self-love to create a world where everyone would fall head over heels for my fabulousness.

I know, it's easier said than done.

Carrie mentioned that she had just arrived in New York and was looking for a place to live. She was couch surfing but wanted to settle in someplace.

"Wait, you're homeless?" I immediately said. "You can't be homeless. Move in with me!"

"You know, Holly, I've never lived on my own. I was thinking now would be the right time."

"No, no. Now is not the time. Trust me on this: you'll have years to be on your own. You need to move in with me."

Okay, there might have been some self-serving intention there, but I was desperate for company. Anyone with a heartbeat was a contender to become a roommate. The thought of having Carrie with me instead of my thoughts and demons was too tempting. Besides, who could turn down a sales pitch from a pro like me? I find people homes for a living. She said yes.

When Carrie moved in, I was genuinely relieved to have her companionship. I told the thoughts in my head that they would have to take up residence somewhere else. Life was so much easier when we could concentrate on Carrie's dating life or any other challenge she was facing. Now, some might call this distraction, but I called it good fortune. As for Carrie, well, she was the lucky recipient of all my attention, because I didn't have the capacity to pay attention to myself.

If she ran out of toothpaste, I'd have a fresh tube waiting for her.

Breakfast? Made to order, every morning.

What to wear on a date? I had loads of unsolicited advice, some of which she even took.

As it happened, I had the answers to all her problems and none to any of my own.

I was living in a state of perpetual avoidance.

Someone once told me that it's easy to spot the flea on someone else's shoulder and miss the elephant on your own. I heard the message loud and clear. I just wasn't ready to ride the elephant anytime soon.

When it comes to endings, whether it's selling your home, breaking up, or losing a loved one, you can't hide from change forever. You must anticipate it, accept it, and manage it, or it will manage you.

I got a call once from a well-known broker whom I'd known for years. He had a famous buyer whose heart was set on a small boutique building in Greenwich Village. There were only a handful of condo buildings in that neighborhood at the time, and this buyer had just lost out on the last sale in the building he coveted. Determined not to let this be the end of the story, the broker was reaching out to me.

"Would any of your clients in that building be interested in selling if we made it worth their while? And, if the answer is yes, can you get us in tomorrow? My client is leaving town, and this is all very time sensitive."

I took a deep breath and said, "Let me see what I can do." Fortunately, my client picked up the phone. I was relieved to get a live person on the other end.

"Jeff, how are you? How's the new baby doing? How old is he now, five weeks? You guys sleeping?" I was doing my best to make quick connective chatter before dropping the bomb.

"The baby is great, the sleep is not," he said in a very exhausted tone.

I had known this couple since they were just dating. They were some of my favorite clients. They were considerate, so damn creative, talented, and absolutely amazing people. I was so lucky to have them as clients and as friends.

"So, we have one of those weird situations where someone might want to pay you a lot of money for your apartment. It might be a lot, or it might be obscene. Either way, they want to get in to see it tomorrow. You interested?" I paused, hoping he would bite.

"Well, this place looks like a tornado went through it and then backed up to go through again, but I'm too curious to turn this person down, so let me talk to my wife. Let's hear what they have to say."

Bam.

The showing took place the following day, and the offer came in twenty minutes later. I was still with my clients when I got the call, and all of us were speechless. In the midst of the chaos of two toddlers, a new baby, and a dog, they locked eyes and said, "Looks like we're moving!"

It was a big rush for all three of us, because it appeared out of nowhere; but then I got a call from Jeff. "Okay, so I think the sticker shock is wearing off, because now we're realizing that we're totally homeless and have less than thirty days to find a place. I'll be honest, we're starting to freak out a bit."

My work was cut out for me. Not only was the clock ticking but this was right in the middle of the holiday season, one of the most challenging times of the year to complete a transaction. If I didn't find this family someplace to move to, I feared that the deal might implode. Clearly an extended hotel stay with three kids and a dog was not happening. Okay, guys, we're just going to figure this out. Sometimes the price can be right but the timing is off. Because of the circumstances, they couldn't be homeless. And though my door is perpetually open to clients in need, I couldn't possibly take all of them in, so we did what we had to do and got to work.

Sometimes people will sign a contract without thinking through the details of what's to come. That's when the fear of being homeless freezes them in their tracks. They're unable to take the simplest steps forward. When that happens, things can really start to unravel. My goal was to keep everything in motion and make this transition as smooth as possible for all parties.

The family fell in love with an apartment that was owned by the lead singer of Depeche Mode, a band I grew up loving. Admittedly, I was a little surprised by the amount of pink in his apartment until I realized he had daughters who had taken charge of the interior design. Clearly it had morphed from his sanctuary into Barbie's dreamhouse. Even so, my family wanted it.

We visited the property several times, and each time we did, they became more and more enamored with it until they were ready to pull the trigger. It was located on one of the dreamiest streets in the West Village. The loft had a big, beautiful kitchen and living room that faced south, with views over the Hudson River. And the real sweet spot was a spectacular terrace that could be entered from both of those rooms. The garden was in full bloom, and the plants were thriving. My clients are both magnificent chefs, and when they saw the big built-in grill, they let out an *ahhh*. It was getting better by the minute. The broker could see their enthusiasm and motioned me over to him.

"You've got competition on this place," he said.

"Okay, I hear you."

We put in a very aggressive offer, but someone had fallen harder for the place and bid way over the asking price. Before we knew it, the apartment was gone. We were heartbroken. It's so hard to emotionally attach like that and really visualize your life somewhere only to have that vision shattered in an instant. Their dinner parties, their grilling fests, playing with the kids on the terrace, enjoying outside life in New York's West Village—all gone up in smoke. Time was running out, too, and the smell of desperation was getting thick among the three of us.

After a lot of tears and heartache over losing this amazing place, it became apparent that any further big decisions needed to be put on hold. It was time to hit the pause button and think about a rental. I didn't want them to pick just any apartment because of their circumstances. We were looking for a real home. And sometimes that takes time—time we didn't have.

We ended up finding them a townhouse also in the West Village, that was marginally ready for occupancy. The family understood that they had to be flexible in their needs, but the townhouse never really felt like home to them. While it was incredibly charming and had a nice backyard, it apparently was a mosquito magnet. I had never even *seen* a mosquito in Manhattan, but evidently they existed. And while the house was charming, it really needed an entire gut renovation. Ultimately, they ended up leaving Manhattan for a while, feeling disenchanted with the city. When they came back, I helped them find their real dream home—one they could settle down in without settling for less.

Panic never pays off—unless, of course, you're being chased by a pack of wolves. Then panic seems like a good idea. Maybe. When making big life decisions, we should never feel like we're under the gun. There are always choices, even if you can't see them or they haven't presented themselves yet, or you've consciously or unconsciously chosen to ignore them. Sometimes, pushing the pause button until you're clearheaded again is the best move you can make. Heated emotion clouds your judgment.

Sure, I had a roof over my head, but it didn't feel like home, and I knew it never would. I had to leave this apartment in order to find peace, even if it took a little while.

CHAPTER FIVE

My Haunted House

Stop cheating on your future with your past.
—Anonymous

JUST AS MY DIVORCE WAS BECOMING FINAL IN 2004, FACEBOOK was really starting to take off. For the first time, we got to see into everyone else's lives. It was eye-opening to have a peek at what others were doing—what I was missing. They were enjoying companionship, dating, love, and traveling. They were having kids, throwing baby showers, and, before anyone could blink, enrolling those same kids in kindergarten. And there I was, picking up the debris around my broken home and feeling very left behind. It was as if the elevator were perpetually out of order and I was stranded in the darkness of the basement. Sure, there may have been other posts about delicious meals at fancy restaurants or pictures of Fido, but the only thing I saw was what I so desperately wanted and felt as though I would never have.

Looking at how happy everyone else seemed to be made me feel like the biggest loser. I'd never really struggled with feelings like that before my divorce. If there was something I wanted, I usually knew a way to get it. Yet finding my soul mate—the most important thing in the world to me at that time—simply eluded me.

Misery never loved company so much as when social media was born and everyone else's joy was out there for all to see.

Somehow, in that dark stage of my life, having people around who were equally miserable brought me an odd comfort. Luckily, I had a group of friends who were all going through challenges of some sort too. A few, like me, were going through divorce, while others were coping with death or loss of other kinds. There are all too many varieties. We spent most Saturdays and Sundays together in the city, and occasionally in upstate New York, where most of them had weekend homes near Woodstock. We would entertain one another, sometimes even competing to see whose life was more pathetic or who had suffered the most gargantuan challenges. With the high costs of Manhattan living, and with each of us coping on our own, we would joke about buying a large brownstone where we would each have our own floor. It would be the chicest communal living around, and we'd call it Bummer Brownstone. When someone rang the doorbell at this tower of sadness, it would make an ominous *whaa, whaa* sound (think Charlie Brown). All deliveries would be things that we didn't want or were just wrong in general. The co-op board would be easy to win over, as long as you weren't hopeful, cheery, or enthusiastic. Every happy hour would be whine with wine.

When you get right down to it, though, pity parties are no parties at all. Who hasn't let themselves fall into a rut from time to time? And who hasn't thrown the "woe is me" party to end all parties? But when we're dwelling on our losses and failures, we tend to wear the opposite of rose-colored glasses. I call them "loser lenses" because they make everything appear darker, drearier, and more out of focus. When we see a situation from this point of view, the challenges are automatically magnified.

Everything is too tough to do.

The competition is better than we are.

The city is dirtier.

The sky is grayer.

The deal is dying.

There is simply no hope.

That kind of self-defeating attitude can be felt by everyone and everything around you. You may as well be Pig-Pen, with a cloud of stink all around you.

Phew!

Not really a soul mate magnet. Unless I wanted a soul mate who was a big stinker himself, and I did not. Sure, the Law of Attraction is in full force—except it's working double time against you, attracting negative things.

The Bummer Brownstone collective gave each of us permission to be competitively pessimistic. If negativity were an Olympic sport, we would have been the A team. I'll admit that sometimes it was funny. Okay, lots of times. Laughter is amazing medicine, and these people were hilarious. Especially Aimee, who was not only stunning but also one of the funniest women I know. She certainly kept me laughing, sometimes so hard I cried. But behind the tears of laughter, there was a real sadness. And it could be downright depressing; while it's true that camaraderie is important, Bummer Brownstone wasn't really helping any of us move past our hurt. If anything, it was keeping us mired in it.

My brutally blunt mom gave me advice during that time that I'll never forget. She said, "Holly, it's hard for you to celebrate your wins right now because, well, you don't have any. So go out there and celebrate other people's wins until you have your own. And really be a part of those wins; feel their happiness alongside them, and then hold on to that feeling, because it will stay with you."

I knew my mom was right; not only was I not helping anyone celebrate their wins, I was the host of a big loser party. The inhabitants of Bummer Brownstone weren't losers, but we were definitely in recovery from losses. There was no denying that I felt like a victim. It was as if I were the only person on the planet going through a divorce. Naturally, I knew that wasn't true. I also knew that embracing that lie didn't help me feel any better, especially because it only kept me wallowing in my pain. Bathing in it, in fact. My only relief was work. I could disappear into my clients' lives, even if only for the day. My job was helping them to be happy, and when I was giving them peace of mind about the largest purchase they might ever make, I had peace for a moment too. Still, I couldn't make my world all about real estate, could I? I needed to celebrate other people's wins in all arenas. It wasn't easy, but then again, nothing worth pursuing is. And just like exercising, the more I did it, the stronger I got.

I had married earlier than most in my circle of friends. Now, as a fresh divorcée, I was faced with the golden age of weddings. Putting on a happy face and attending all those nuptials took a lot of energy and effort. My pregame warm-up usually started with a cocktail. I was never in a hurry to be on time. Ever. I wanted to be happy for the couple getting married, but I had temporarily lost my belief in "happily ever after." I looked at every wedding as if the couple were buying a home they'd live in for the rest of their lives. Had they done all the inspections? Tested the soil? Checked the roof? And what about that furnace? Would it *really* be good for another fifty-five years, or would they need to replace it within the first six months? I wanted to see the cup as half full, but I couldn't. I was questioning everything I once believed in. I grew up viewing weddings as joyful occasions, situated at the pinnacle of all celebrations. Getting married meant that you'd finally found true companionship, a love that would last through sickness and health, for better or for worse. Having experienced the other side—the pain, the loss, the sorrow—I now viewed weddings as kryptonite. Whenever I received an invitation to one in the mail, I'd shudder and begin thinking of all the reasons I would RSVP no. Just being in that environment felt awful. And, worse, I was scared for my friends as they entered into this sacred bond, knowing full well that their chances of succeeding were less than 50 percent. I simply didn't trust myself to be anything other than a full-blown pessimist at this point. Not what you're typically looking for in a wedding guest. I worried that when the minister asked if anyone knew of any reason these two should not be joined in holy matrimony, I'd jump up from the pew and scream at the top of my lungs, "Don't do it! Marriage sucks!" I just wanted to tell them to turn around and run, as if Michael Myers from *Halloween* were chasing them.

Who wants a Debbie Downer at their wedding anyway?

No amount of alcohol helped the situation either. The more I drank, the harsher the critical commentary inside my head became. I couldn't help feeling that marriage was a lot like the evening commute on the subway: everyone on the platform is dying to get on, while everyone on the train can't wait to get off.

There was no question I was living in a haunted house full of ghosts from my past, and they took turns being my raucous plus-one at parties. Had I become the Ebenezer Scrooge of marriage?

The thing about living in a haunted house is, whether or not the ghosts are always present, you wonder if you manifested them. In my case, there were spooky signs about my marriage from the start; I knew it, and so did the few people who were really close to me. On my wedding day, my mother took me aside and said it wasn't too late to change my mind. In that moment, I thought she was just being protective. But deep down, I knew she sensed what I sensed: that this was not the right match, and I might be making a huge mistake. But as is so often the case when it comes to love, we tend to see what we want to see, not what is.

Some people live with other people's ghosts, like their ex's. Some create their own ghosts. Out of those people, some will burn the sage until the presence is no longer felt, while others simply mask the obvious or ignore it until it becomes unbearable.

I'm one of those people who's willing to try anything and everything until I get the result I want. When I'm marketing a home, there is no bad idea—only ideas I'm willing to try. Some will work, and others won't. So when it came to exorcising my ghosts, I brought in every expert I could find. I feng shui'd, I went to therapy, I went to Reiki, and I burned sage to exorcise negative energy. I sought out all kinds of gurus to help me get past this slump. Nothing was too silly or too hard, because I was on a quest to get my life back and my home in order. In real estate, you have to disclose if a house is thought to be haunted or if a murder was committed in the home.

When you're in this mindset, patching the walls doesn't really fix things. Like it or not, you're in the depths of a full-blown reconstruction. Everything needs to be ripped out and taken down to the studs before you can work your way back. Cutting corners will only result in a defective product that will ultimately lead you back to where you started. A quality reno takes time, patience, and skill.

When I first started in real estate, I had a friend who was buying outside the city, so I wasn't representing him. On the day of his closing, he discovered a leak coming through the ceiling. As a result, the closing was postponed, and the seller agreed to fix the leak. The buyer and seller knew each other and shared friends in common, so my friend didn't pay as close attention to the finished product as he should have. Worse, he chose not to have another inspection performed, trusting that the seller had properly fixed the leak. Unfortunately, that wasn't the case. She had simply thrown paint up to cover a much larger problem. When he did the final walk-through, everything looked fine—but underneath that paint, the problem still existed, and it reappeared seven months later, teaching him to always trust but verify. That little leak was not a little leak at all but a huge structural nightmare that cost him $40,000 to correct.

Quick fixes are like Band-Aids: they may stop the bleeding and bind the skin together, but they really aren't what heals the wounded tissue. That's up to the body. I realized that I had a lot of work to do inside my house before I could even begin to think about any type of showing.

I was trying to follow my mother's advice by doing my best to find joy in other people's happiness—to be glad for them, regardless of my situation. This might sound simple, but when you're in a rut, digging down deep to feel good about anything, let alone someone else's blessings, is a tall order. It requires practice. Lots of it.

My therapist, Jane, had been to the Esalen Institute many times. It's a retreat center in serene Big Sur, California, that attracts a wide international community. I had heard about it from my friends in San Francisco, and when I mentioned it to Jane, she thought it might be a good idea for me to go there.

Esalen focuses on humanistic alternative education. Its innovative focus on the mind-body connection, use of encounter groups, and ongoing experimentation in personal awareness introduced many ideas that later became mainstream.

Esalen may not be all things to all people, but there are a few things you cannot contest. First, the real estate is jaw-droppingly gorgeous. The facility sits high atop bluffs overlooking the Pacific. It's absolutely breathtaking, and the most perfect spot I have ever sipped my morning coffee. Second, the food—mostly vegetarian and grown on the property—is some of the best I've ever eaten. And third, there's no judgment. It's full of people who are there to better themselves. I'm well aware that Esalen may not be for everyone, and it shouldn't be confused with a high-end spa. It's really anything *but* a spa. I'd call it more of a glamping experience, sort of. Sure, you can get a massage, but the prevailing idea is to tune in to yourself, your feelings, and what's holding you back from living the life you want to live. You must enter with an open mind. When I visited for the first time, it was clear that I had some friends with whom I could share this place and others who, if they came, would likely never leave their room, as they dread the smell of patchouli—and it was everywhere. I get that. But for me, Esalen was a beautiful place for reflection and seeking answers.

On my first trip to the center, I stayed in a beautiful home that looked as if it had dropped out of the sky and landed on the edge of a cliff overlooking the sea. Seven women I had never met before were sharing the house with me, and we got to know one another during the week we were there.

Esalen is all about stripping down, literally and figuratively. I was never comfortable being in the buff in front of other people. I'd hide in the changing room or in a bathroom stall at the gym. I'm just not a big naked person. I don't want to see other people undressed, and I don't want them to see me undressed. So when I learned that there would be public nudity in the natural hot springs at the Institute, I knew I would never go there. The other women staying in the house went a couple of times a day, however. They were always raving about how free they felt, how healing the springs were, and how the views were so spectacular. Admittedly, I grew curious. Not enough to check it out au naturel, of course, so the first time I went to the springs I wore my bathing suit. I decided to go in the dark of night so no one could see what I was wearing. If you're the only person wearing a bathing suit in a tub full of naked people, you can become as self-conscious about that as you would if you were naked. It goes over like a fart in church. While the pools were beautiful and I was proud that I'd forced myself to go, the experience wasn't especially comfortable. What I will never forget, though, was the full moon that night and the sound of the ocean waves crashing against the shore. It was truly peaceful.

At dinner one night, I met a guy who asked me out on a date ... at Esalen. I didn't see that coming. Anyway, we made a plan to meet the next day to go on a hike. When the time came, however, I was in the middle of a class, and there was no way to reach him. Cell phones don't work at Esalen; there's no signal. I'm not sure whether that's by design or default, but either way, I was going to be a no-show. I was getting stressed out about the situation when I realized that I wasn't at Esalen to meet guys or to go on dates—I was there to work on me. I was annoyed that I felt guilty about standing him up. That's when I decided to let go of everything that was out of my control. Sure, in different circumstances I would have loved to go on that date, but this was neither the time nor the place.

After six days together, the eight of us at the cliff house had all grown very close. It had been a very relaxing and eye-opening week of learning and contemplation. We had bonded tremendously, taking turns sharing stories of our lives while sipping tea and watching the dramatic crashing waves below. The others were determined to help me "get over" my modest New England ways. This group of women helped me believe that I could get rid of my bathing suit. They were cheering for me to have the whole experience. On the last night we were there, the girls pushed me to join them in true Esalen fashion—naked at the hot springs, underneath the beautiful starry sky.

While it was dark at the baths, the lights were on in the foyer where you take off your shoes and drop your towel. The girls had gone ahead of me while I mustered up the courage to let go of my last bit of cover. I never felt so attached to terry cloth. I felt like Linus and his blanket, terrified to leave mine behind. Just as I had finally gathered the intestinal fortitude to hang up my towel, I turned around and saw the guy I was supposed to meet the day before—in all his glory.

"Hey, what happened to you? I waited for you," he said, standing there unclothed yet looking happy to see me. Very happy.

I was mortified. I immediately crossed my arms to cover up, but it was too late. I felt very awkward. I couldn't have scripted a bigger nightmare moment. This was exactly why I never liked being naked. What if *you* were nude and bumped into someone you had just stood up? I didn't really want to stay there making small talk. I wanted to run away as fast as I could. I threw my head into my hands and looked away.

"I can't have this conversation right now. I'm sorry," I cried over my shoulder, scurrying past him toward the tub. Thankfully, he was just leaving, so I didn't have to endure his getting into the tub with me and the other girls. I jumped in, naked and proud that I had broken that barrier. With the help of the other women, I'd pushed myself to do something I never thought I would do. And, as it turned out, it was nice. Everyone was very supportive and understanding. I liked feeling such a strong bond to these women. There really is something about being in the company of strangers that allows you to be free. Esalen is a pretty damn good place to embrace that feeling.

As I mentioned, the center offers a variety of courses during your stay, but for the most part, before you arrive, you choose one general course to attend throughout. I signed up for a five-day raw foods class. All eight of us ladies had committed to the same course. A chef came to our house and showed us how to prepare meals in which nothing is heated above 100° Fahrenheit. The chef was known all over the world for his incredible healing ways with food. He had worked for many people with terminal illnesses and had seen and performed miracles through his food preparation. His stories of these cures were astonishing. I came to call him the Wizard of the Woods of Big Sur, not only for his magical powers but also because he actually looked like a wizard. He stood about four foot eight, with a gigantic smile and brightly shining eyes. He had a full head of wiry gray hair that stood straight up like a gnome's. He was gentle, kind, and spiritual, and seemed to have so many answers locked up inside his head. Our conversations were purposeful, meaningful, and everlasting. We talked a lot about the power of food and of placebos. Was the healing he did for people truly about the food alone, or was it their mindset? We have an incredible power to heal ourselves of just about anything with the right tools. It was my opinion that his presence alone would have had a powerful impact on anyone. He certainly had an impact on me.

Once I'd implemented my new raw-food diet, the toxins began making their way out of my system. On the sixth day of that diet, I found myself doubled over in pain. I was unable to walk or stand. It felt like I needed to go to the emergency room. I was lying on the floor of the room where our classes were held. The Wizard knelt beside me and gently whispered, "These are all of the negative emotions leaving your body. Let me help you move that energy."

At that moment I was willing to let him do anything to relieve my suffering. He felt around my midsection and asked if it hurt there. It did. As I cried out in pain, he began rubbing his hands together and then slowly waving them over my body. I'd heard about Reiki but had never tried it before; it's an interesting system, in that the practitioner never actually touches your body. The Wizard's hands hovered over the areas that hurt, and through his wizardly ways, he succeeded in easing my excruciating pain. In fact, when I finally stood up, I felt much better. I joined our cooking class, and by the end, I was feeling better than I had in as long as I could remember. The next day, I was completely pain-free. It felt as though I had been through an exorcism. The chef truly was a wizard (my Dumbledore), and I felt like Harry Potter. The "slithering" darkness was gone. After a full week at Esalen, I began to feel as though so many of my ghosts had been vanquished by the Wizard, by the work he led me through and that we had done together. I was ready to harness my magic—or, at the very least, try to.

When I left Esalen, I drove up to San Francisco. I was going to visit with Mindy, Heather, Laila, Gina, and Ceci. Ceci and Mindy are both originally from Oregon; however, I met Ceci on my first day of real estate school in Manhattan, when I was around twenty-five years old. She then went into get her Masters in social work and then decided to go to clown school. No, really. A lot of my close friends are hysterically funny, and Ceci is one of them. She started doing improv theater and studying humor and comedic timing. She loved it so much that she went to actual clown school. When we met, she was dating a man that we all referred to as Fat Meltin', a playful twist on his real name. We called him that because he had discovered the Atkins diet and was losing tons of weight—which was incredible, because he ate chicken wings and ranch dressing all the time. If I had been on that diet, I'm certain the effect would have been the exact opposite. He was in commercial real estate and lived in New York City. To give you an idea of how fun-loving my friend Ceci is, the first time she flew from Oregon to see Fat Meltin' in New York, she brought a Wonder Woman outfit with her to wear for Halloween. The plane she took was full of rugby players headed to a tournament. Ceci, who's a lot like Forrest Gump, always finds herself in outrageous and unpredictable situations, and this one was no different. She began partying with the boys. About halfway through the flight, she said, *I've got a surprise for you guys.* She grabbed her bag, disappeared into the bathroom, and emerged to run up and down the aisle, arms outstretched, wearing the best Lynda Carter–era Wonder Woman suit you've ever seen. Ceci nailed it. Now, this was long before 9/11, when the rules of flying were a lot more relaxed. The rugby team loved it, and so did Fat Meltin', who met her at the airport. All the fellas were begging her to forget about the man she came to New York to see and join them instead. I absolutely love her free spirit and the joy she expresses in everyday life. It's contagious—at least, I was counting on it to be.

Ceci and Fat Meltin' were together for a while. They lived a few blocks away from me in the city in a big, beautiful loft—an apartment that was much bigger than mine. In fact, they did everything in a big way. When I would go to their apartment, Ceci would say, "Help yourself to some wine. We just bought that case at the Sotheby's rare wine auction." Okay, first, free alcohol? Count me in. And second, top-notch vintage? Now we were speaking my language.

Anyway, Fat Meltin' wasn't going to be present at this get-together in San Fran; it was ladies only. Each of my gal pals was funnier, wittier, and happier than the last. I couldn't wait to see them and for them to see me. I hadn't been "me" for some time.

It was a picture-perfect California day. I rolled down the windows and turned up the radio. I was on a super high. Was it the raw foods? The nakedness? The revelation of my weaknesses? The Reiki? It didn't really matter what got me there—it mattered that I was there. I felt the most optimistic I had been since before I got married. I had renewed energy and hope that I would not only survive this period in my life but actually come out of it better than ever. No more loser lenses for me; I had put those down once and for all. I knew I would find love again, have children, and manifest my dream life. I was able not only to see it but also to feel it. I was ready to usher in this new beginning. It was perfect timing too; as I was driving there, I knew these were the ideal people to celebrate my new outlook on life with. The next three days were full of laughter, crazy antics, more laughter, and shared hopes for the future. The weekend was such a success that we vowed to come together as a group as often as we could.

CHAPTER SIX

Better Homes and Gardens

Doubt kills more dreams than failure ever will.
—Suzy Kassem

MONTHS BEFORE I WENT TO ESALEN, I DID MY BEST TO approach the jungle of Manhattan with optimism but I couldn't always get there. I just wasn't ready. I imagined that at some point I would be interviewing some very well-qualified candidates to share dinner with, but I wasn't likely to be a fun date. There were sunny days and stormy days, all of which I needed to reconcile as they came. Neither lasted very long and it felt like a never-ending rollercoaster of emotional highs and lows. My first peek at the savage world outside, though, scared me to death. I'm certain that that was when I first turned to Ina Garten for support. Audiences love her for more than her celery-root remoulade. I, for one, was nourished by the steady diet of hope she fed me. I believed, because of her, that someday I too would live in a home surrounded by people I cherished. Her show, underneath all the deliciousness and calories, was really about celebrating loving relationships.

Because my friends all knew I was getting divorced, I heard every joke and one-liner there was on the subject. P. J. O'Rourke once said, "Staying married may have long-term benefits. You can elicit much more sympathy from friends over a bad marriage than you ever can from a good divorce." But sympathy, attempts at humor, and just about everything in between wasn't what I wanted. I just wanted to sit around the table and freely laugh again with my loved ones.

When you go through a divorce, it can be difficult for friends and family to know how to handle the changes that come with the process. Maybe they have a subconscious fear that it will rub off on them. Divorce is like death, and we all know what a conversation stopper that is. Many people are often at a loss for words or say the absolute wrong thing in a genuine effort to console, distract, encourage, or help you see some kind of upside, of which there is none. Of course, there are also those well-intentioned friends who might say things such as, "Well, at least you now have the whole bed to yourself" or "Don't be sad—he wasn't *that* great anyway." Oh sure, now you tell me.

I've been told that grief is a natural part of the process and, eventually, a positive part of the healing. I also remember reading a quote from Carl Jung that said, "Even a happy life cannot be without a measure of darkness, and the word *happy* would lose its meaning if it were not balanced by sadness." I can appreciate the wisdom now, and certainly the intentions of people who were less eloquent, but I couldn't then. The lesson here is that when you lose the future you were counting on, it can have a powerful ripple effect on everyone around you too. Divorce is never what we plan for when we say "I do," and it's not something your family and friends plan for either. Learning to cope is something you have to discover how to do together. A divorce is really a bit of a family affair.

If it's hard to talk with your inner circle during a time like this, imagine how hard it is to talk with any of the new men you may be meeting. What was worse than being at a loss for words about my situation was the way my home signaled things about me that weren't up for debate. When I got divorced, I really should have sold my loft and moved into a studio apartment. If a man owns a big, beautiful loft, it's attractive. When a single woman is the homeowner, it's a turnoff. Why? It's seen as straight-up competition. No man wants to feel less than. If I had moved into a studio, potential suitors would have felt like saviors, like knights in shining armor scooping me up and rescuing me from squalor. The knight always saves the damsel in distress from certain death, eternal sleep, and fire-breathing dragons, but never from a big, beautiful penthouse. And you thought only women fell under the spell of fairy tales! Men have bought into some of those notions too.

When you're of a certain age, I think your upbringing leads you to believe that your man should be big, strong, and brave, and he always has to be the breadwinner in the family. A woman's role is to support. It's a picture straight out of the 1950s, when women wore pearls and maintained perfect coifs and immaculately painted lips. The wife was always expected to have dinner ready and to look elegant when her husband came home from work. My father used to carry around an article he cut from a popular women's magazine about how to be a good wife. While it was meant to be a joke, and we all got a good laugh out of it, somewhere back in time, those rules and words were legit. They were practices to live by if you wanted a good marriage and a happy family. The article made a point to express how important it is for a wife to receive her husband correctly. This meant having a tidy home, bathed children, dinner in the oven, and a freshly baked dessert cooling on the counter. The wife had to be dressed well, have a feminine ribbon in her hair, be perfumed, and be ready to hand her husband his slippers and a drink to help him recover from his hard day at work. I think men wanted and needed to feel strong and very much like the head of the household. Of course, that's not necessarily the way things are today, but I believe most men still don't want to feel competitive in their relationships.

Even though my father was the primary earner in our family, my mom always worked part-time teaching French, Spanish, and piano. She also volunteered at various organizations and still had dinner ready for our family every night. While I'm definitely someone who can't sit still, my mom was always going a million miles an hour. My parents were an awesome team, something my dad always spoke of with great pride and affection. He stressed the importance of having a partner. And while he certainly believed a woman's place was in the home, he also wanted a wife who could take over and sail the ship if need be.

A lot of strong men and women have something I like to call Broken Bird Syndrome (BBS). They love to feel like they saved someone. They're especially drawn to vulnerable people who are needy. Will this person be forever loyal if you save them? Maybe that's the wish. Or maybe there's a sense of power they derive from being the rescuer. The problem is that desperate strays often bite—and how fair is it to rescue a wounded bird that's free and then cage it and keep it? Is that even rescuing? It's more like trapping.

Generally, people who are struggling aren't capable of loving with a full heart. There's too much fear and pain for them to be truly available. I don't think they're able to love themselves in their state, so it becomes virtually impossible for them to truly love you. Their struggle demands their full focus, and sometimes you can get in the way of their growth. It's not personal; they love you the best they can, albeit sometimes in a flawed way. There's always collateral damage after a battle. And sometimes it's impossible to bounce back, to trust, or to even want to help.

I was introduced to Big D through a friend. He lived in Hadley, Connecticut, and was a developer with buildings in Boston, Philadelphia, and various cities in Connecticut. He was blond and a little pudgy—not the look I'd ever gone for in the past—but he was hilarious. I'm a sucker for a wicked sense of humor, so the laughter tipped the scales in his favor. At the time, I didn't really trust anyone. If I was dating someone and it had gotten beyond the first few dates, I needed to know that we saw eye to eye on certain things, especially on financial matters. He didn't have to be rich, but he needed to understand money. I wasn't looking for someone who carried a lot of debt or made irresponsible financial decisions.

Big D fell head over heels within just a couple of dates; like a lesbian, minus the U-Haul and cats. He was constantly professing his admiration for me, saying things such as, "I can't believe we're together"— which often then made me think the same thing, only not the way he thought it. On our second date, we went for drinks at a bar in Back Bay, near Boston Common. It was around the holidays, and the city was full of festive decorations and cheer, meaning drunk Bostonians singing Christmas carols up and down Beacon Street. As we sat sipping our cocktails, D kept telling me how lucky he was to have found me. And then he threw his hands up in the air and said, "Get everyone in the bar a drink on me! I'm celebrating this beautiful woman." While I was flattered, I didn't feel the same way he did. It was too much, too fast. We barely knew each other, which made me hesitant and a little confused. Everywhere we went, he was, well, *big*. When the valet brought the car around, he handed him a hundred-dollar bill. If the maître d' walked us to our table, he handed that person a hundred dollars too. Okay, so it was the holidays; maybe D wanted to play Santa. He certainly had the belly, which left me wondering if he had a "dick do"—that's when, as some might say in the South, a man's belly sticks out farther than his dick do. But there was something about all of that flash and cash that didn't feel right to me. Not that I don't believe in love at first sight, but the chemistry must be there. I'm not saying there was no spark between us—there was. And, slowly, I began to feel something for D that surprised me. What I fell for was the way D liked me. I was a little suspicious at first, but I'll admit that it was nice to feel worshipped. (Now I understand why Elizabeth Taylor got married eight times.) I didn't, however, need to be saved. There's a difference.

Big D wanted to save someone, anyone, and it disappointed him that I wasn't a willing participant. When he tried to pay for a trip to Aspen, I was reluctant to let him cover everything. We were just testing the waters. I didn't expect him to take care of all the expenses. I insisted on paying for my own plane ticket. When I playfully asked if he was going to embarrass himself on the slopes and whether I'd see pizza or French fries as he headed down the mountain, he recoiled.

"Why, are you a good skier?" he asked.

"I can ski," I said, knowing I would likely be a bombardier compared to his technique. I could hear in his voice that it freaked him out. *Are you going to be better than me?* I guess we were going to find out.

An hour later, he canceled the trip.

When I teased him about skiing, I could see his insecurity and panic surface. This funny, confident guy suddenly turned into a scared little boy. My intention wasn't to hurt his feelings so much as to bring on a friendly challenge. To me, it was all fun and games, something meant to spice things up a little bit. To him, not as much. At the time, it felt so frustrating. I needed to be who I was, not who someone else wanted me to be. I couldn't and wouldn't make myself smaller for him, and he needed that; he needed to be Big D and to run the show. I thought it was really weird that he pulled the plug on our trip. As surprised as I was, I also began to recognize that Big D didn't like to be challenged—in any way.

The first time D came to my apartment in New York, I could immediately see it was threatening to him. The expression on his face told the whole story. He looked like a deflated balloon. I'd gotten used to this reaction, because the apartment certainly was dramatic. I was hoping and waiting for the day that someone would walk in and be unfazed. *That* was the guy I was looking for—someone who wasn't intimidated by where I lived. Someone who saw the whole me and was good with that. I was looking for a partner, not a patron.

As big as D was, he couldn't handle anyone else being bigger. When he started spending more time in New York, it became obvious to me how fragile he was. If we had dinner with clients, it always turned into a contest of some sort. Who drove the most exciting car? Who had the bigger home? Who was wearing the nicer watch? None of this stuff mattered to me, but it surely did to him. And more times than not, the outcome was not in D's favor.

After Aspen was canceled, so was our relationship. I didn't want to be with someone who didn't need me. I wanted to know my role, and I needed to feel important. Big D did make me feel important, but he didn't make me feel needed.

And I need to be needed. It's part of my caretaker DNA.

And it's part of suffering from Broken Bird Syndrome.

I only came to realize that I suffer from BBS after collecting enough birds. I'm attracted to dynamic people who can entertain me. I like characters who aren't run-of-the-mill. To be blunt, I like a little crazy. The spicier the better. But what sometimes happens with this is that I find myself involved with too much spice. At the end of the day, crazy is crazy—yet we still worship those broken birds in society. Look at Marilyn Monroe and Princess Diana. Both seemed tortured and alone. Marilyn, struggled with depression and substance abuse, unable to feel truly loved. Princess Diana struggled with bulimia, lack of self-esteem, and lack of love from her husband, Prince Charles, who'd never stopped loving Camilla Parker Bowles. What is it about us and our culture that compels us to give our hearts to people who are broken? I can't imagine what these women must have endured. On some level they were the most beloved women in history, yet they both died tragically, and, many would say, lonely.

For me, taking care of a broken bird helps me feel less broken. My best friend growing up was crippled by shyness, but when we were together, she didn't suffer from timidity. She felt safe, and that made a huge difference in how she responded to the world. I enjoyed giving her that security. Sure, it made me feel important, but it also helped my friend grow. When you have these types of relationships, you hope that by changing the other person's path there will be a level of loyalty that never goes away. But that isn't always the case. Sometimes people get what they need and then move on. Fixing the broken bird is intimate and fulfilling, but birds are meant to fly. If you aren't willing to take the risk of someday having that bird spread its wings, then don't rescue the bird.

Not long ago I came to the realization that BBS is not too far off from the codependent triangle; it's just more disguised. Here's what I mean: the codependency triangle points downward at the role of the victim; at the top are the roles of rescuer and persecutor. The victim is always in a state of "poor me." The rescuer says, "Let me help you," and the persecutor says, "It's all your fault." The rescuer is usually an enabler, the persecutor has a need to be in control, and the victim feels helpless. A person can shift from one role into another, depending on where they are in the moment. If you're a caretaker—a rescuer—like me and don't understand your limits and boundaries, however, you can overextend yourself and eventually run out of steam. Often the person you're rescuing doesn't understand when you're on empty, and they push back. They can feel resentment and frustration that you stopped helping. This can cause you to resent their lack of gratitude for all the help you've given them already. This can cause drama on both sides. When things got dramatic for me and I wasn't able to do more to salvage the relationship no matter how much I loved it, I would feel guilty and sad. After that came the inevitable climb back up and the belief that I could save this—I could do more.

A friend of mine acted this out with a stray dog. The dog had no collar and looked as if he hadn't been fed for quite some time. My friend invited him into his home. He named the dog Mutthead. Mutthead was thrilled to be inside and out of the cold. He made himself comfortable by the fire while my friend cooked him a hamburger and some rice. After the hearty lunch, my friend, who lived in a no-pet building in New York and so couldn't keep Mutthead, called the local dog pound. When the person from the dog pound drove up the driveway, my friend went to bring the dog to the door. Not so fast. You see, Mutthead liked the warm fire and the delicious food he'd eaten. He had no intention of leaving. When my friend reached out to grab him, Mutthead bit him on the hand. We dubbed this the "desperate stray syndrome." It's an affliction that affects animals and, yes, sometimes people.

I will always be inclined to help people. It's my nature. But I learned to be aware that there's a big difference between helping someone to help themselves and diving in and taking over for them. When that happens, you run the risk of being bitten. My challenge was identifying the difference, which all goes back to connecting with myself. The more time I spent relating to myself, the less distracted I was by trying to fix others. You know the saying "Those who can, do; those who can't, teach"? Clearly, I was leading that parade. I had to stop the noise, the distractions, and the constant urge to dive into someone else's challenges and just face my own issues.

I've known that I'm codependent for as long as I can remember. My therapists make it a point to remind me too.

For many years, I found myself surrounded by gay men, because they're generally so engaging. I was investing in relationships in which there were no roles and no expectations. These men entertained me, made me laugh, and always made me feel special—not to mention the fabulous birthday gifts, the help with my hair, and the fun gossip. The point is, they weren't threatening or dangerous in any way. They didn't want anything from me, and, more important, didn't need anything from me. They just liked me for exactly who I was. They provided a soft landing for me when I was the one who felt like a broken bird. For a long time, those were safest relationships in my life.

There were definitely times I would travel with my handsome gay bestie and no one would hit on me. It took me a long time to realize I was walking around with kryptonite. Why would Superman come near me when his nemesis was by my side? Even so, those friendships filled my emotional bucket in ways my relationship with my ex never did. And I was so grateful for that, especially while I was healing my wounded heart.

CHAPTER SEVEN

The Summer Rental

*The women I love and admire for their strength and grace did
not get that way because shit worked out. They got that way
because shit went wrong and they handled it. They handled
it a thousand different ways on a thousand different days,
but they handled it. These women are my superheroes.*
—ELIZABETH GILBERT

*B*Y THE SUMMER OF 2004, I WAS OFFICIALLY BACK ON THE MARKET, even though I had hardly dated and wasn't really sure I was ready to in any big way. I still had a lot of healing to do, and I knew in my soul I wasn't up for anything serious, but I was open to testing the waters.

Is there any better place than the beach to recharge and renew during the hot New York City summers? Not that I'm aware of. So I did what most young, single, successful Manhattan women do—I went in on a share house with sixteen people in the Hamptons, and just a couple of blocks from one of the most beautiful beaches I've ever seen. A share house is when a group rents a home together, usually a nice house with a pool and several bedrooms. Depending on your arrangement, you either spend every weekend or every other weekend of the season there. Some shares include your own room; others require that you share a room. In our house, no one had their own room. Since we were all single, we were encouraged to bring friends. The room allocation was made on Friday nights when everyone showed up and we knew how many attendees there were.

The people I connected with that summer were all really nice and well on their way in life. Everyone in the house was incredibly warm, well-educated, and fun. And I certainly needed a dose of that in my life.

We'd take turns cooking and making the house feel like home. We threw big dinner parties, and people would bring their friends. We would set up a long table in the living room, but sometimes we had to combine several tables and place them outside on the terrace. There were already sixteen people in the house, so with friends, it was common to have over twenty-five people.

The dinners always started the same way: newcomers had to sing for their supper. We would go around the table and ask everyone to share their most embarrassing story. This always evoked a lot of good laughs and some really witty comments, and it set the tone for a very enjoyable weekend. It was a wonderful icebreaker that always led to unexpected places. I may have shared my naked Big Sur experience. I can neither confirm nor deny.

I made a commitment to myself that I wouldn't wallow in my pain that summer. Any sulking was to be done only in the ocean. I just wanted to have a good time. I didn't want to talk about anything having to do with the demise of my marriage. I needed to breathe in the fresh air, smell the ocean breezes, and feel the warm sunshine on my body. I chose not to drink a lot either.

I was looking to sort out my emotions and knew that drowning them in alcohol wouldn't be productive. I also wanted to keep my emotions completely contained. I didn't want to share how I'd been feeling with anyone. Not even a little bit. And there's no question that alcohol isn't conducive to that degree of masking. Faking it till you make it sometimes really works, so I put on a big smile, adopted a cheery outlook, and decided that I was game for anything. Underneath it all, though, I was a little overwhelmed by the need to go with the flow of everyone else's plans. The truth is, I'm not that flexible. I can be pretty opinionated about scheduling and how things are executed. Even so, I knew it was neither the time nor the place to be the leader. That summer was about getting in tune with myself and not necessarily taking care of others, as I so often did. When it came to dating, I was open to the idea, but I definitely wasn't looking for anything serious or heavy. "Light and easy" was my summer mantra.

Frankly, I was in no shape for anything more.

We all got together in Manhattan to meet before we kicked off our first official weekend out East. (That's what you call the Hamptons when you're living in Manhattan.) That was the first time I met a guy I call Dickey. He was very cute, but I could tell he wasn't necessarily the cool guy growing up. I like smart guys, and a little geek never turned me off, though too much nerd wasn't my thing. I remember meeting him and thinking, *My parents would love this guy.* My father always told me it was a big mistake to only go for the outgoing type, the one who's always the life of the party or tearing up the dance floor. He said, "It's the ones watching from the sidelines who make the best husbands." After my marriage fell part, I think I finally understood what that meant. History would not repeat itself—not that summer, or ever again.

I grew up in a very conservative home and community, where it was frowned upon to be promiscuous. I was told that bad girls slept around. My mother always said that men would never want a girl who was all used up. She said that girls like that would quickly develop reputations for being loose, and while they might have had a steady flow of dates, that made them less desirable as wife material. Boys, on the other hand, were encouraged to get out there to sow their oats. Boys will be boys. My dad was, like a lot of parents, biased in that he gave boys more freedom than girls, but, to his credit, he was always very vocal about being respectful to women and never, ever doing anything that would directly hurt a woman's feelings or self-esteem. I never liked the disparity and always thought that if women save themselves for their wedding night, how the hell do they know what they're looking for? It's like buying a house you've never been in.

In our family, if you had a long-term boyfriend and it was clear that you would marry each other eventually, my parents might (and that's a big *might*) look the other way if you were sleeping together. You could get a pass for just one boyfriend, and only if you'd been dating for several years, but that was it. So I was never the loose girl; I cared about what other people might think, and I appreciated the message my parents instilled in me, even if I didn't agree with it. I knew that if I wanted to move on from my ex, I was going to have to live a little. I'd have to get out of my comfort zone, which meant dating, and all that comes with it. A southern comedian I know always shares some advice her aunt gave her: "The only way to get over one man is to get under another." Clearly, our families were very different. It feels like the truth may lie somewhere in between. But this much I knew: I needed to move past that first encounter and not be weighed down by the next. In addition to vowing not to get seriously involved with anyone, I also vowed to get out of my head—basically, to just stop thinking so much. My only goal was to have some much-needed fun!

And that's where Dickey comes back into the story. He and I started hanging out almost immediately. In real estate, sometimes location and timing matter more than the property itself, and that's what Dickey was all about for me. He could get out of work early on Fridays, around 1:00 p.m., so that made us driving buddies. I had a car and would meet him outside his office in Midtown; he drove out to the house while I worked. We would get to the house well ahead of the others, so we'd play tennis, go for a run on the beach, or have an early cocktail, and, yes, by the middle of summer we had gotten romantic. It had been many years since I'd been with another man. I wasn't sure how I would feel about it. Truth be told, it felt amazing—freeing, actually. Freedom is a beautiful thing, isn't it?

I wanted to keep it casual, with no expectations and no commitments. Thankfully, he agreed. I told him from the start that I was a little bit broken and that this would be nothing more than a summer fling. By design, I didn't get into my story at all. No one wants to hear about your tragic breakup—it's not an aphrodisiac. Ever. At the time, I was like a home with really good bones that needed a lot of work, and I was willing to make a modest investment to spruce things up a bit because I knew I would be flipping the place anyway. Perhaps sooner than expected.

It didn't take me long to discover there was a darkness around Dickey. You see, I'm an inquisitive woman by nature. I love asking people a lot of questions, and then I listen and watch carefully. I think it's the best way to get to know someone. I do this all the time with buyers and sellers. The more questions I ask, the better I understand their needs. It's important to be a good listener and a good observer, because people will always show you who they are. You just need to be patient.

Curious about who I was spending my weekends with that summer and bored of small talk, I conducted a similar inquisition with all of the boys in the house to see what they were made of. It was always late at night and usually after they'd had way too many drinks, so their defenses were down, which meant that they gave me all I needed to know … and then some. I could probably have worked for the CIA if I hadn't taken my chosen path. Whenever the guys would see me, one would usually say to the others, "Don't get pulled into the Holly web. She'll make you spill your deepest, darkest secrets." It's true; I was like a late-night Barbara Walters. It was my game to see what these boys were really afraid of and what was holding them back.

I've never had a high tolerance for small talk. I really can't stand that first-date routine of endless questions about where you grew up, your family, and, yes, your past relationships. Don't you wish we could put all of that into a dossier and send it ahead before the first date? I'd much rather find something meaningful to talk about. A topic that might evoke a debate is always good. Anything that creates deeper engagement than "So, what do you do for a living?" Oh, I'm sorry. I'm sleeping already.

Listening to Dickey talk that summer I realized he had some deep-seated issues, and they concerned me. I noticed how he loved to toy with me, sometimes doing things he no doubt knew would hurt my feelings. There were times when he'd bring other girls to the house, shooting me a look to see if I reacted. I let him know his behavior wasn't escaping me. I wasn't jealous—I had no reason to be—but I did feel that it was more than impolite. I may not always notice when someone is intentionally trying to ruffle my feathers, but I always notice rudeness. It was disrespectful. He liked making me feel uncomfortable. While I was under no illusion that we were anything other than friends with benefits, I knew I'd never parade another man in front of him. I thought we were friends, and why would you want to make your friend feel uncomfortable other than to feel powerful yourself? He deliberately tortured me. It was on a small scale, but I didn't have that game in me. If he wasn't respecting me as a friend, it was painfully obvious that he would never truly respect me as a girlfriend. While I enjoyed his company on the weekends, I knew he wasn't great boyfriend material. I wasn't interested in being mistreated, especially not by him. I asked nothing from him except that we keep it simple. I wasn't looking for drama on any level, and certainly not in my dating life. This seemed like an attempt at causing exactly that.

I decided to spend the rest of the summer studying him. It was a bit of a science experiment. And the more I watched, the less I liked. If you're a *Seinfeld* fan, you know that Jerry always found something that turned him off about the women he dated. Maybe she had big hands, ugly feet, or a funky smell. That's how I felt the longer I observed Dickey. So why did I keep seeing him? I feel so shallow admitting it, but he was tall, hot, and a great tennis partner. But let's be real: Who wants a bad home even if it's in a good location? Unless you're willing to do a complete teardown, and I wasn't. There was no need to; I was living in New York City.

When summer came to an end, everyone from the house got together in the city for a charity event at the Gramercy Park Hotel. Overall, it had been an awesome three months, and this was our last hurrah. A group of us were standing near the bar when Dickey made his way over. I looked at him and softly whispered, "You've got everybody fooled. They believe that you're just a nice guy, but I see you. You're a wolf."

He shot me a wicked grin—the same one the Big Bad Wolf might have given Little Red Riding Hood before he ate her.

Did he think I would fall for that?

Was he going in for the kill?

Not this time.

"I know who you are," I said. "I see you! The real you."

It was fine to play with the wolf, but I was never going to stay with the wolf.

Shortly after Dicky arrived, his sister joined us for drinks. I had met her several times during the summer and liked her, but much as I don't enjoy chitchat on first dates, I had very little desire to engage in small talk with her. When the bill finally came, Dickey turned to me and said, "Can you put that on my tab?"

Okay, so I knew he was a cheap bastard. I'd seen that behavior all summer long.

I can't stand that!

Game over. We were through.

I suppose Dickey served a purpose. When you find yourself back on the market, you need a transition person. Dickey was never a real contender, but he most certainly helped me turn a corner. He was like the brownstone my clients moved into, the one with all the mosquitos that made it clear to them they needed a break from the city. When they returned, they found the perfect place. The important thing with transition dating is that you remember *not to buy.*

STOP.

Hear what I'm saying.

You're in temporary housing.

Don't get lazy and concede or make unnecessary sacrifices you'll regret later.

As with real estate, once you're displaced from your last home, you just rent until you can move into your next home.

To be certain, I would have run in the other direction if I had dated anyone who truly was a contender that summer. I needed to know that the first person I was with post-divorce, even casually, had enough flaws that they never had a chance of winning my heart. Sometimes in real estate you tour a home you know you won't buy. There's a kind of safety in the fact that it's out of your price range, it's not in the neighborhood you prefer, or that it will take too much work to fix up. I look at these tours as education or entertainment. Either way, they rarely turn into sales.

CHAPTER EIGHT

Mi Casa Es Su Casa

*If you want something you've never had, you must
be willing to do something you've never done.*
—ANONYMOUS

DESPITE HAVING LOADS OF FUN DURING MY SUMMER ESCAPADES,
I must confess that I also spent a lot of time bawling my eyes
out. I mostly cried on Sunday nights. The moment I walked into my
empty apartment, I burst into tears. It was such a contrast from all the
camaraderie I'd enjoyed at the beach.

Once, right after I left the share house, I began sobbing on my way
home. There were so many times when I felt my emotions building
up that I had to tell myself to hold it together for just a couple more
hours. Then I could get into the car and cry all I wanted. I didn't want
to break down in front of any of my housemates, and this time was
no exception. The faucet opened wide the minute I left the driveway,

letting all the sorrow flow out after forty-eight hours of wearing that smiling mask. It was exhausting. My tears caused me to somehow lose my way; this was before GPS, so I had to stop on the side of the road and ask a woman for directions. I had no idea how I'd gotten myself so lost. The woman's eyes widened as she looked at me. She seemed extremely concerned and a bit frightened. As I drove away, I looked at myself in the mirror to see what was the matter. My mascara and makeup was everywhere—and I mean *everywhere*. My happy mask had literally melted all over my face. Laughing and crying, I drove myself back to the apartment that never felt like home.

Yet no matter how lonely I felt on those nights, I did have one constant companion: pain. It was there like an unwanted guest who never gets your cues to leave. As many times as you say, "Well, that was fun, but I've got to turn in now," that bastard just won't go. So there I sat in my pajamas waiting for the pain to retire for the evening.

Some Sunday nights I would lie in bed and think, *What if?* It's such a dangerous game to play. *What if I never slept again? What if I never had kids? What if I couldn't do my job anymore? What if I couldn't pay my mortgage? What if I had to move home with my parents?* And, finally, *What if I were eaten by wild dogs and not found for days?* Or, wait, maybe that was just Bridget Jones. But still, it could happen, couldn't it?

When you start relating to Bridget Jones, it's time to go to therapy again.

I had already started seeing Jane by then, which was helping me a lot. But turning the lens inward was brutal. She forced me to look at everything, everyone, and every excuse I had in my arsenal. She also helped me see my distractions for what they were. I was looking from the inside out.

When searching for a new home, clients sometimes come to me with what I refer to as their "best-of" lists. They rattle off all the high-lights from the properties we've toured, like the wraparound terrace with views of the park, the beautiful finishes in that loft downtown, and the brand-new amenities in the newly built Midtown high-rise, saying, "*This* is what I want." It's their greatest hits, like a compilation of all the most amazing songs. When it comes to apartment hunting—and partner hunting—it's a pipe dream. No musical artist is perfect enough to have every hit on the Top 100 charts. It's just not realistic. Likewise, the chances of one person possessing every attribute—being six foot two, incredibly handsome, insanely funny, charming, worldly, entrepreneurial, athletic, crazy intelligent, artistic, good with numbers, a champion masseuse, *and* a world-renowned chef, for instance—are pretty slim. The same goes for a home. It's unrealistic to take all the "best of" qualities you've ever seen and think that they can all be found under one roof. It's important to dream, but it's also important to understand that there's no such thing as perfection. If you look only for that, you'll never be content. More likely, you'll be homeless and alone.

The reality is, to quote the Rolling Stones, "You can't always get what you want."

But as Mick would have you believe, you get what you need.

Which is better?

Sometimes we get one or two things on our list, sometimes none. Rarely, if ever, do we get a life built to spec. Nobody gets the best of everything. There are no perfect houses any more than there are perfect children, perfect parents, or perfect partners. You have to pick the items that are most important to you and focus on them. And then, as I always tell my clients, let the rest go. When they do that, we can find them the ideal place to call home.

By the end of the summer I felt exhausted. Some people look forward to the fall because it's when they go from playtime back to real life, but I wasn't so happy about the change of seasons. I felt very disconnected after the party was over. Parties are great, but the next day, when you have to face those empty wine glasses and cigarette butts, it's no fun at all. What life was I going back to?

I didn't have anything to rush home for.

Jane lived through the Dickey experience with me. She knew the lack of respect he showed, and how I felt like a living, breathing bummer after that. I didn't really want to invest my time in a series of flash-in-the-pan boyfriends, dates, fuck buddies, or whatever. It took work to do that, and frankly, it wasn't filling my emotional tank.

So, what do you do when you're trying to rebuild a life?

According to Jane, you stay busy!

I started reaching out to people, trying to connect on some level, looking for anything that felt real or fulfilling. I called an old friend from boarding school who was working as a film director. He was very good-looking, smart, and fun to talk to. I think he thought I wanted more than good conversation, but I didn't. I wasn't ready for more.

One night over dinner, I told him I was thinking of leaving New York for a while. I was toying with the idea of living somewhere else, a foreign country perhaps. He looked at me and said, "What are you waiting for?" As in, what the hell was keeping me in New York City?

I didn't have an answer.

Outside of my career, there was nothing keeping me there at all. Maybe he was right. I decided to take a look at my options, not over-think things like I usually do, and just pull the trigger.

The next morning, I tallied up my frequent-flyer miles to see where they could take me. I had forty thousand miles, enough to get to Buenos Aires, a place I'd never been but had always wanted to visit. My ex and I had planned to go there a few years before we separated, but that was around the time the Argentinian economy had fallen apart. The span from 1998 to 2002 was considered the Argentine Great Depression, but it was around 2001 when the economic crisis really crippled the country. We were going to visit Esteban and his wife, Vicky, friends we knew from my ex's class at business school. Just two weeks before our expected departure, everything fell apart. There was a run on the banks, forcing the government to freeze accounts, which resulted in riots. Esteban told us not to come because conditions were too dangerous. He and Vicky are very generous people and wanted to show us a good time, but the turmoil would have prevented us from doing anything fun, so we canceled our trip.

When I met Esteban and Vicky, I adored them instantly. They were so warm, festive, and enthusiastic about New York. Their romance began the summer before Esteban came to the States. It was just months after they had fallen madly in love that he left the country to pursue his studies. Devastated that she might have lost him forever, Vicky shed many, many tears that first semester he was away. Esteban too was heartsick. He made a plan to surprise Vicky over Thanksgiving break. Without her knowing, he flew back to Argentina and called her from outside her home. They talked as if he were still in New York. When they hung up, Vicky broke down crying. She was overwhelmed by how much she missed him. Then the doorbell rang. When she opened the door, she was stunned to see Esteban standing there with a bouquet of flowers and a ring in his hands. He could see that she had been crying. At first, she wanted to kill to him. But things quickly progressed from a heated hello to a very spicy one, just the way Americans picture love in a Latin soap opera. The two were married months later.

Vicky is ten years younger than me, and also ten years younger than Esteban. She went from living with her parents to becoming Esteban's wife at twenty-one. I mean, who was I to judge? I had been just twenty-five!

We became fast friends with Esteban and Vicky. They had amazing energy and hearts as big as those of anyone I've ever met. Their family and friends were everything to them, and they would always so eloquently let you know how special you were to them. Vicky was hot, sophisticated and spicy with that "it" factor, that charisma that kept everyone laughing. Especially me. My ex and I did our best to play tour guides while they lived in the US. We showed them all our favorite spots around

New England. I took them up to my family's place by Cape Cod after graduation. We spent endless days riding bikes and taking long boat rides, and we showed them how to eat lobsters and clams, New England style. It was sad to see them return to Buenos Aires, but we promised to make our way down to visit them when we could.

Since then, the idea of traveling to Argentina had always been in the back of my mind. We'd hit the pause button back then, but I was eager to go now.

Esteban and Vicky were the only two people I knew in Argentina. When I called Vicky to ask what hotel I should book, she insisted that I stay at their apartment.

"No hotel, Chhhollee," she said with a beautiful, sexy accent that made her sound so much like Sofía Vergara. "Come to my apartment and we will figure it out." She was adamant. "*Mi casa es su casa.*"

I hung up thinking two things. First, I loved the way she said my name. It was as if she had merged the words *holy* and *challah*. And second, I was so appreciative of the invitation.

I secured my ticket and packed my bags, and, within twenty-four hours, I found myself on a nearly empty plane to Argentina.

I was both nervous and excited about my great adventure. The plane was empty mostly due to the fact that the Argentinian economy was still struggling. There were only a handful of passengers, seemingly all of whom were in the bar watching the Red Sox game before the flight. It looked as if the Sox were going to the World Series that year. By the time we got on the plane, we had all bonded, and I had promised that I would come visit several of them for a drink when we were in the air.

Once we were in flight, I popped around chatting with one person after another, and before I knew it, we were landing. Where did the ten hours go?

My decision to travel was spontaneous and not especially well thought out. I had clients to serve and homes to show. The good news was that the Manhattan real estate market was incredibly strong. And I had Morgan, my fabulous and trusted assistant. With his boots on the ground and my voice on the phone, we could get our clients to the finish line on any deal. Morgan and I planned to talk several times a day. He'd make all my calls, and we'd handle any hurdles together. If anyone asked me where I was, I'd simply say, "I'm here." Total truth, right?

It couldn't have worked out any better. Apartments were selling almost as quickly as we listed them. The market was hot, and the men in Argentina were even hotter. I guess you could say I had the privilege of closing deals on both continents (if I wanted to!).

We touched down at ten in the morning to the most spectacular day in Buenos Aires. The jacaranda trees were all in bloom, with the most beautiful purple flowers I'd ever seen. We don't often see that color purple in the Northern Hemisphere. It had been only a handful of minutes since my arrival, yet Argentina had already stolen my heart. I immediately understood why they call Buenos Aires the Paris of South America.

As soon as I arrived, Vicky and Esteban welcomed me like family. She took me to lunch at a charming restaurant in Palermo Soho, a hip, trendy shopping neighborhood downtown. Everything in Argentina was new to me—the smells, the atmosphere. Although Buenos Aires is a city, it felt soft and inviting. The use of materials was so organic and earthy. The beautiful wooden tables, the stone bar, the wrought iron fixtures, and the beamed ceilings in the restaurant were simply perfect. It's not often that I feel especially comfortable in a new environment. I usually have to move several times. Whenever I check into a hotel, I typically start the conversation with the clerk at the front desk by saying, "Show me the third room first." Yes, I'm that person—I want the best room, even if it takes three tries. Yet here I was, far from home, feeling an immediate calmness, as if I belonged. I was in a SoHo—just Palermo Soho. Already, everything seemed better. Some people call it running when you escape to a different locale. For me, it always felt like beginning again. While we sat outside under the beautiful trees, Vicky shared her own challenges with me. She had faced a significant one over the past few years. She told me about a surgery she'd had to remove a growth on her brain. She was suffering from severe headaches, worse than migraines, and no one could tell her why. They were debilitating; when one came on, everything had to shut down. She had to be in a dark room in complete silence until the headache passed. After she had the surgery, she felt like her life was paused. She wasn't sure about anything. She was living one day at a time.

It didn't take us long to discover that we were both at a crossroads in life. I was in emotional pain, and she was in constant physical pain. We didn't know it then, but cementing our new friendship would become the healing gift we both needed.

When I arrived in Argentina, I spoke enough Spanish to get by. My goal was to become conversational. I helped Vicky with her English, and she helped me improve my Spanish.

Vicky and I spent our days shopping, touring, eating wonderful authentic Argentinian food, and drinking lots and lots of delicious local wine. We talked endlessly about what we both wanted next in life. We wrote down affirmations and goals, keeping the list with us at all times so we could edit it as we went along. Vicky is a wonderful cook who spent time teaching me all about her culture. On most days, we'd stop in local shops to look for items to decorate her beautiful home. We'd often end up at the Four Seasons in Buenos Aires for a late lunch or cocktails. One day our conversation turned toward dating and men. I asked Vicky who her "celebrity hall pass" would be. This is a term I use with my married friends, meaning who would they choose if they had a pass to go out on just one date with a famous person.

"Robbie Williams," she said, with a big, toothy grin.

"*Robin* Williams?" I asked. I thought that was so random, but maybe hysterically funny, hairy men were her thing.

"No, no. Robbie Williams, the singer."

I had no idea who he was, but the mere mention of his name made Vicky blush. She sang a few bars of one of his songs, "Angels." It was his biggest hit. It sounded familiar, but I wasn't sure I knew it. And I really didn't have a clue what he looked like, so for me, there was no visual when she spoke of him.

One afternoon, as we drove up to the Four Seasons, we noticed a large crowd that stretched for blocks. The streets were clogged with people.

"What's going on?" I asked Vicky.

That's when we saw people holding signs that read, "We love you, Robbie!" There were throngs of screaming girls standing around a roped-off area.

"What should we do?" I asked.

"I still want my apple martini, so let's go in!" Vicky said. Oh yeah, she had the right idea. We drove her car right up to the door and handed the keys to the valet.

When we entered the hotel, much to our surprise, it was quiet and relatively empty. We couldn't understand why the fans were lined up outside when they could easily have walked in and sat at the bar.

We made our way to the restaurant, which was also completely unoccupied. Not a single person was seated there. Given the crowds outside, it felt awkward for the place to be so uninhabited. I'm not sure what stopped the others from venturing inside, but we certainly weren't going to be deterred. In life, you have to break away from the crowd to get what you want. If you believe in yourself enough, you'll always be able to saunter into the Four Seasons as if you belong there. Besides, I never really understood the point of screaming for someone's attention when they can't even hear you. We ordered our drinks and laughed about how random this all felt.

I could see that Vicky had spotted someone she knew out of the corner of her eye. At first I wasn't sure if this was good or bad. Her face looked frozen with fear. Suddenly she said, "Oh, my God. There he is! That's him!"

I turned around to look. "Who?" I asked.

"Robbie. That's Robbie!"

"Your hall pass, Robbie?"

"Yes! Shhhh. Oh, God. He's coming over here," she said.

And he did.

Robbie Williams walked over to our table, stopped, and said, "Hi, I'm Robbie. Do you mind if I join you for dinner?"

And just like that, Vicky's dream date was sitting with us.

Gotta love the power of manifestation. And hers apparently worked fast.

He was ruggedly handsome, with lots of tattoos. Not what I'd expected at all.

We played it cool, or at least as cool as we could. I could see Vicky was smitten. And I'll admit, he was damn sexy, in a bad-boy biker sort of way.

"I'm performing tonight. Would you two like to come as my guests?" he asked.

"We'd love to," I said before Vicky had a minute to second-guess herself.

Robbie ordered dinner while Vicky and I drank. Before leaving for his show, he said he would leave two tickets for us at will call.

When we picked up the tickets, we discovered that he wasn't actually performing a concert—he was the musical guest on a local late-night talk show. Somehow, we'd expected to be sitting in the front row of a sold-out arena, with backstage passes and the full VIP treatment. Instead, we were sitting twelve rows back from the stage in a small television studio, with no other access. We weren't groupies! Looking back, I don't know why we were so offended. I suppose we thought that since we'd had dinner together it was going to be a red-carpet experience. What we got were linoleum floors.

CHAPTER NINE

Sprawling Glacier Views

If you combine wine and dinner, the new word is winner.
—Anonymous

VICKY AND I BECAME INSEPARABLE. SHE KEPT ME LAUGHING AND entertained day after day. She's one of the most genuine, authentic, and kind people I've ever met. The love she exudes is so great, so strong, and so pure. There was no competitiveness between us as there some- times is among women, and that was refreshing. Her honesty, beauty, and transparency were like a breath of fresh air. If she was ticked off at me, she'd just say it.

"Chhhollee, don't be such a beech. I'm hating you right now," she'd say, just putting it all out there. It was like a splash of cold water in your face—kind of refreshing.

Vicky quickly became my touchstone. If I was going down a rabbit hole, she'd grab my hand and pull me out. "Chhhollee, come back to me, what are you doing?" She grounded me in a way I hadn't felt in years, if ever.

We didn't talk about Vicky's illness a lot, because there were no answers. The doctors weren't giving her any new information. She didn't know if having kids was possible or if it would kill her. She didn't know how long she might live. And she couldn't work until they knew more. She taught me to live life in the moment. So often we get mired in the past, and give credence to the stories we tell ourselves, even when they're not rooted in any shred of truth—stories such as we're not good enough, we're not smart enough, or we're not worthy of being loved by someone. Vicky didn't get stuck in the minutiae. When you're on the other side of brain surgery, the here and now is as real as it gets. She was living day by day, fighting for her life, and every second of every hour mattered. She put everything into perspective. Why would she waste time being angry, hurt, or negative?

I needed someone to see me—the real me, not the broken bird. Vicky saw *me*. And I saw her. And through it all, we forged a lifetime bond that could never be severed.

We spent weeks together, touring her beautiful city. She taught me to drink yerba mate at polo matches and to dance until dawn at the hottest clubs, and about the value of a disco nap and the joys of eating dinner at 11:00 p.m. We'd take long walks in the most magnificent parks. She'd show me the landmarks and historical places, and we'd talk about life, love, and everything in between. Perhaps the greatest gift we shared was laughter. We could find humor in just about anything. And I believe that laughter is the best medicine.

After several weeks, I grew restless and curious about the rest of Argentina. I also wanted to give Vicky and Esteban time to be on their own. Besides, no one likes a houseguest who overstays their welcome. What's the old Ben Franklin saying—"Guests, like fish, begin to smell after three days"? Not that I felt I was in their way, but I was there for adventure, and I wanted to see everything. That wouldn't happen if I stayed in Buenos Aires.

Google and even the Internet were not as widespread back then, so I didn't have the necessary access to research various destinations the way I would today. Luckily, Esteban had an aunt who was a local travel agent. She set me up with what appeared to be the perfect itinerary. My only directives were to show me the country as she would see it, and to book me into the nicest hotels. Admittedly, I'm a bit of a hotel whore; I love a luxurious environment, and I'm so much more comfortable in an aesthetically pleasing place. Since I'm in the business of service and beautiful surroundings, it's always inspiring to stay in a place that just nails it—the lighting, the music, the architecture, the interior design, the amenities, all a symphony of perfection. I return from such trips motivated to re-create those gorgeous experiences for our buyers in New York.

My first stop was El Calafate, a town that sits near the Southern Patagonian Ice Field in the province of Santa Cruz. Its main claim to fame is as the gateway to Los Glaciares National Park and the Perito Moreno Glacier, a popular hiking and sightseeing destination. I stayed at the Hotel Los Notros, about forty five minutes from the center of town. According to Esteban's aunt, the hotel is arguably one of the greatest not just in South America but in all of the Western Hemisphere too. Yeah, she may have overshot that one just a little bit. I'll admit, it was breathtaking, and the setting was very romantic. Let's just say, though, that the appraisal value on this place was inflated. A buyer like me has different criteria. There were no televisions, no phones, and only one computer for guests to check e-mail.

It also didn't take long to notice that there weren't a lot of single people around. I was definitely the only person going it alone. It was fucking Noah's Ark—everyone was traveling two by two. I was the freak solo act. This was definitely not the hotel for that type of sideshow. At this point I had half a mind to call Aunt Torture—I mean, Aunt Theresa—to let her know what I really thought about her "vacationer's paradise." It had obviously been many moons since her single days.

Everyone there was either a newlywed or celebrating a golden anniversary. They weren't really looking to chat with anyone else because they were having their own special moments. I felt like a unicorn at a horse farm. The worst part was that I was slated to be there for five nights. It was a constant reminder of exactly what I was missing. If I didn't know better, I would have thought that my worst enemy or an assassin who was plotting my death by humiliation had planned my trip instead of a friend's well-meaning travel-agent aunt!

Still, I was determined not to be self-conscious, even though it was painfully obvious that I was the third wheel everywhere I went. I was, after all, in one of the most beautiful places on earth. There was too much to do and see to let my marital status stop me from having a good time.

On my first day there, I went with a tour group to the terraces of the glacier. Our guide showed us how to use crampons—bear claw–like metal clamps that attach to the bottoms of your shoes to help keep you stable on the ice. We took pickaxes with us too. The axes came in handy when we got to our first rest stop, because we used them to crush ice for a cocktail. *Now* we were speaking my language.

When we got back to the hotel, I was ready for a good meal—I just didn't expect it to be seven courses! Considering the fast pace of New York, everything in the South American countryside seemed slow. But somewhere between courses five and six, I started to think of watching paint dry as an action sport compared to getting through this tasting menu alone. I actually jotted down on a napkin, "Note to self: bring a book with you tomorrow night! Or an icepick to stab your eye"; that's how long it was.

The endurance test continued on day two. As the sun rose, the tour guide announced that we were going to see the glacier by boat.

Okay, I thought I'd seen the glacier yesterday, but hey, I was game. So off I went with the group to the dock. We got on the ship and, yup, there it was, the glacier. This time, we were underneath it. Same glacier, different day. Oh, look, everybody is getting their picture taken in front of the massive mountain of ice. And guess who became Annie Leibovitz when someone had to snap pictures of the happy couples. My cold, lonely heart had seen enough.

By day three I was over the glacier. I mean, how many times can you look at a giant slab of ice? I'd seen it at sunrise, midday, and sunset.

Are you feeling me here?

Been there, done that.

It's big. It's frozen.

Move on.

I had just come off the most amazing experience with Esteban and Vicky in Buenos Aires, and had arrived in El Calafate feeling really good. But El Calafate went over like a debutante with pit stains. It's easy to say don't sweat the small stuff, but this was a big deal. I had traveled six thousand miles for an uplifting experience, and now my positive energy was melting faster than those icecaps.

A very kind couple I'd seen over the past few days could tell I wasn't having the greatest time. "Honey, what the hell are you doing here?" the husband asked in a deep southern drawl.

"I'm the poster child for taking bad advice from a travel agent. Look up 'disastrous vacations' and you'll find my picture there," I shot back.

The husband looked at me and said, "This is not what a young girl like you should be doing. Join us for dinner tonight."

I immediately accepted his invitation. I was genuinely excited to finally have people to talk to. To be honest, I would have dined with polar bears if there had been any wildlife on the glacier.

We met at the hotel bar, because they must have picked up on the fact that I was in dire need of some action. From where we were seated, we had a view of the open kitchen. I had been staring at one of the chefs there, as the food wasn't the only thing that was *muy caliente*. God, the men in Argentina were gorgeous, and this one was especially hot. After we'd had a drink or two or five, the chef made his way over to us. To be honest, he was really responding to the One, Two, Three. Oh, have I not mentioned the One, Two, Three?

That's a move I've had in my back pocket since I was a kid. In fact, it's so old that at this point I automatically kick into the One, Two, Three.

It goes a little something like this.

One: you lock eyes.

Two: you hold him in your gaze for a beat. When he looks at you, turn away quickly like you're embarrassed you got caught staring.

Three: look at him again. When he looks back, flash a great big smile like you just can't help it, like you can't fight it anymore.

That's it!

And if that baby is single or ready to schmooze, he'll be caught hook, line, and sinker, and you won't have to lift a finger.

The One, Two, Three is foolproof.

And voilà! There he was.

I hadn't even realized I was doing it, but before long Chef Calafate Cool was standing beside me, gorgeously at my service.

My southern dinner date loved it, and wanted to spice up this dish even more.

"Hey, buddy, where's the party tonight? Where do you and your friends go when you finish here?"

Had my life really come to a random stranger trying to hook me up?

I felt like I was suddenly in a scene from *Dirty Dancing*, because he'd ordered the chef to take me wherever he and his friends were going that night.

"Do you understand what I'm saying? I don't want you to leave this young lady here after work," he said.

All I could think was, *No one puts Baby in a corner.*

Under any other circumstances, I would have been horrified. I would have wanted to shrink into a small ball. But I knew he was right: I needed to get away from the couples and the lovers and have some fun. I didn't care who it was with, as long as they weren't another married couple. The chef seemed not to mind his customer's request and wore a smile like the cat that ate the canary. It seemed like this was a made-to-order that he could handle.

After saying a grateful goodbye to my southern gentleman friend and his wife, I was off. We piled into the chef's car and drove to El Calafate. Everyone had a cocktail in their hands as we made our way into the national park which separated the hotel from the city. I swore to myself that if one of the guys mentioned the fucking glacier to me, I would jump out of that moving car.

A few minutes into the trip, the driver turned off the headlights and kept driving. So, for a couple of seconds on that back road toward the city of El Calafate, I began to say goodbye to all the people I had loved.

Car games have never really been one of my favorite things, but I'd asked for action, and I supposed this was their idea of fun. As long as they didn't kill me, I decided I still preferred this to taking pictures of glaciers.

When we got to El Calafate, we went to a party. The venue was a far cry from Tequila, a club I loved in Buenos Aires. This place was such a sad runner-up that I started to regret my One, Two, Three maneuver. Aside from the boys I came with, I didn't know a soul. Oftentimes, these types of nights lead to long-haul commitments. The party doesn't even get started until early morning. Loud Latin music was blaring through the speakers, and the drinks weren't very good.

An hour in, I was out. Done. "When do you think we'll head back?" I asked the chef, hoping that I wasn't screaming too loudly in his ear over all the noise.

That's when I found out that these guys usually stayed until 4:00 a.m. or so.

At that point, I just wanted the comfort of my hotel. There was no way I could get through another four hours.

The chef could clearly see the horrified look on my face. "We could go back to my place," he said.

The hotel was an hour away, and there were no taxis. Would I really need to stick it out until dawn? My options were to stay at that lame party or leave with the chef.

Easy. He was cute. It would be fun, and everything would be fine. Or he would murder me, and I would wind up on that fucking glacier again, with people standing over my body saying, "That's the lady who was alone."

"It's not far from here. We could have a drink and relax," he said. "You never ate your dessert. I could make you something yummy."

"Let's go," I replied.

His place wasn't prime real estate, but he lit a fire that helped take the chill out of my otherwise dampened travels. When I opened my eyes the next morning, I glanced around the room and for a second didn't know where I was. I looked at him as he slept, and even though we'd had a great time together, I knew my morning exit was not going to be a smooth one. Coyote arm was the perfect term for my situation; that's when you wake up in the morning and someone is sleeping next to you *on your arm*. You would rather chew your arm and make a quiet getaway than wake him up.

Oh, God, what a disaster.

I had a flight to catch later that morning. How was I going to get all my stuff from Los Notros? I really didn't have time to pack my things.

I woke up my sexy friend and called the hotel concierge to ask if they could gather my belongings for me. Could they possibly put my luggage in a car and bring it to me in El Calafate? The idea that I would do that was unfathomable to my new friend. He handed me an incredible cup of coffee while shaking his head in disbelief.

"I've never seen anyone come to Los Notros and not stay at Los Notros," he said to me.

I didn't care. Last evening had turned out to be a nice reprieve, and I actually really loved meeting this sweet and gorgeous creature, but I couldn't wait to get out of this town!

It would take some time for my bags to arrive, so I found an Internet café nearby. I sent an e-mail to a friend that simply read, "Help me! I'm being held captive. The only thing to see is ice, and I can't do it anymore."

Once the car arrived with my things, I was off to Ushuaia, the next stop on Aunt Theresa's torment tour. Ushuaia is near the southernmost point in South America. It doesn't get more south than that.

My sojourn there was further evidence that Argentinians really don't understand the concept of traveling alone. Whenever anyone realized that I was by myself, they looked as if they'd smelled something rotten.

"*Sola?*" they'd ask, as if I might have a communicable disease.

"*Si. Fucking sola. Solamate una persona. Comprende?*"

When I got to my next hotel, I felt like I'd walked into a geriatric convention, or onto the set of *Cocoon*, the South American version. Those who weren't bald had gray hair. I seriously don't think there was a person in the lobby under the age of ninety-five. The only thing worse than being single in a sea of young couples is being single in a place where Grammy and Gramps are getting more lovin' than you!

Traveling by myself among so many couples was truly an isolating experience. It was like living in a small studio apartment while everyone else around you is living large in a duplex.

I was ten days into my trip and wanted to cut it short. Maybe I should have gone someplace like Ibiza. Instead of meeting new people and having stimulating conversations the way I'd hoped, I was eating dinner at 5:30 and working my way through an entire book at each meal. It turns out elderly people from all over the globe like to eat dinner early. I'm still surprised no one invited me to watch *Los Jeopardy*.

I will give that travel agent credit for one thing: my hotel room in Ushuaia was stunning. So nice, in fact, that I didn't want to leave. So, I did what came naturally to me and just started working. I would call my office and have them conference me in with clients so the number would come up with a 212 area code on their caller ID.

Working helped me feel grounded. It gave me a sense of purpose, and something to do. Whenever I had a rough time with anything, work was my anchor. It's like when your home is being renovated and you keep at least one room intact, like a bedroom. You may climb over workmen for your morning coffee, but once you're back in your bedroom, the "normal" is restored. That was what work was for me, my slice of normal. I didn't know a lot about myself back then, but I did know that. Once I regained my equilibrium, I could see that isolating myself wasn't good. I had to seek out some company.

I headed to the lobby for the first time in days and signed up for as many activities as I could. I needed adventure. I needed conversation. I desperately needed something, anything, to feel alive and good about myself.

ATV ride in the mountains? I'm in!

Hiking? Absolutely.

Horseback riding? Love it.

A canoe trip on the river? You betcha.

A walk up the glacier?

No fucking way. I just . . . couldn't. I couldn't even put ice in my beverages for a month after that trip.

It turned out that I was the only person who signed up for horseback riding, and that became one of the highlights of my travels. When I arrived at the stable, a girl who was about my age walked out. We saddled up our horses and went for a long trek through the high country. It looked like something from the film *A River Runs Through It*. There were looming mountains, lush fields, and a crystal-clear river. No Brad Pitt, but I'd had already had my celebrity encounter on this trip. (I still kept an eye out; lightning can sometimes strike twice, can't it?) We rode our horses through the water and up really steep trails, talking the entire time, mostly in Spanish. My guide didn't speak much English, but we tried our best and struggled through. She did a wonderful job sharing the history of the area we were riding in. She said the indigenous people never wore clothes because they went into and out of the water so much that they couldn't be wet all the time; so they just adapted to being naked and learned to exist in the raw. They collected and ate oysters and piled the shells up on the beach. These shell towers are still intact hundreds of years later. She told me about her boyfriend, we talked about dating, and before I knew it, I was relaxed. By the time we reached the top of the mountain, I felt as though I had made a new friend. We stopped to have lunch at the highest point of our ride, overlooking Chile. It was a view I will never forget.

Much to my surprise, lunch was spectacular too. We set everything up on a large blanket that my guide pulled from her saddlebag, then noshed on some gourmet treats, drank, and laughed hysterically for hours.

I felt as though I had climbed a mountain that day, both literally and figuratively. And I did it on my own terms, at my own pace. It felt monumental. I thought about the indigenous people and how they learned to adapt. If they could do it, then so could I.

And even though I spent a good part of my overall Argentinian tour feeling frustrated, I also spent time healing, thinking, and planning. What else do you do with that much time on your hands? It turned out that that was exactly what I needed. I didn't know it at the time, but that solitude was actually the medicine I required.

CHAPTER TEN

As Is

Life isn't about waiting for the storm to pass ... it's
about learning to dance in the rain!
—Vivian Greene

Once I'd returned to New York, I was determined to use my newfound confidence to keep from falling back into a rut. I wanted to move forward with intention. I wasn't exactly market ready, but I was ready to take some risks again. In real estate, a property marketed "as is" can mean a few things: that the seller is unwilling to make necessary repairs, that the asking price is lower than the market price in the area, or that the property will be sold in its condition at the time the offer is written. Visiting with Vicky had helped me see that there was a light at the end of the tunnel, but I also knew there was a lot of work I needed to do on myself if I was to truly get this property ready for market and not put it all out there "as is." When I was in Buenos Aires, I had updated my wardrobe. As a thriving designer, Vicky loved to dress me before we'd go out for a night on the town. It didn't matter if we were heading to dinner at some hot new restaurant or to our favorite club, Tequila. I've always enjoyed dancing. So as long as there was lively music, I could be found on the dance floor. Even in high school, I'd turn every party into a dance party. And there I was, in one of the sexiest cities in the world, full of beautiful people, and not only was I dancing, I was feeling really good too. Toward the end of my stay at her home, Vicky turned to me and said, "Chhhollee, we have to get you ready for the next phase. We'll hire a stylist, and you'll go home with brand-new clothes to match your brand-new outlook on life." No more mom jeans. No more office Martha. It's boring! These looks die in Argentina.

Two friends of Vicky's had just started a personal shopping business to help clients, especially foreigners, spiff up their wardrobes. Everything was so inexpensive in Argentina that they anticipated Americans flocking there for great deals. They knew all the best places to shop, and I was going to be their first customer. For me, it was a chance to rebrand myself, starting with my look. Up until that point, I never spent money on anything other than work attire, and even then, I was conservative about it. I bought my shirts at Pink and my suits at Theory. My weekend wardrobe was made up of "who cares," because I was married and didn't mind being in casual, comfy clothes. Everything had a purpose.

I made up my mind then and there: no more conservative suits. I wanted to look as lively on the outside as I was beginning to feel inside. I wanted to be excited about getting dressed, and, for the first time, have a little fun with it.

The two consultants—a tall, very handsome gay man and his female business partner—came to the house. They were both immaculately dressed. They took one look at me and said, "Oh dear. Yes, Vicky, we see what you mean." Then the man circled me, only hmm-ing as he took it all in.

That's never good.

I'd never been more ready for anything in my life. It was time to finally make an investment in something new, something far more valuable than real estate or the stock market. I was making the most important investment of all—in myself. I'd had that conversation with sellers so many times: "You need to make some investments if you want to sell your property." Once they put a little love into the place they had become so familiar with and even begun to take for granted, they often paused the sale for a while to appreciate their home again. So it really didn't take much convincing. I was ready.

"Bring it on!" I said.

And with that, we pounded the pavement for a week. Every day I'd head out with these two fashion mavens, stopping only for lunch and maybe a glass or two of wine. They picked out fun party clothes, pretty dresses, and sexy outfits galore. We went all over town. These two were extremely professional and made me feel like I was an absolute princess.

They had put together a folder of images of the look that they were going for, including the eye shadow, the lipstick, and the hairstyle. These two were not fucking around. I got my hair cut and colored, had a facial, got my makeup done, and enjoyed a particularly luxurious manicure and pedicure—the whole works, all while the two of them were standing close by, monitoring every move. The timing was perfect, because on the same evening they were planning their unveiling of the new Argentinian me, there was a huge party at Tequila. Everyone was dressing up in costume. Vicky had been working on ours all week and was visibly stressed about it. We all went as Egyptians. Esteban was King Tut, Vicky was Cleopatra, and I, well, of course, I was the third-wheel slave.

Our costumes were *amazing*. Vicky had done an incredible job. When we arrived at the club, I suddenly understood why she had been so intent on getting everything just right. People were wearing some of the best creations I'd ever seen. This place was like the famous Met Ball in New York. Everyone who was anyone in Buenos Aires was there, in full fantasy fashion mode.

When Vicky saw me taking in the sight with wide eyes, she shot me a look. "See? Now you understand why I was such a crazy lunatic this week. These Argentine women take this very seriously," she said.

And boy, was she right. One had painted herself solid gold, with tiny green leaves covering only her nipples and thong.

Wow.

I had never seen so many stunning people in one place before. In that moment, I was eternally grateful for my two-week makeover. Talk about fantastic timing.

So many of Esteban and Vicky's friends were there, including one in particular whom I had met several times before. I don't know if it was the costume, the makeover, or the One, Two, Three, but he wasn't leaving my side. "He's so hot, but, honey, he's just a puppy ..." Vicky whispered in my ear with a laugh.

I have to say, this puppy was adorable, and a fabulous dancer. I felt as if I were in high school again as we made out on the dance floor to Coldplay's hit "Clocks." From where I was standing, it sure looked like this puppy wanted to play. As the night came to an end, he asked for my number. Spending more time with him was a great way to wrap up my last weeks in Buenos Aires. Sure, I had to survive the constant teasing from Esteban and Vicky, but they were like proud parents, just happy that I was having fun. It was so light and innocent, and he made me forget about my heartbreak for a while.

Okay, so what if he still lived with his mother? I'm sure many powerful men have lived with their mothers from time to time, right?

Well, maybe not. I think this was a case of a near perfect house in the wrong location.

Time to start thinking of getting back to the right location. While I was sad to say goodbye to the puppy and, of course, to Esteban and Vicky, who had become my family, I had to get back to New York. While unpacking the several extra suitcases I returned with, I realized that tucked inside all those gorgeous garments was the confidence I had been hoping to find. Maybe, just maybe, I would be able to steer my ship away from the iceberg I'd felt like I was headed for every day since my divorce. It was as if a heaviness had lifted and I could breathe again.

I was determined to hang on to the ways of my beloved Argentinians, celebrating life daily, enjoying the simple things, and not sweating what I had no control over.

The holidays were coming, and I couldn't wait to show off my new look. No one loves Thanksgiving more than my father, Artie, and so this is one of my favorite holidays too. My parents' home is always full of love, laughter, and radical candor. That kind of warmth goes perfectly with impeccably roasted turkey and delicious apple pie. The trifecta is basically flawless. And, for many reasons, this would be a Thanksgiving not to be missed.

I was always in charge of making the pies. Apple pie is my secret weapon. If anyone is mad at me, I bake an apple pie. It's pretty hard to stay pissed off once you taste the flaky homemade crust that tops my buttery cinnamon-baked apples. The sweetness in every bite melts away any sour feelings that might linger. To be fair, though, I don't always bake a pie to smooth things over. Often, I make them by popular demand. When I created my first pie masterpiece, there was an audible gasp from my dad. It was meant in a good way. He sat back in his chair and declared, "Holly, you are gonna fetch a good man someday with that pie!"

I had to laugh. If only relationships could be saved with apples, flour, and sugar.

This family function would be the first of many that I would attend as a divorcée. I didn't like the feeling, let alone the word. And though I was more optimistic about my life at this point, deep down I wasn't sure I was ready for the family circus that is the Parker Thanksgiving.

"Honey, you can't run away forever. We'd really like you to come home for the holiday," my dad said.

I knew he was right.

How could I turn down this request? I couldn't say no.

I have two ancestors who came over on the *Mayflower*. We once visited Plimoth Plantation—on Thanksgiving. We even found the house of one of those distant ancestors, Stephen Hopkins. Inside, an actor was dressed up in period clothing from 1620. We all took turns posing with him outside his mud-and-thatched-roof dwelling. Now *that* was a fixer-upper that could've used a little staging before showing!

Yes, we are *that* family, and *this* is our holiday. Looking back, I guess you could say that we've always been a bit pilgrim obsessed. When we became full-blown members of Old Sturbridge Village, we were invited on the VIP tour, drank hot cider, and ate spice cake with other descendants of *Mayflower* passengers. WASPS and their pilgrims are a thing. One year my sister, Heather; my two roommates, Jenny and Amy, and I even hosted a pilgrim contest in Plymouth— you know, the place where the landing on Plymouth Rock is reenacted every day of the year. From start to finish, people were *into* it, and we were duly inspired by their enthusiasm. We had dressed up in our best pilgrim clothes. Okay, so they weren't really pilgrim clothes, but big buckled shoes were in that year, so I bought a pair to boost confidence in my pilgrim strut. There was no doubt I would win "Pilgrim Mania." The game went a little like this: the first person who could successfully pull a pilgrim actor out of their circa 1620 character and into the present day would win the game. Those pilgrims didn't have a chance with the One, Two, Three. It was a long battle and the competition seemed to escalate with every minute, but those pilgrims wouldn't budge. Regardless of how crazy our distractions were, they stayed in character the entire time. Despite our best efforts, all four of us struck out. The pilgrims wanted nothing to do with us hussies. They seemed more eager to put us into the stocks. Come to think of it, maybe that was their thing.

I knew it was definitely time to get my butt back to New England to celebrate this massively sacred holiday with my clan.

We were gathering at my sister's house in Winchester, Massachusetts, about fifteen minutes north of Boston. Winchester is the quintessential New England town, and one of the cutest I've ever seen. Everything looks perfect: the charming cafés, sweet little shops, old churches, and, of course, the beautiful houses all surrounded by white picket fences. It's straight out of a Norman Rockwell painting. Wherever I looked, I saw families of four, and when I'd see that perfect little family dog in tow, I let out a deep sigh. It looked like Mister Rogers's neighborhood. That fleeting thought gave me some comfort. While I never saw an episode in which Mister Rogers visited a divorced princess puppet who ran away to South America, I hoped that, because he embraced us all, he would have embraced me too.

I'd returned from Argentina feeling pretty good about next steps, for the most part. And yet nothing threatens progress like an impending holiday with family, no matter how loving they are. Because we always want to experience the ideal despite the fact that there's no such thing, occasions like these typically end up pressing buttons. Trust me: Thanksgiving can be a hot button for anyone, not just those who are mildly dysfunctional. So there I was with the perfect outfit in hand, getting ready for this much-anticipated event, and all I could see was a big scarlet letter *D* on my chest.

Although deep down I knew that I was in charge of how I responded to whatever came my way, I really hoped that being with everyone for the weekend wouldn't undo the work I'd done on my travels.

Good news! I was greeted at the door by my adorable nephews, all three of whom came running toward me. I bent down to hug Nicholas, who was five, and the twins, Colby and Tyler, who were three. Honestly, they were the best hugs I'd had in a very long time. My heart was instantly full of love and gratitude. I was happy to have my family around me, celebrating this holiday we all cherished so much together.

Of course, this year I'd decided to forego my traditional garb and dress with a little Argentinian flare instead. Yup—I wore a feathered scarf, a bright pink silk tank top, big dangling earrings, the works. As I passed the cranberry sauce, I couldn't help but feel like a modern-day pilgrim embracing my very own new beginning . . . or at least like the hostess at a flamenco club. Either way, I was on new ground, and, like my ancestors, I was determined to carve out a new life in unchartered land.

Now, if you live in the city and have ventured even fifteen miles outside of its radius, then you know that the suburbs can really fuck you up. In the city, people run around with cats on their heads, snakes around their necks, and dogs on skateboards. The city is a place where people feel comfortable and free to wave their freak flags. At least they do in downtown NYC. It's why I've always loved Manhattan: it's hard to feel like the world's biggest oddity in a place with a lot of competition for that title. Crazy in New York is just part of the stamp on your passport.

In the suburbs, however, the opposite is true. Everyone's inner freak is well hidden in the attic, in the basement, in the brand-new pool house—wherever. Everyone and everything seems perfect and flawless.

But stop right there.

What family do you know that's perfect and flawless?

Like the Abominable Snowman, no such thing exists.

Yet when you're driving through these enclaves, you really do get the impression that life's storms happen only to you, leaving a messy trail of destruction in your path. Humans are pack animals, and no one likes to feel like an outlier; but suburbs, with their picket fences, can make you feel that way. That's why I don't sell real estate in the suburbs. They're a pressure cooker.

Most New Yorkers don't pretend to be perfect. You can't become a full-fledged citizen of the city without a standing appointment with your therapist. Neurosis is a prerequisite. It's those flaws that keep us interesting and the city vibrant. Every time I see someone doing something unbelievably weird, my heart fills. It really does. I love watching people just doing their thing, whether they're playing guitar in their underwear in Times Square or they have a cat on their bike wearing its own helmet. Expanded mind plus expanded community equals an expanded life. When people are tapped into who they truly are, it not only creates joy for them but also vibrates that joy out into the world. And for that, I love my city. It somehow gives us all permission to be who we want to be, and that kind of freedom is contagious.

So, although the holiday went phenomenally well, I couldn't wait to get back to New York, where I needed to hit the ground running again. Argentina was amazing, but it was time to put the pedal to the metal and get to work. I had a lot of catching up to do.

CHAPTER ELEVEN

Abandoned Property

Always focus on the front windshield and not the rearview mirror.
—Colin Powell

I N REAL ESTATE, THE TERM *ABANDONMENT* DENOTES THE FAILURE to occupy and use a property, which may result in a loss of rights. In the late 1980s, many homeowners found themselves financially underwater when the value of real estate fell to all-time lows. They owed more on their mortgages than their homes were worth. For many, it was easier to walk away from their properties and start over. In New York, people from other countries, especially those who owned co-ops, closed their doors, got on a plane, and never looked back. They knew co-op boards' legal arms didn't have deep-enough pockets to chase them overseas. In the process of abandoning their homes, they left their neighbors on the hook for the joint mortgage for the entire building. As I've explained, in a co-op, you don't own your apartment outright; rather, you're a member of a corporation that owns the entire building and you own shares based on myriad factors. If one person leaves, the overall mortgage is still due. If a person falls behind in payment, their deficit is picked up by their neighbors. So many buildings suffered these occurrences that 90 percent of co-ops still will not allow foreign purchasers today. Most sellers and brokers won't even consider foreign offers because there's very little possibility of getting them past a board. The pain of that abandonment and the memory of the financial burden it left are still fresh thirty years later.

In life, we enter into all types of relationships. Some are business relationships, others are personal, and still others are romantic. Some blend all three. These can be among the deepest, richest, and most painful relationships of all.

With divorce rates hovering around 50 percent in the United States, topping 60 percent in some European countries, including Spain, Portugal, Luxembourg, the Czech Republic, and Hungary, and peaking at 70 percent in Belgium, there's no doubt that a seismic shift in our romantic relationships is occurring worldwide (with the exception of China, where the rate is just 3 percent). First, women are through putting up with shit they no longer wish to tolerate. Second, women are more financially independent today than ever before, unless they've consciously entered a relationship in which they and their resources are controlled. (And by the way, I know as many men in this kind of relationship as I do women.)

There was a time when women really couldn't leave their marriages because men held the financial reins, owned their homes, and ran their businesses. If you wanted to leave your husband, you either ran out and abandoned your children or killed him. There weren't a lot of logical choices. Today, of course, things are different. Or are they?

I think we all believe that we'll somehow land safely on the positive side of these numbers. Surely we enter our relationships believing we'll never become statistics. The new trend in the United

States, perhaps because of the divorce rate, is a steady decline in weddings. Evidence shows that people are choosing not to get married. In the same way that many women don't want the government in their wombs, they also don't want the government in their beds. And now they have the right to say so. It's safe to guess that this new generation of young girls doesn't daydream about what their wedding will look like but rather what their Nobel prize or album cover may look like. When gay marriage became legal in New York, I joked with my attorney, Jerry, "Well, it's about time you guys started dealing with the same challenges. Welcome to your nightmare!" Now gay guys and gals are getting divorced too. That should keep the economy afloat! Do you think it's a coincidence that women are lured into marriage with a sparkly piece of jewelry, a flurry of parties, and the promise of a fabulous vacation? What really drives me crazy is the notion—the absolute belief—that the institution of marriage will make them happy. For many, it's more about the ring, the flowers, the parties, and the cake than it is about a lifetime of commitment. Marriage is not a verb. It's not going to do the work for you. In fact, it's a lifelong job—until it isn't. Sometimes it works, and sometimes it doesn't. It's a lot like the weather: you'll have your sunny days, rainy days, gloomy days, and storms. And like the weather, April showers bring May flowers. Your storms, if traversed correctly, will bring you closer with your loved one. If disrespect and dishonesty are elements in those storms, however, the marriage likely won't survive. Neither will you if you don't remind yourself that there can be sunny days again.

When my marriage ended, there's no question I felt abandoned by my ex—although it wasn't a new sensation. My ex checked out long before we separated. From the beginning, I was trying to create a new life for us, and he was often cruising on autopilot. It felt as if I were putting boards on the windows and gathering extra water while he was just looking at me as if to say, "This is just a hurricane *warning*.

What's wrong with you?" The thing is, before a natural disaster occurs in your life, there are always warnings. I'm not saying every storm in a marriage is a potential hurricane, but why not google how to navigate through the foul weather?

All relationships require sacrifices and work. It doesn't matter whether you're married, you're co-parenting, or you're just close friends; relationships of any kind can be tough.

We don't tend to enter friendships with the same cautionary tales in mind as we do romantic relationships. But maybe we should. Our time and our hearts are by far our two most precious commodities. One we control, and the other, not as much. A breakup of any kind, whether it involves a friendship or a marriage, can cause absolute devastation. It can set you back mind, body, and soul. Therefore, all relationships need to be analyzed and evaluated from time to time. Make sure the retaining walls are strong and the foundation is safe. While we all have our needy moments, relationships must maintain a rhythm, a dance, a back-and-forth that keeps things moving in step. You give; they give. It's true in business, love, and friendships. A true relationship won't survive without it. As Alan Watts once said, "The only way to make sense out of change is to plunge into it, move with it, and join the dance."

People love to talk about breakups, but they don't like to talk about loss—what it means, the holes it leaves, or the scars that will always be there afterward, even as time goes by. The older I get, the more I believe that friendships come and go. I see people all around me who are able to maintain relationships for years, and yet there are so many of us coping with the loss of someone we really cared about. Logic tells me that most of the time, it isn't necessarily about something we did as much as something else going on in the other person's life. But love isn't logical; it's emotional, and therefore, even when it's about friendship, it defies logic. Everyone wants to believe that they're the star of every story in their life, but sometimes they're a secondary player in someone else's story. You can't always be Carrie. Sometimes you're Miranda.

Are there rules to friendships?

There are. And they seem to change over time.

Do you know yours?

I've learned that I require the art of celebration. It may seem trivial, but I also feel it's essential in relationships. While it's understood that we're there for each other's lows, being there for each other's highs can sometimes be even more important.

What is the art of celebration?

It's being around people who want to celebrate your birthday, a promotion, or some other big life event. They show up without obligation. They smile, they laugh, and they enjoy the milestone we're sharing. They understand, in part, what the trek up the hill was for, and they take a moment to pause, look at you, and say, "I am so fucking proud to be your friend."

There are only so many soul mate friends who can make you feel completely seen. Mine all have the same common denominator: they make me laugh hysterically. What is it about laughing out loud, especially when it's not appropriate, that makes you feel like a child again? You know what I mean. Your body shakes, and you fight every instinct to let out that irrepressible giggle. It's naughty, fun, and contagious. And let's face it: anyone who can make you feel like you've turned back time is immediately a friend, at least in my eyes. For me, humor is the ultimate drug. If you can make me laugh, then we're off to a great start and a fabulous new friendship.

When I first decided to make real estate my full-time job in New York, I took a position at one of the top luxury real estate firms in the city. I worked directly across the aisle from someone who at first glance looked to be much older. He had (prematurely) gray hair. As I would soon discover, he was only seven years older than me, to the day. Yup—we shared the same birthday. I like to say we were twins born seven years apart.

We got to know each other and became fast friends. He had a quick wit and became the Will to my Grace, except funnier because we weren't limited by broadcast network standards. I'd say we were more HBO when it came to humor. We had instant chemistry and a dynamic rhythm. I was never funnier than when we were together, and neither was he. One plus one equaled one hundred. Everything just clicked.

This man quickly became my hero, mentor, and best friend. In real estate, people tend to use the term *rare gem* loosely, but he was just that. A rare gem.

When I think about it, he was more than just a best friend—he was my gay husband. We did everything together. Well, almost. You see, he wasn't one of those friends who understood the art of celebration. In fact, he sucked at it. He may as well have been a Jehovah's Witness.

In many ways, we grew up together. We leaned on each other. When his boyfriend of fourteen years cheated on him, he moved in with me. It was my home where he sheltered for nine months. And despite his sadness over the loss of his relationship, it was a beautiful time in ours. So good, in fact, that we wondered why we hadn't cohabitated before.

Oh, I know why.

I was married.

And he may as well have been too.

We met for the first time when he offered to split a brownie with me. Turning down food of any kind has never been my strong suit. Feeding me is a great way to win my friendship. A shared brownie turned into fifteen years of having lunch together every day. His was the first call I would get in the morning and often the last I would make in the evening. He kept me learning and, for sure, laughing through most hours of every day. He was my everything. I grew dependent on him for advice, fashion consulting, help navigating challenges, and picking hotels and restaurants. It was as if he were the oxygen in the air I breathed. We were inseparable. In fact, it was rumored that we were more than friends. We, of course, thought that was hysterical and went out of our way to egg people on. I would mess up the back of my hair and smear my lipstick, and he would untuck his shirt as we came back to the office from lunch. You could see the wide eyes and the hot stares of scandal. Whenever we met on the street from different directions, we would hail a cab and pretend to have a huge fight over who got it. The poor cabdriver didn't know what to think as we both slipped into the back seat, still arguing until we cracked up laughing. We might not have been amusing to others, but we certainly entertained each other.

While my marriage weakened over the years, he was the one pillar I could really depend on. He would help me find humor in whatever pathetic, devastating circumstance I found myself in. And by now, you know there were many.

After twenty years of friendship, my friend moved on with his career and life. He was in a new relationship and moved to a new company, and that was enough for him. I wanted him to be happy, to have love and companionship—I just never thought that would come at such a high price. I didn't understand the 180-degree turnaround on a two-decade relationship. He stopped speaking to me. Really. And when I did speak to him, it was brief and cold. Surprisingly enough, this was the hardest divorce of all.

When I tried to talk with him about it, I never really got any explanations for why we went our separate ways. His only response was, "I have my boyfriend now. Life is about chapters, and this is just a new one."

I didn't realize I was merely a placeholder until he found happiness. Twenty years is a long time to be a seat filler. Wow! He even gave Connie a run for her money. I thought "my little gayling" and I were family. In some ways we were, but when he found a husband to make a nest with, this dear bird had to fly. Whether I liked it or not, I needed to accept that.

Now I was left to make myself laugh. I'd lost my comic relief. My safe place, my happy place, my "she shed" was burned to the ground.

And speaking of shed, you've all heard of the divorce diet, right? You shed weight like it's your job, and you look the best you ever have. Well, that doesn't apply to gay divorce. In gay divorce, the opposite happens. I blew up like a tick in the heat of summer. Seriously. Can you imagine a better gay man's revenge than watching your ex of sorts pack on the pounds?

I have a close friend who shared a similar story with me. She was friends with a woman for years. Both single, they became inseparable, traveling and enjoying many interests in common. But one day my friend noticed that the other woman was starting to be reluctant to make plans. And when she did, it was usually something along the lines of, "I can see you tomorrow from nine fifteen to ten o'clock, in between yoga and my next appointment." This wasn't just a onetime occurrence either. Their friendship somehow shifted from plans almost every weekend to a forty-five-minute time slot every few months.

Who likes feeling like they're being "fit in," especially when it comes to best friends?

And if they were such good friends, why weren't they having a conversation about what was happening? Even if it was a difficult task, good friends rise to the need. True friendship is rooted in being able to talk about the hard stuff. It feels like everyone is playacting these days. Has hiding behind our devices really become our out? It just doesn't seem like anyone wants to have real conversations anymore.

I don't know about you, but that makes me bananas. I'm involved in a busy, twenty-four-seven business, and *somehow* I find time for the people I want to be with. Always.

When my friend broached the subject of whether anything was wrong or if she and her friend needed to talk through anything, the other woman simply said, "That's it. I'm done."

To this day, she doesn't know why the friendship ended. She's reached out a few times only to have her concerns fall on deaf ears.

Does it bother her?

She says it makes her sad, but she also understands that sometimes relationships run their course, and sometimes there's more to the story. Unfortunately, when it comes to friend divorce, you may never know the reason for the breakup in the first place. And that's tough. *Really* tough.

Relationships are always going to change. Someone might suddenly be down on their luck, and you find you need to be there for that person a little more than usual. Maybe one of your girl-friends is going through menopause, and suddenly all they do is complain—about everything! Or perhaps you're going through a life-altering event yourself and you suddenly feel as though no one is there when you need them most. One of my favorite clients had a business partner who was dying of cancer. He decided to write a book full of life lessons that he wanted to share with his friends and family before he passed. One of his lessons was, "Get sick every seven years to weed out who your true friends really are. It will most likely surprise you."

Hopefully, the tide changes without washing that friendship out to sea. Whatever the reason, it's a challenge when the going gets tough and others seem to get going as far away from you as they can. Maybe you lost your job and can't go out like you used to, or you're now in a relationship with someone, leaving little time for the old gang. So many successful women talk about their disappointment in relation-ships—all relationships. Some people can't handle success. Some can't support it in others. And there are those who don't want single women around their husbands. I get it—all of it—and yet it doesn't diminish the anguish you feel when someone you've been friends with for years suddenly stops talking to you and you have no idea why.

We've all had friends who simply don't show up when we think they should, or who only come around for the fun times and are totally out of there when things in your life change. Whatever those things are, they just don't work for them anymore. I didn't grow up believing that friendships are disposable. I realize that sometimes life takes a sharp left turn that we didn't see coming—but isn't that when we need our friends most? We never expect to say goodbye to these soul mate friends, especially ones in whom we've invested decades. No one ever warns us that giving so much of our hearts to a friend could be dangerous. You're supposed to be safe from heartache with friends, especially those who will be with you until the end. They're supposed to be part of your foundation. There's nothing you shouldn't do for a best friend. It's the call you'll take in the middle of the night. It's the person you'd drop everything for when a crisis happens in their lives.

But friend divorce can and does happen, as it did for me and my little gayling. Why couldn't we have the hard conversations? My friend and I had been best friends for twenty years, half my lifetime. It's been ages since our divorce, and I still can't tell you why it happened. Would you simply pack your suitcase and disappear from a relationship one day? Just walk out the door and leave your ex wondering what the hell happened? Sure, people do it, but you don't often hear that story. Although I think we did in the film *Kramer vs. Kramer*, which is one of the saddest movies I've ever seen. You don't do that in romantic relationships, because it's cruel. Plain, hard, cruel. So why is it tolerated in other relationships? I'm taking a stand to say no more bad behavior. If you have to make a break from a best friend, then do it like you're breaking up with a boyfriend or a girlfriend. Let them know what's going on and why it's not working. And be honest, no matter how awkward it may be. They deserve the respect you would give to a romantic partner. Friendships are an investment of the heart and of your precious time on this earth. You can't just drop from one hundred to zero with no explanation. There's too much hurt and pain in the world. We need more relationships with empathy and love. I'm not saying you need to keep friendships that are hurting you or don't serve you anymore; I'm saying the right thing to do is to let someone you loved understand why you're moving on. Ghosting someone is worse than telling them to fuck off. It says, "You're ether to me; there's no way back in, and I'm okay with that." It's abandonment in the worst form. When you abandon a co-op, you leave the board with the burden of figuring out why you left and what they must shoulder now. When you abandon a person, you do the same thing.

Not understanding the reason for the abandonment is the most painful part of divorce. In my case, I already blamed myself for everything. But having this soul mate not address the elephant in the room has been one of the saddest and hardest challenges of my life to navigate. The irony of that really kills me; how could that one person you loved so intensely be the same one who put the biggest hole in your heart? Not knowing the how and the why can be nothing short of devastating. It sure was for me.

And even now, I keep thinking about all the years I lost with my friend. Yes, I think of them as lost. Twenty years of my life went up in flames. People come into our lives for a reason, a season, or a lifetime, and I was investing in a lifetime with him. I thought it was something real, something that could weather challenges and storms. But that's the heartache of divorce. It was the biggest outlay of time and emotion, and I never expected it to stop yielding a return—or, worse, for there to be a net loss. A loss that felt 100 percent catastrophic.

Another friend had a very best friend growing up. They were inseparable. They spent their youth spying on her three older brothers, making forts, giving each other makeovers, and attending many fun preschool, elementary school, and high school events together. They were the ultimate side-by-side, ride-or-die duo. Or so she thought.

After having grown up with this person, my friend was ghosted like something right out of the bad first date handbook. Really? No discussion? No explanation after more than a decade together?

It's not normal!

Or is it?

Does this happen more often than anyone thinks?

Maybe the pain, blame, and shame are too much to share with others, so it remains underreported.

This was the first real heartbreak for my friend, and the most impactful one. She set off for college with a heavy heart knowing that something special would be missing from her life for years to come. Could someone who would do that to another human really be that special after all? You don't think to ask that when you're shattered.

I've thought a lot about why people don't talk about this more. I think it's for two reasons. One is our feelings of shame. Why does someone's best friend suddenly abandon them? They must have done something horrible, like cancel the Fourth of July or outlaw popsicles. The wounded party might not want to draw attention to the fact that their best friend just up and split, so they carry that secret around with them silently. It's embarrassing and humiliating to admit that truth to anyone.

The second reason we don't talk about friend divorce is that, in my belief, that type of loss and pain never completely leaves you. In fact, it permanently marks you, like those tiny little fractures that weaken the whole foundation of a house.

When I announced my divorce from my prince, some of our friends said, "I'm with you!"

My reaction was stern. "Oh no, you don't have to pick sides here. There are no sides; we weren't even fighting. I would love for you to stay in both of our lives." And I meant it.

Many responded by saying that was too awkward, believing that there are always sides to be taken, while a few understood where I was coming from. But just like that, lines were drawn, and like our belongings, some went to him and some came to me. Any way you slice it, there was loss.

Almost all our long-term friendships stayed on their respective sides, but that's not always the case. A friend I work with used to be a psychiatrist. She and her very best friend did absolutely everything together. They had babies at the same time. They lived around the corner from each other. They did toddler and ballet classes together. They traveled together, and each was the other's coach, confidante, and cheerleader. After twenty-five years of marriage, my friend got divorced from her husband. And when she did, just like that, her very best friend stopped returning her phone calls. They would see each other at parties, but it was incredibly awkward. To this day, she still doesn't know exactly what the problem was. And like so many of us, she's been left on her own to try to fill in the painfully bizarre blanks. At the time of the divorce, her husband was significantly wealthier than she was. The only explanation my friend could come up with was that her former BFF followed the dollars. The irony is that my friend switched careers and is now one of the top real estate brokers in the country, literally a real estate rock star, while her ex has since retired.

But then, is that really the story?

Don Miguel Ruiz's enlightening book *The Four Agreements: A Practical Guide to Personal Freedom* taught me to not make assumptions, but when you're left in a black hole, it feels like assumptions are all you have.

Each of us has at least one friend we love but also slightly dread spending time with because they can be energy vampires or drain your emotional reservoir. If you're in your thirties, forties, or older, you've met a lot of people along the way. Sometimes a long, amazing friendship just ends; other times you have an inkling about which relationships won't last; and sometimes you have no idea, and the end hits you like a two-by-four across the head. Or you have an inkling but choose to ignore it like a squeaky screen door you hope will somehow oil itself.

For the most part, we all know it happens, yet we say nothing in the aftermath. But we should. Especially when the abandonment leaves us feeling so completely sideswiped. Endings stir up difficult feelings and often force us to look inward. Is this part of a pattern? What responsibility do you need to take in the demise of the relationship?

Saying goodbye to someone we love is difficult under the best of circumstances. The older you are, the harder it becomes. It's important to remember that it takes confidence and a strong sense of self-worth to make a decision like friend divorce. There will be anger and sadness all around. You're losing someone who once meant something to you. That's super sad, and it's supposed to be. It isn't easy, but it's sometimes essential. Whether you're on the receiving end of the news or you're the one delivering it, my heart goes out to you.

So once it happens, how do you invest in another property? Whether you did the abandoning or got stuck with the abandoned property, how do you trust yourself to invest in another property, or trust another buyer who claims to want to invest in yours?

It's not easy, that's for sure.

But I've thought long and hard about this one. For me, friends and family are my central focus, the reason I'm here. Every time I suffer a fractured relationship—and I've had a few of them—I feel as though I'm moving further and further away from my purpose.

When that happens, I inevitably ask myself, *What am I doing here? What's the point?*

Evolving into the best human beings we can be? But what happens when your friends and family let you down? I mean, none of us is perfect. We're going to let one another down; it's inevitable, the way a storm will bring rain. Am I right?

At some point, everyone and everything will disappoint you.

The sooner we can all accept that—in fact, the sooner we *expect* it—the better we can prepare for such storms and weather them when they happen.

I don't pretend to know how the future will play out. I'm not Nostradamus. I've been hurt more often than I ever could have imagined by those whom I thought would always be by my side, protecting me. When you have my loyalty, I'm such a dutiful soldier. I'm fiercely protective. If I had lived in Roman times, I'm certain I would have been a bodyguard—oh, wait, I meant to say empress. I would have had a centurion guarding me; yeah, that sounds more like it. If you had gone after someone I loved, I'd have had you taken out with a quick snap of my fingers. I'd have given the order as fast as a Roman chariot race in the Colosseum, and believe me, I would have had no problem releasing the lions on you.

Going through friend divorce is humiliating for two reasons. First, because my friends and family are the most important things in my life. Second, because communicating difficult topics is what I do for a living. Put those two things together, and please tell me why I have relationship troubles in my life!

I used to say that any friend who stayed with me longer than seven years was tenured, which meant I would put up with an enormous amount of shit from them because of the years I'd invested in the friendship. The longer the friendship, the more flexible I was. After twenty years of friendship, I believed I could weather a tsunami of bad behavior from my rare gem. But there comes a time when respect is crossed not once, not twice, but too many times to count, and you start to say, "That's not the relationship I signed up for." When you think about it, we're a collection of experiences we're willing to tolerate.

I don't have the answers here. I'm not sure I ever will. I do think that we're living in a time when communication is breaking down everywhere. We're all texting and writing in acronyms. Who picks up the phone or shows up in person to have the hard conversations?

Not many people.

I can speak only for myself, but I see the inability that so many others have to effectively communicate the hard stuff, especially when it comes to their emotions or something that's detrimental to their closest relationships. There used to be a silent code regarding what was expected—the ten unspoken commandments, lines you would never cross. Duties that were expected. And now it's the Wild West. No one knows the rules, everyone is connected, and yet loneliness and anxiety are at all-time highs. The world is indeed evolving. Am I just one of those old women sitting on the sidelines muttering under her breath that this isn't how we used to do things in my day? Maybe so. But I don't think I'm alone in seeing the deterioration of communication as an epidemic. So please reach out to your friends, family, and loved ones and have those difficult conversations. They don't come easy. Nothing does. One of the best things a coach said to me when I told them I wasn't good at something was that I wasn't good at it *yet*. We need to keep looking for the similarities, the things we have in common, the positive thread that connects us. And, when appropriate, we need not only to say the difficult things but also to listen—*really* listen—listen not to reply but to understand. We also need to look for the pearls of wisdom. What is my takeaway from this? How can I grow, change, and get stronger? Because then the growth will be worth the pain. Look for these lessons in everything.

As a self-confessed control freak, when a deal goes south, I always ask, "What's the takeaway? What could I have done better? What could I have anticipated to ensure that things went in another direction?" If I'm a victim, I have no control. If I'm the one creating the error, then I can fix it. This has always worked well to improve my performance in the office. The problem is when it seeps out into everything else I do. I tend to take on the fault in all that goes wrong. I bathe in the blame. And sometimes that's a lot to carry. My friend's absence was an enormous void, and my foundation was certainly cracked. But from that destruction came one of the most valuable lessons in my life. I finally learned not to take action but to be silent and allow myself time to heal. I meditated more than ever. The absence of this best friend led me down a path back to myself. When I started examining all the blame I'd taken on, trying to find a reason he left, I began to stick up for myself. The more I thought about it, the more I realized that faulting myself for his actions was horseshit, and I knew it. I was an amazing friend, and I was proud of that. I didn't want to beat myself up over this anymore. I was done feeling bad. I had been carrying around too much hurt. It was time to turn all of that pain into petrol.

For the first time in my life, I didn't need a sidekick. I didn't need a workout partner or someone to desperately seek advice from. I had connected to myself in a way that brought peace. True peace. And that connection is the best investment I've ever made, because it can never be taken away. When I'm around friends or find myself in situations where I start to feel disconnected, I pull back, take a beat, and then reconnect with myself. I now understand that true happiness all begins and ends with my own connection.

Growing up, I was taught that thinking about yourself was being selfish—even self-obsessed. That idea was drilled into me. One time at my own birthday party, I stood first in line to play pin the tail on the donkey. My dad shook his head and said, "Back of the line, my dear. You're the host. The host always goes last."

"But it's *my* birthday!" I cried.

"Back of the line!" he repeated sternly.

And when I stood my ground, he sent me to my room.

It was my seventh birthday, and I spent it in a time-out.

And so I learned a hard lesson, but an important one. My father wanted me to understand the value of putting others' needs ahead of my own. He wanted me to think about someone else's feelings and not just my own. There certainly is merit in this and it has served me well over the years. And still, while it's nice to be a caretaker, and I've enjoyed it, I have also come to understand there really is nothing more important than taking care of your own needs. It took me many years to understand that good manners are one thing and self-preservation is something else. Self-care is the oxygen and the true foundation for any relationship. So yes, while it's kind to show others that you care, it's so important to take time for yourself—time to think, time to learn, time to grow. It's a necessity. Without it you can lose yourself. And after my friend divorce, I promised myself I would never be lost again.

CHAPTER TWELVE

Launching for Sale

Don't blame a clown for acting like a clown. Ask
yourself why you keep going to the circus.
—Anonymous

Aﬀter so many disappointments, it's only natural to
wonder if you'll ever feel hope again. There were twinges of it for
me, especially after returning from Argentina, but the feeling would
come and go.

At some point I realized that hope is nice, but it's rarely a plan. I
knew that if I were ever to experience the sensation of optimism again,
I would need to start purposefully building the life I deserved. So, I
began making a conscious effort to engage in activities that made me
happy, or at least happier. I determined that I was going to give my
fabulous bathroom a run for its money, and I did. I allowed myself
time to luxuriate in a tub brimming with bubbles. Sure, this was the

place where I'd cried my eyes out, but now it would also be the place where I pulled myself together.

Just after my divorce, I would sometimes flip over in the bath and see how long I could hold my breath, wishing it could be forever. I wasn't trying to kill myself or anything like that; I just wanted calm all around me. It was like returning to the protected space of the womb. But after my epiphany about crafting an action plan, I was no longer holding my breath. I was above water now, able to breathe easier again, this time in rhythm with soft music and the flicker of candlelight. I knew I had begun to heal, albeit slowly.

Instead of watching cooking shows on TV, I signed up for them. I started volunteering with the Make-A-Wish Foundation, which I found both humbling and fulfilling. I hired a life coach to hold me accountable. No more tears, and no more feeling like a victim. I declared all my woebegone days to be over. It was time to take serious action and move myself out of the dark and into the light. I saw the holes in my life, and I had a strategy to fill them.

It's incredible what a regimented routine can do for the body, mind, and soul. Working out became my lifeline to feeling good about myself. It created the road map for the kind of day I would have. If I missed a workout in the morning, I made a point to get to the gym at the end of the day. I knew this time was critical to my mental state and well-being. I never wanted to give it up. If the body is the vehicle, the mind is the steering wheel. Everything we do—or don't do—begins and ends in the mind. I always feel better when I adhere to this routine. And when I don't, I find myself slipping down the rabbit hole remarkably fast. The only way to dig my way out is to keep moving.

After meeting with a seller and walking through their home, my team and I would create a marketing plan for the property: Who is their buyer? Where is this buyer, and how are we going to reach them? Is it a family with kids going to the nearby school? Or is it a groover?

(That's my term for the "too cool for school" bachelor who wants only sleek, modern places.)

We often need to have a come-to-Jesus moment with the seller. Are they being realistic, or do they really believe they've created the Taj Mahal?

Launching is game time. This is when you need to be realistic—what I like to call *optimistically realistic*. You never know where your buyer is going to come from. Even though our website statistically has the largest reach, we keep many different avenues of communication open.

When selling a property, I work on descriptions for days, and sometimes weeks. I take notes while I walk through the property, and I always list the best qualities first. Many buyers don't read past the third sentence, so you need to make sure you get the best attributes into the first two sentences.

What makes your listing special?

What sets your home apart from the other listings?

Build on your strengths and know what they are.

There are questions that most buyers ask, and it's important to have well-thought-out answers ready.

Two of the most frequently asked questions I hear from buyers are, "How many other buyers have seen this house?" and "How long has it been on the market?" Buyers want to know that information. Remember, real estate is all about the dance of attraction. Can I really say four thousand people have seen it and absolutely no one wanted to buy it? That I'm on my knees praying that somehow I'll get lucky here today?

Yeah, that wouldn't fly.

But I can say, "We've been on the market for a couple of months, but the activity and energy around the property has really picked up in the last couple of weeks."

And then there's my favorite question: "Why did this house fall out of contract?" Which is really another way of saying, "What's wrong with it? Why did the buyer walk away?"

This is when you must have your concise, two-sentence answer ready. This is especially important when dating after a divorce or a breakup. Inevitably, your next suitor will ask what happened, so be ready with a brief answer. Mine went something like this: "Unfortunately, we weren't able to be married anymore, and we were both very disappointed about it. Maybe if tonight goes well and we get to know each other, I'll share some of that with you, but for now, I want to hear about you."

In life and love, sometimes you have to spin it to win it.

Create the energy, create the excitement. Remember, you're always in demand, even when you're not. Everyone wants what they can't have.

Anticipate the future. Don't report on the past.

In new construction and development, we spend years getting a building just right before putting the first units on the market. When I work with developers, I always advise them to know their product, know how it will stand apart from the competition, and understand what will excite, motivate, and inspire buyers who want to make this their new home. You don't want to build a big, sleek, shiny building in Alphabet City, because people go there to escape sparkly and shiny. They like that there are no chain stores there. Those buyers are fleeing SoHo to get away from the influx of commercialism. You might end up with an inventory of unsold apartments, something developers who haven't done the proper planning always worry about.

It can take years to find the right land or opportunity. Designing the right apartment configurations counts too. How many one-bedrooms, two-bedrooms, and three-bedrooms will there be? Which apartments get the view of the park? And what's the top price for them?

If it's a new building, we try to determine *everything*. For instance, we contemplate how high the ceilings are going to be, because if we make them twelve feet, we have the potential to lose a whole floor at the end of the build. We conduct a complete analysis of the benefits and the drawbacks. Does the price increase resulting from the extra ceiling height justify the loss of a floor? You get the gist. We continuously tweak these projects until we feel we've perfected them. A lot of thought goes into each building, home, or new development long before a buyer does their first walk-through. *We* know what they want before *they* do. It's our job to know.

In the movie *The Devil Wears Prada*, there's a scene in which Andy laughs about two belts looking exactly the same. Miranda Priestly, the fictitious boss of *Runway* magazine, looks at her and unleashes a verbal lashing about the work that goes into creating trends in fashion. She basically dresses Andy down for her naiveté. Priestly tells Andy that while she may believe her lumpy blue sweater suggests to the world that she doesn't take herself too seriously, its very color tells a different story. It's not just blue; it's not turquoise; it's not lapis; it's cerulean. Priestly goes on to inform her that in 2002, Oscar de la Renta did a cerulean gown, and Yves Saint Laurent also featured a cerulean military jacket, causing a run on the color for the season. Cerulean showed up in the collections of eight different designers before everyone else in the fashion world adopted it too, including the Casual Corner where Andy thought she'd found her very own fashion statement in a clearance bin. My takeaway from this: behind every buying decision, even the ones you think are arbitrary, there's some level of commercial strategy. A single luxe color, in this instance, had influence. Applied at every price point, it subliminally helped to move units across the board.

Fashion, real estate, and any other consumer-driven enterprise goes through a similar process before product gets to the market. Those toys your children beg for in the lead-up to their birthdays or Christmas are meant to be begged for; manufacturers create market trends. People love to have the latest and greatest. They want the hottest products. Think about Apple and how they market the newest iPhones. It's as if you can't live without it, right? The phone you waited all day in line for only a year ago is now complete crap! Of course, you *can* live without the newest model, but you don't *want* to. And when you're one of the first to have that newest phone in the latest color, with all of the bells and whistles, you feel special—for the moment, anyway, until the next one comes out. The fact that the phone recognizes your thumbprint, face, and voice make it personalized to *you*, and that's intentional.

When it comes to marketing, the energy must be positive and exciting. It needs to create a buzz. Renderings and pictures tell the story for buyers near and far. This isn't an area to overlook, and definitely not a place to underspend. These are some of the most important tools we have to sell new construction. Why? People can't see what isn't there. They can't imagine the lifestyle that's being sold, so we present it in a visually appealing manner. We want them to envision themselves in the story, enjoying all the amenities, beauty, and serenity of this new home. As with anything, if you love your product, you can sell your product. The challenge is matching the product with the right person.

So one of my biggest challenges working in sales—and, quite frankly, with being human—is how to manage rejection. I work in a business of "No." I still have to get up, dust myself off, and be positive and confident every day. It's really the only way I can reach my clients' goals, and my own, time after time. Not only do I have to take rejection, I must then deliver it to my clients and convince them (even when it's hard to believe) that we're just facing a bump in the road. I have to be an eternal optimist with a plan. The amount of rejection a real estate broker has to endure is massive. Sometimes you're rejected after a pitch. Sometimes you're rejected before you even get the opportunity to pitch. You're rejected by buyers who don't call you back. You're rejected by sellers when you bring them an offer they don't like—or, worse, when you bring them *no* offers.

One thing is for sure: you'd better be able to stand up to all that rejection, because there's no avoiding it. Every time a deal doesn't go our way, what do I do? You've heard me say it before, because it's a strategy that's important and that works. I look at it and ask, "What is my takeaway from this? Where did I go wrong? Where could I have done better?"

That's how I continue to learn, get stronger, and navigate through difficult landscapes. It's all part of the process of bettering myself.

The way I've ultimately learned to manage challenging situations and to improve my life is to have so much going on that I don't have time to focus on the negative signals or the letdowns because I'm too busy fielding the positive ones.

New agents tend to think it's easier said than done. Some look at seasoned brokers and assume they manage so well because they have an established business to fall back on. But I believe everyone has the ability to fill their days with opportunities and possibilities; it simply requires shifting your focus to the positive things that are happening. Because when you have a lot of possibilities, losing one is not that big a deal.

When I was finally ready to launch the new me, I realized that one great thing I had going for me was my career. Real estate had prepared me better than I could have imagined. I had dealt with rejection, learned how to market a property effectively, and come to understand my value. At thirty-two, I was one of the most successful agents in the country, and I *loved* it. One day, while I was giving a colleague of mine some advice about his business, he asked me about being single. The conversation that followed was laced with sadness, humiliation, and fear. Then the subject switched back to real estate for a minute, and I was instantly someone else, someone with confidence, strength, and power.

"Wow!" he said. "Do you hear the difference in your voice? You sound like two different people. You're a whole other person when you're speaking about real estate."

When he said that, it was like a switch was flipped and a light came on. I knew what I needed to do. It's not like real estate doesn't have a million challenges. Of course it does. You name an absurdity, and I've seen it, dealt with it, and sold it. I've gotten my sellers out of not just one bad decision but several. I'm a problem solver and caretaker and one hell of a salesperson. And now I needed to find a buyer for the best property of my life: *me*! I was the crown penthouse, the double-wide brownstone, the classic six over the park. I was the luxury property, and I needed to approach this entire situation differently. I had to become one of my clients. I was a *great* property. I had suffered many blows but still stood beautiful and intact. I had landmark status, baby! The value of this property was only going up.

I had watched dozens of buildings launch throughout my career, but I had never given much thought to the similarities between getting them ready to enter the marketplace and getting myself ready to do the same. It occurred to me that the crossover was both relevant and necessary if I were going to launch the new me successfully. Just like I understood everything about a new building, I needed to understand who I was now and how I wanted the world to see, feel, and think about me. Yeah, I was no longer married, but who had I become since then? A single, successful divorcée? Sure, that was true. But what else was I? I'd have do the analysis. I'd have to identify what I wanted, what I didn't, and how to achieve my goals.

What did I want?

I was looking for someone with an open mind, someone who loved life and the many varieties in it. Someone who enjoyed dancing, great food, and skiing. At his core, he'd be a real family man. I wanted someone to say, "Yes, sounds great. Let's do it," and mean it. Charisma and style were important too, but I truly wanted a lifelong partner with a deep well of integrity and loyalty, and someone who was a student and always hungry to grow and improve in all areas of life.

What I didn't want was judgment, closed mindedness, or laziness. I didn't want to be in a loveless relationship—the kind where two people coexist but never come together as a team. I wanted to grow a relationship *together*. I didn't want to show up to a six-act play that was already in progress. I wanted to be a part of the fabric, to weave in and out of my partner's strengths and weaknesses.

If you don't have a dream, you can't create a plan. And if you don't have a plan, chances are you won't get to where you want to go. Your dream will become just that—a pipe dream. It's critical to remember that a dream is not a plan. Neither is hope.

With my list of nonnegotiables in hand, I needed a plan to find my buyer. I mean, I wasn't looking for someone offering six goats and three cows for my hand in marriage. I was determined to find the one, and I knew he was out there. There were many times when I questioned my list and worried about where I'd have to make compromises. It's hard to get everything you want on the island of Manhattan. It's not impossible, but it certainly has its challenges. And if he did come calling offering livestock, well, that was just a bonus.

Since my divorce, I'd referred to myself only as a divorcée. That was the story I was telling myself. And while it may have been true, it didn't have to define or limit me. I'm also a skier, an adventure seeker, a tennis player, a chef, a daughter, a sister, and a friend. I didn't want to go on dates and cry over my soup. I wanted to throw back a few cocktails and have some fun. My story was sad to me, but certainly not uncommon. Statistics told me one thing, but my mind was saying something completely different. When negative things happen to us, we often feel as if we're the only ones suffering that plight. Even if we know that isn't true, it's how we feel. It's a grand illusion, one that plays a dirty trick on us. I had to figure out how to control those thoughts whenever they popped up. I now had a handle on my narrative and wanted to tell a completely different story going forward.

The thing about healing is that you have to actively participate and do the work. It's not a quick fix. For many, it can take years. And for redheads, even longer because we take longer to heal. As far as I was concerned, I was doing it in relatively record time. I had made a lot of progress since the separation, and certainly since the divorce. I was no longer looking to someone else to complete me. I was doing a pretty good job of that myself. I was laughing, stimulated, and learning all the time. It felt liberating. And necessary.

The steps that we follow before we launch a property are designed to plant as many seeds as possible across many different platforms. And that's what's critical when reintroducing yourself into the community as a single person: as fabulous as you are, not everyone is looking for a penthouse over Central Park. Some people know that they can't afford you, or they might be scared that they won't be able to afford you in the future. It's simply not comfortable for them. Maybe that studio in Midtown is better. It reminds them of the best times they had as a child visiting their grandmother. It just feels like home to them. The reasons we're attracted to the people we're attracted to are complex and layered. They're often reflections of our past and cycles that are repeated over and over again. That person just feels familiar. But I wasn't looking for the same thing I'd had in the past. I had shed that skin and was ready to start anew.

The day had finally come when I felt that this sexy, sleek penthouse was ready to launch on the market. Up until then, you could say I was still under construction. Buyers who wanted to pursue this listing had been turned away; even if they were qualified, this unit wasn't available yet.

As with any launch, a brochure precedes a showing. It includes beautifully shot images of the space intended to seduce a prospective buyer into thinking this could be the one. Every brochure tells a story of what life might be like if you called this space home. If I were creating a brochure for myself, what story did I want to tell? What pictures would I include? What would my tagline be?

I needed to figure all of this out. I sat dumbfounded and dazed, staring at the homepage for Match.com—the one where you fill out your personal profile and upload pictures that tell the story of who you are. Both in real estate and in online dating, you share imagery. In real estate, however, everything is shot with a wide-angle lens, while in online dating photos often require a "skinny filter."

The pressure from friends and family to join an online dating site had grown intolerable. It was easier to just join than to avoid any more dialogue on the topic. My brother, Matthew, and a few close friends insisted that I do this, as they knew lots of people who had met their significant others this way. The alternative wasn't necessarily better; so many of my waking hours were spent working that I wasn't sure how I would ever have enough time to go out and randomly meet someone. I was being social, but until now, I wasn't being open. I was hoping my new receptiveness would help. I can't say that the idea of online dating entirely appealed to me. In fact, it sent me into a state of panic. Who would see me? Would anyone recognize me? It felt like the land of the lost, the home of losers. It felt like TJ Maxx: good fashion at an affordable cost. Did I want to be a markdown? Did I want to be in a relationship where I would be constantly looking for the red tape that was hiding the other person's fatal flaw—the crack in the foundation that made them such a bargain to begin with? Okay, I realize that I was one of them too, so, no judgment. But to put us all together in one location seemed to amplify that even more. This must be what people look like after they've blown up their lives.

Did I really think I could be the off-market listing that so many sellers dream of carrying out? What I'd learned in the real estate market was that it takes all eyes on the property in order to understand its true value. If this was this case, there was no denying that I needed to go online. Yet it was such a completely new concept to me. At the time, other than real estate, the things that were sold online were old pairs of shoes, baseball card collections, or antique furniture.

Was this really the point my life had come to? Sticking a price tag on my head and sending it out into cyberspace for all takers? It felt desperate, especially after I'd gone online to see what was out there. How many times have you heard stories about how a handsome six foot two, dark-haired fella your friend was chatting with on a dating site turned out to be a bald hobbit? The thought of that was scarier than *The Blair Witch Project*. And like the Blair Witch, I went around and around, wrestling with this dilemma.

Aside from the urging from friends and family, the only other reason I agreed to go online was because of real estate. Here's what I mean: most buyers do their search online, at least at the start. They eventually need to find a broker to really figure out what they want and what they can afford, but they surf the Internet first. Basically, I couldn't be on the market if I wasn't listed. And there it was: the truth. The hard, cold, awful truth.

Occasionally we come across sellers who feel too vulnerable having their homes publicly on the market. This mainly happens with very high-end real estate. The sellers explain that they're too private and they don't want the way they live to be available for all to see. They tell us they want to be a "pocket listing," a listing only we Realtors know about. But by doing this, they're severely narrowing the market. I understand that putting a price on your home and your life and sticking it up online is asking a lot. But if you expect a lot, you'll be asked for a lot, and when it comes to luxury real estate, it's important to get the word out to get the price up. If that's what I preached for my business, how could I possibly argue that I was different?

I finally came up with a compromise: I hid my profile. People couldn't see me, but I could see them. I would make the first move. I'd unlock my account for a few hours so they could see me, and then I'd make it private again, until the next time. This was how I dealt with my discomfort.

Because I knew from my experience in real estate that every picture must tell a story, I selected mostly photos of me diving, skiing, hiking, and traveling—all my way of saying that I needed someone active and adventurous. But before I actually posted them, I paused. As Stephen King once said, "The scariest moment is always just before you start."

Now, *that* guy has known a lot of frightening moments in his life, so take it from him. Those seconds before you launch are going to be scary, scary, scary. Did I mention they'd be scary? King has created an entire career out of playing to his readers' fears, understanding that the unknown is by far the most terrifying thing of all. That which we cannot see becomes the fear we create.

Feel that fear and know that it's perfectly normal to be petrified. And then acknowledge that it's all in your head. It's the story you've been telling yourself. When you're frightened of the dark, turn on the light; it's as simple as that. And so, I dove in, head first. Initially I think I was too specific about what I wanted. I wasn't open to anything that wasn't on my trusted list. No open house for me. Maybe I was being too narrow minded, or perhaps I was just not willing to settle.

The thing about launching anything is to make it fun and exciting. What's the best way to do that?

Throw a party!

My friend Suzi said, "I got this. I'm handling the guest list." And that she did. My loft seemed more like a clown car, with an endless stream of colorful people squeezing in. As they say in Hollywood, "Lights, camera, action!"—except on this night there was more action for other people than there was for me. I was okay with that, as I felt more like a debutante coming out than anything else. There were well over a hundred people in my 1,600-square-foot apartment, new faces in addition to old friends. There were lots of guests to meet, but I cautiously took my time. We tend to always be rushed in life, especially in this city, but I love moving slowly when something is important.

Online dating was such a new concept for me. I don't think I was very good at it, but I wouldn't have changed a thing about it. I did meet some very nice guys. I didn't find a match, but none was a total waste of time. They were good picks and great guys . . . for someone, just not for me. I considered each encounter an exercise that would help me get stronger and further hone in on what I really wanted. After a while, it didn't freak me out as much as it had in the beginning. It started to feel somewhat normal. Besides, every date was a way for me to practice my pitch—and in sales, it's all about the pitch! Open houses don't always find you a direct buyer, but they're a great way for a broker and seller to learn how the property is being received.

In real estate, you can't sell to no one. My general rule is, take the showing. If it's not for you, you might have a friend, family member, or neighbor who is a good fit. Referrals are everything. The same philosophy holds true in dating: even if you have reservations, take the showing. What's thirty minutes, which was always my limit if I suspected it would never work?

Whenever I was in the midst of coordinating a date, whether by e-mail, text, or phone call, there was always a moment I worried about. It was like the sound of the guillotine for me; the inevitable, "Where do you want to go?" It was a deal killer. It may seem small to you, but to me it said everything. Why was this person handing me the reins before I was even on the horse? We would never get on the range, at least not the way I wanted to. I may be modern in many ways, but for the first steps of this dance, I'm not flexible: the man needs to lead. He needs to have a plan and be confident about it. Let's meet here for coffee; Joe's makes the best cup in the city. It doesn't need to be fancy, but it has to be his, and he's got to have a story behind it—I like it here because the room is so beautiful, the biscotti are delicious, or the bartender makes the best margaritas. It needs to be thought out, or at least appear to be. I guess you could say I need a man with a plan.

While it seems so simple, it was an expectation that was rarely met. It was as if I were asking for a personal outdoor swimming pool in the middle of Manhattan. While there are a few, the likelihood of owning one is small.

Knowing very well where the conversation would lead, whenever I heard, "Where should we meet?" I would blurt out, "Giorgio's on 21st Street. It has the best atmosphere."

I mean, how hard is that?

Giorgio's was a block from my apartment, and Brad, one of my best friends, was a waiter there. He was an actor by day who worked tables at night and was like my annoying little brother who never missed a chance to rib me. It was always great to have an audience for what usually ended as a Shakespearean tragedy. The staff got to know me quite well, as I became a regular, accompanied by one "no-plan man" after another. They held back their smirks whenever they'd see us walk in the door, knowing this poor shmuck didn't stand a chance.

If I was stood up, the staff kept the drinks coming.

If the guy was gone in thirty seconds, dinner was on the house.

And if by chance the date was going well, Brad's annoying menu innuendos were endless. "May I bring you some oysters? They're particularly flavorful this evening," or "I'd recommend the salty prosciutto and succulent peach salad this evening. It's gotten rave reviews." Of course, my date had no idea I knew the waiter, or that he was speaking to me in code. A highly tuned-in date might have questioned Brad's behavior, but most didn't even notice. As for me, well, it was always fun, and usually the best part of my date.

I really appreciated having that backup for what was often a tiresome showing. The point is that I never regretted my choice to be there, not once. As in real estate, when you find the right match, you know it; and when you don't, you keep searching. Sometimes it takes lots of showings to understand what you're actually looking for. It's all part of the process. Just remember, if you take the time to pick a meeting spot that reflects a little something about you, it's as good as baking cookies before a potential buyer arrives to see your home. It sets the mood and says, "Hey, this is a cozy place." Even if the showing is a bust, you'll have fresh cookies when they leave.

CHAPTER THIRTEEN

Curbside Is King

Use your eyes to see the possibilities, not the problems.
—Anonymous

So often, when we find ourselves back on the market, we get too close to the flame to stay out of the fire. We cannot be objective and suddenly forget—or forgo—the rules of engagement. We don't fix our foundation, we think curb appeal doesn't matter, and we refuse to spend the money on staging, thinking that buyers should be able to see beyond that. But humans are shallow. Attraction is always with the eyes first; the mind and the soul follow, but the eyes always do the leading. Some properties are worth restoring, while others are teardowns that you must rebuild entirely from the bedrock up. Assess your property and come up with a strategy for making the best use of the new you going forward.

I had a neighbor who was single for years. At one time, she had been a beauty pageant winner. She fell in love, moved to the suburbs, and had babies. But then her husband cheated on her and broke her heart. When they divorced, she moved back to the city, which is where we met. During that time, she let her gray hair grow in and her waist grow out. She went from wearing fashionable couture to Uggs and sweats all the time. And she didn't care, which is admirable in some ways. She gave off an aura of nonchalance, though I knew she was hurt, sad, and lonely deep down. It was painfully obvious that she was broken. She had let the weeds grow and the paint chip. The lights inside were dimmed, and not in a good way. If you were indoors you could see what a great place it was and what great potential it had, but she had no curb appeal, which meant no one was going to stop to go inside. They would draw their own conclusions about the interior based on the dilapidated exterior.

We'd spoken many times about how badly she wanted a companion to share her life with. I always felt her pain and would try my best to steer her out of her melancholy ways. The reality was, she first needed to find herself. I've always believed that a smile is the best accessory, and just like Annie says in the Broadway musical, you're never fully dressed without one. Similarly, a lot can be forgiven when there's light pouring through the windows or beaming out from the soul. But when you're walking around looking like the love child of Pig-Pen and Eeyore from *Winnie the Pooh*, life will always be messy on the outside and gloomy on the inside. That's a really tough combination. Only Pooh and Charlie Brown will seek your company, and sadly, they're just make-believe.

There was no pep in my neighbor's step. She wasn't happy, and her hair looked crappy. She needed to reconnect to her property and remodel, renovate, or rebuild it, love it, and highlight its strengths so she could show it with pride. Paint the front door, plant some flowers, trim the ivy. Skip those steps and you'll skip the sale.

Let's face it: an overgrown bush is never attractive.

Light is one of the most important and expensive features in a property. If a home has light streaming through the windows, it can completely change the feel of the place. A good agent knows the exact time optimal light shines in the property they're showing. When a buyer calls and asks for a 12:15 appointment and the agent knows the light is perfect at 1:00, you'd better believe that the 1:00 slot is the one that's pushed.

So how does a person turn on their lights?

Is there such a thing?

I found that my lights came on when I connected to myself. The more I practiced self-care and the more I catered to my own passions, the more my lights glimmered. With a smile on your face and light behind your eyes, you can absolutely to take on the world. If you're not feeling hot, it's time to turn up the heat. Turn your light on!

Many times, people form their opinion based on curb appeal alone. They'll say, "We can skip this one. I don't need to go inside. It's not for me." The least one can do is spend a couple of minutes breezing through the place. No one has ever said at the closing table, "I wish we didn't see some of those other apartments." It happens all the time in job interviews. The resume got that person through the door, but the interview is where I separate the "appearance" of being right for the position and the reality. I look for passion, persistence, integrity and above all, whether the candidate will be a good fit for our team.

A great agent knows that showing a home is about the whole experience. It's finding the right balance between livable and must-have. It should smell inviting, fresh, and polished. Whenever I suggest painting the walls, I almost always get some type of pushback because the owner loves the violet or the powder blue that's currently there.

Really?

Did their grandmother own the home before they did? The walls should be neutral. A prospective buyer should remember the space, not the color. The paint choice isn't really the issue so much as the owner's perception. They've lived in their home for so long that they don't have the ability to see it as a new buyer does. They just think, "I love my home the way it is. There must be at least one buyer out there who will love it this way too," or "A real buyer will be able to see past all of this." I've heard these cries of denial from reluctant sellers all too often. I've even made that mistake myself. In assessing my own property for sale, I thought it was okay to just paint a couple of walls and not the entire apartment. When the sale was complete, the new owner, who bought the property as an investment, asked me to rent it for him. The first thing he did was paint the entire place. Wow! I had been *way* off the mark. It made a huge difference, one I couldn't—or wouldn't—see when I'd owned it. I wanted to believe that painting a couple of walls was enough, but it wasn't. The new paint totally transformed the space. How many times do we convince ourselves that the easier way is good enough, when making that extra effort is really the best way to achieve our goals?

Ah, yes, the stories we tell ourselves.

When I went back on the market, I had a rule—just one, but I followed it religiously. Never turn down a date. To clarify, the buyer needed to be fully vetted and the recommendation had to come from a top broker, but if they got past those gates, what was the harm in giving them a few minutes?

But being me, I would know from three hundred feet away when they had no curb appeal. In fact, they lost me before they got through the front door. Ninety-nine times out of a hundred, I'd see the person and I was out. There's no crying in baseball, and no crime in chemistry. When it's there, it's there—and when it's not, it's not. When friends complained they weren't finding anyone, I would joke, "You're clearly not drinking enough." But there are no beer goggles that will fix someone's curb appeal.

The way I navigated this awkward introduction was always to refer this buyer to another property. I did this to avoid any embarrassing follow-up—the lean-in kiss I didn't want or the unnecessary and unwanted text. The referral took care of all of this before the bill arrived. Clean, kind, and a small investment to make. There was one date where the guy was so nice and so accomplished, but he really wasn't my type. Always the dealmaker, I suggested that my friend Nancy would be a good fit for him. I genuinely thought she would be, but he shook his head in disbelief. "Why are you fixing me up? Aren't you interested?"

"You're great, but I match people for a living. You and Nancy are a much better fit."

As time went on, there were a few more of my friends I tried to fix him up with. He'd take them out for a spin, but no one seemed to be the right complement. At least I got him a lot of tail!

This wasn't a rarity. In fact, it became a habit. For the most part, every date I went on, at least at that time, turned me into a matchmaker—so much so that I genuinely contemplated starting my own dating service. In my mind, it was the same as selling real estate. It's all about chemistry and true pairing. It didn't matter to me if I was matching people or places. I loved making people's lives better.

Admittedly, it got awkward from time to time, but only for a second. The potential of a true match always overcame any sense of rejection. The promise of tomorrow outweighed the disappointment of today, so it really was a win for everyone.

I never questioned my friends' taste. I knew all too well that one person's frog is another person's prince. What appeals to me might not appeal to others, and vice versa. Sometimes, however, my friends really missed the mark. A colleague fixed me up with a man whom I'd heard a lot about from various people. I was intrigued, because he was a well-known bachelor in Manhattan. He still is. You get the point. Anyway, we met for a drink at Perry Street in the West Village. When he walked in, he was sweaty and late. After apologizing, the second thing out of his mouth was, "I forgot my wallet." I've seen this movie more times than I care to recall. And still I stayed, because we had mutual friends and I had long been waiting to meet this man about town. I found him to be distinguished-looking, although totally not my type. Within minutes of our hellos, he began telling me about his brother's apartment, which was under construction across the street. He wanted to give me a tour and get my take on it. We had barely touched our drinks before we were out the door. We did a quick walk-through of this amazing space. There wasn't a lot to see, since it was being renovated, but it didn't take much to understand that this was going to be a real showplace. His brother was combining two floors with endless views of the Hudson River. Even in this state, it was majestic. When we left, he hailed a cab for me and said, "It was nice to meet you." For a moment, I thought we were going to another place. Instead, he ushered me into the cab and said goodbye. I guess this was his way of referring me to someone else. When I looked at my watch, I saw that it was twelve minutes into the date. I called my colleague from the car to give him the report.

"Aren't you on your date?" he asked.

"It's over. Done."

"Done? You couldn't possibly be done."

"I assure you; we are absolutely done. He actually stuffed me in a cab and sent me on my way."

"Was that really a twelve-minute date? What did you do to him?"

Good question!

I thought it was hysterically funny. From that day on, I've referred to him as the "cab stuffer." I wasn't asked on a second date and didn't get the listing, but I got a pretty good "bad date" story, and he got a nickname that would someday be published.

Someone once asked me about the proper etiquette for a buyer looking at a space they know isn't for them. If it's a townhouse do they really need to climb to every floor when they know from the curb it's a pass? No one wants to have their time wasted, and yet I believe that sometimes the unexpected is just that. Whether it's real estate or dating, curbside is king. You can bet people will judge appearances. I later found out that the cab stuffer preferred petite, ninety-pound, racktacular women, which wasn't me. And that's okay. Looking back, I see that there really was no reason to prolong that date. It wasn't going to work, and we both knew it inside of five seconds.

I once had buyers who were looking for an apartment. We'd seen everything on the market in their price range except for one apartment that was like a time capsule from the 1970s. I called it the Austin Powers Palace. I set the expectation going in that the décor was beyond tacky. The master bath, which opened onto to the master bedroom, looked like a Roman bathhouse. Clearly, free love reigned supreme here. If the walls could talk, I'm sure the things they would have said would've been filthy. I'm certain we wouldn't have wanted to listen. The suggestion of what type of lifestyle had been lived here gave me the creeps. When the buyers had pushed to see more listings, I'd warned them as strongly as I could that this apartment would need a total gut renovation, starting with a massive amount of dynamite. Yet upon entering, the wife saw the bathroom and exclaimed, "I love how open this is!" While she ogled the golden commode in the center of the room, the husband was fixated on the mirrored ceiling above the bed, saying, "Well, this could be a lot of fun."

I wanted to hurl.

It was just way too much information for this pilgrim to handle.

I learned a valuable lesson that day: this couple wasn't looking for an investment, they were looking for a home. It was early in my career, and I hadn't read them right. I was talking, giving my opinions, and not listening. Guess what? I got it all wrong. But I also realized that even though the home didn't appeal to me, it was their dream come true. Everything I hated, they loved. It was clear that these weren't clients who would become friends, since I had never owned a fondue set or thrown a key party. And so I came to understand more fully the expression "to each their own." A mistake that makes you humble is better than an achievement that makes you arrogant.

I love the optimism of "it just takes one." But when you think about it, that's really what people say when they don't want to do the work. It's the lazy battle cry for the army of denial. As I've said, hope is not a plan, but it is an ingredient in a recipe. This is especially true when it comes to dating and real estate. When people don't want to do the work, is it laziness, ignorance, or fear that holds them back? Or is it really just an excuse?

A job well done is a job worth doing. Why not do your best? If you don't sell, at the very least, you've cleaned your shit up. You've gotten your affairs in order, your space organized, and your life decluttered. Okay, well, at least your home.

Sometimes exceptions are made. There is a yin to the yang. But these exceptions are rare and cannot be used as a road map to get you to where you want to go. If I got a Prada purse at Bergdorf's at 60 percent off, the likelihood is that I could go back searching for that same bag at the same discount a hundred times and never find it. Some people just have good karma in love and in real estate. They defy the odds, and the stars align for them. It happens. But you can't count on that any more than you can winning the lottery.

For most people, though, appearance is everything. This explains love at first sight, or that familiar feeling that you've known someone or someplace forever. You've been there before. There's a comfort that just feels like home to you. And you'll know it when you see it.

When heading back onto the market, there's no time like the present to adjust, fix, and finesse your problem areas. If you truly want to get to the closing table and to move forward in your life, you must tackle these challenges. No amount of camouflage will disguise them. You must deal with each one. Now, more than ever, the world is at your fingertips, and if you can't DIY, there are specialists you can bring in for everything.

A common mistake I see all the time is the equivalent of putting lipstick on a pig. Here's what I mean. To put lipstick on a pig is to make superficial or cosmetic changes in a futile attempt to mask the true nature of a product or person. But the truth will come out during the inspection.

When someone discovers that you've just painted over the problem—and they will—you've lost their trust forever.

I have a good friend who always says, "When people show you who they really are, believe them."

Eventually, we all walk our talk, even when our talk doesn't at first match up with our walk.

We've all seen early signs of decay, damage, and leaks while dating someone but have chosen to ignore the obvious signs of impending problems. Why? We didn't want to believe them. We saw them for who we wanted them to be and not for who they really were.

My dad always said, "Watch how a man is with his mother and his dog, and you'll have a road map for how he'll treat you."

And if he doesn't have a dog but does play golf, hit the links with him and watch how he acts. Does he cheat? Throw his club? Get pissed when he misses a shot? Oh yeah. It's all there to be seen.

I've always had a very high level of emotional intelligence. I can read a lot from people's behavior, body language, breathing, and energy. Since 90 percent of communication is nonverbal, this opens up the conversation tremendously. All the things and feelings we don't say out loud but say clearly in other ways are what I hear. It's a huge advantage in a business where I need to "predict" buyers' and sellers' next moves, and it has always served me very well. But like many superpowers, there is, of course, a downside to this. Sure, I pick up on the positive signs, and there are many—for example, the body language that tells me a buyer will keep pursuing a bid. But this ability also automatically opens me up to the challenging things as well, such as when a buyer is thinking, *She's talking too much. I don't even like this penthouse. When is our next appointment?* or *I can't stand brokers. This whole song and dance is a lie. Brokers never tell the truth.* Sometimes I take those cues and address their concerns directly. Other times I recognize that stereotypes and beliefs were formed long before I came on the scene, and I have nothing to do with the story that's been created in their minds. I get all the intel—the good, the bad, the ugly. There are certainly exceptions to this rule, but in my experience, having this type of sensitivity requires your nerves to run close to the surface so they can act like little antennae picking up others' frequencies.

While emotional intelligence is one thing, actions often speak louder than words. Our behavior is also part of our curb appeal. While so much of our appearance comes from within, how we carry ourselves, what our bodies are saying, and whether our lights are on speak volumes. I'm not just talking about what we see on the facade; I'm talking about what we see in the property as a whole. I've gone on early morning walks past a gorgeous, historic brownstone with window boxes full of bright spring flowers. A big, glossy-painted door opens to reveal a mom who's a natural beauty in a cashmere robe. She holds a golden retriever puppy and hands a book bag to a delightfully disheveled tween boy eating a piece of toast. He starts down the stairs, then doubles back to give his mom a quick goodbye kiss on the cheek before she heads back behind that glossy door. Curb appeal. The action on the inside matches the beauty of the outside. I tell myself, *I want this! I MUST have it!* This is what we're looking to make all buyers feel. And the same holds true with personal relationships. How many really attractive people become ugly because of the way they act? This scenario wouldn't have been appealing if that tween boy was mid-tantrum when the glossy door opened, or if the mom was drunkenly hanging out of her bathrobe and throwing the boy's backpack at him while cursing at the puppy. What looked beautiful before the door opened has left you running toward the next block. And, by contrast, how many less physically attractive people do you find beautiful because of their kind deeds, overall aura, and good behavior? Curb appeal is personal but critical. It shouldn't be overlooked, especially when you find yourself back on the market like I was. I had to constantly remind myself of this. The dating world felt so superficial to me, including and especially my own responses at times. This couldn't really be what life was all about. Or was it? Could a haircut, a toned body, or a fashion trend really make that much of an impact? It just felt too thin to be meaningful, and yet attending to image is a necessary aspect of getting your listing sold. Like it or not, that's the way it is. And the more I fought the tide, the harder I had to swim.

Sometimes, however, you need to give in and learn to surf, and for me, that meant getting my house in order, inside and out—literally and figuratively. If I wanted to have love in my life, I first needed to love myself. When you do that, there's a light that shines through, and no one can dim it except you. I wasn't quite there yet, but I understood what needed to be done. I've always been a very confident person, but self-love is more than confidence. It's a connection with your spirit, a knowledge of how to nurture and feed your soul. The ability to laugh at and with yourself. To work on this, I began practicing meditation in the morning. I started off with just a few minutes each day, taking a few long, slow breaths while cycling through all of the things I was grateful for. I always started with my parents, picturing their sweet faces laughing with joy. I felt my love for them, and that warmed my heart and soul. I then felt the love they have for me. I would progress through each member of my family like that. Next, I expressed gratitude for my career, my amazing friends, and all of the support around me. Finally, I pictured myself on a paddleboard. Instead of standing on the board, I saw myself lying down. I was definitely not exercising or exerting a lot of unnecessary energy in these visions. I was relaxing and allowing the imaginary waves to gently rise and fall as they quieted my brain.

The whole meditation took no more than fifteen minutes, but some days I was so relaxed that it lasted longer. Before opening my eyes, I would ask the Universe to fill my heart with love again. When you have a heart full of gratitude, there's no room for fear and anger. It's like pouring water on a hot fire. I learned that loving myself meant sometimes just being still with myself. How ironic is it that the best action toward love was actually no action at all?

There is a voice that doesn't use words. Listen.
—Rumi

CHAPTER FOURTEEN

_____

First-Time Buyers

May your walls know joy, may every room hold laughter,
and every window open to great possibility.
—MARY ANNE RADMACHER

MUCH OF MY BUSINESS IS BASED ON REFERRALS FROM PAST clients and friends. One particular fall morning, I was just sitting down at my desk with my coffee when my assistant, Morgan, said, "Holly, you have a call on line two. She says she was referred by Andrea Boccaletti, your friend from boarding school."

I picked up the receiver and said, "Hi, this is Holly." Now, sometimes these calls are nothing more than advice-seeking, while other times they're buyers or sellers ready to go.

"This is Cristy, a friend of Andrea Boccaletti, who said I absolutely had to call you."

"So nice to meet you, Cristy. I love Andrea, so any friend of his is a friend of mine. How can I help you?"

"I'm looking to buy my first apartment. I love the West Village, with all the tree-lined streets. I need at least two bedrooms, I'm looking for Old World charm, a fireplace, garage, and private outdoor space, and I would love it to be somewhat modern too. A doorman would be great, and I would love a gym. I was picturing a couple of floors in a brownstone."

"Great. I can definitely help you. How much can you spend?"

"I could go up to $450,000, and stretch to $500,000 if I got everything on my list."

"Can you hold on a second, please?" I asked before pushing the "Pause" button to scream. There was no way I could deliver a fraction of this list at that price. "Okay, sorry about that. I'm back. To get started, I'm going to send you some recent market reports so you can begin familiarizing yourself with prices in the city. Then I'll send you the best options for your price and priority list." I explained that the most important thing on her list was location, location, location, and by wanting to be in the West Village, she had chosen an A location. But A also stands for something else: "When you're talking about location, it also means *a lot* of money."

Whenever I work with first-time homebuyers, I always sit down to discuss their expectations. Occasionally, a first-time buyer gets it right. They actually understand their limitations and therefore have a realistic outlook. Most of the time, though, first-time buyers have very unrealistic expectations. They all seem to have the same theme song, "To dream the impossible dream!" Their feet are not on the ground. They're often disconnected from their needs and wants and what this new home will bring them. Most come to me having done very little research about how much things actually cost in Manhattan.

There may be markets in the country where half a million dollars will get you everything you want, but New York City isn't one of them.

Not even close. I couldn't find a decent studio for that kind of money. So this is when I have to explain that this isn't going to happen. I explain that there are only a few thousand townhouses in Manhattan. Of those, perhaps 150 have garages. Those townhouses start at $10 million and up. So, let's talk about what $500,000 *will* buy in New York City.

It's a harsh wake-up call.

A reality check.

A kick in the groin.

Eventually we come around to what will work, and I can provide my buyer with appropriate choices that fit their needs and budget.

It's all about setting expectations. Finding your dream home is a lifelong journey. I've always wanted outdoor space and a fireplace, but after investing in eleven homes in Manhattan, I still haven't had either. I realize this sounds absurd, but I've always looked at real estate as an investment in the future. Whenever I've bought, the value and investment opportunities were greater without those two things on my list.

Still, I love how first-time buyers come at this with so much excitement and so little research. So often I felt like answering their calls by saying, "Hello, Dream Killer of Manhattan speaking, how can I help you?"

When you think about it, what first-time buyers truly need is a step-by-step plan and a realistic budget—not just for what they're buying the first time around, but a longer-term budget and plan so they can achieve what they really want over time. Strategy without a plan is still just a dream. I want to be a dream maker, not a dream taker.

As frustrating as it can be, I absolutely love working with first-time buyers. I love slowly educating them tour by tour. We talk about their goals, their lifestyle, and the ways this purchase can support both. We talk about their home as an investment and all the tax advantages they could have in making the right decision. How $250,000 of the profit they could make on the resale would be tax free, and how, if they were in the top tax bracket, they'd have to make $500,000 at work to equal the same. We prioritize and find them the right investment they can live in, improve upon, and hold on to when the market rises—and it *always* does. On this tiny, crowded island of Manhattan, they'll be in a perfect spot to make that profit.

Suspend reality for a moment and try to envision yourself as someone who's spent months couch surfing and sleeping in friends' spare rooms. Suddenly, your fairy godmother appears and creates your dream penthouse overlooking Central Park. First, she conjures up the most magnificent facade, with beautiful, intricate details that you see only on buildings that are more than one hundred years old. Then she waves her magic wand and creates a spectacular interior consisting of brand-new everything—all new pipes, amazing amenities, fabulous outdoor space, and four glorious exposures so you can enjoy both sunrise and sunset. It's truly a rare diamond in a city full of jewels.

Okay, so that's the dream, right?

When I married my prince, we were just like first-time buyers.

We imagined the pie-in-the-sky fairy tale home. But take it from someone who's now been working in the Manhattan real estate market for two decades: that's all it is. It's just pie. No matter what your budget, the combination of all things incredible under one roof is as fictional as Sneezy or any of the other six adorable dwarves. Now, I'm not saying that Snow White and her prince can't find their perfect slice of that pie, but it will be just a slice, and sometimes it may even just be a sliver. They'll find it tasty at first and feed each other a few bites. They'll find those tax benefits and other perks sweet for a while too. But eventually, they'll decide they no longer want that particular pie. They've had their fill. Maybe it has made them fat. But some other flavor of pie is beckoning them to move on to a different, perhaps bigger slice.

As analogies go, I'm not just talking pie and real estate here. I'm talking pie, real estate, and soul mates. In my mind, finding my soul mate was equal to finding my dream home, my apple pie. I had active lists of requirements, complete with essentials and deal-breakers. I knew there were some traits or ingredients I needed to have, and some I would be willing to sacrifice. All in all, I was still going for a pretty big piece of pie. I call this "first-time buyer syndrome." It's when a buyer has bigger eyes than they do budget.

Nevertheless, I shared my list with close friends, especially my single friends. Do you know a better plan? It might be a little witchy-poo, but it works. Meeting the perfect person is hard. Why? You really have no control over it. You can plan a meeting. You can start a business. You can make a dinner reservation. But finding your soul mate? That takes a helping hand, or lots of them. And as it often happens, the Universe has a hand in it too. That's hard to accept, especially for a control freak like me, but finding the one is serious business, so you do what you have to do. Remind yourself it might just take a village to find that perfect person, and in New York it might take a village from the actual Village.

But back to my client: after exchanging several e-mails and narrowing our search, Cristy and I were off to the races. I met her on Charles Street, one of the most picturesque blocks in the West Village. I watched her walk up the block. She was breathtaking. She was in her late twenties and had long red hair, piercing blue eyes, and an incredibly fit body. She radiated warmth, especially when she smiled. She gave me a big hug, and I felt as though I were meeting an old friend.

While it's true that Charles Street is definitely an A+ location, there would be no doorman, and we were looking at a third-floor walk-up. When we entered the apartment, we were overcome by the smell of animals. The owner had a dog and a cat and was clearly against bathing either of them. The dog had white hair and the biggest, blackest balls you've ever seen. The cat was clearly turned off by him, as any self-respecting cat would be, shooting a disgusted look in his direction more than once. The hair from both animals was everywhere—all over the couch, the bed, and the floor. And you just gotta love a litter box in a room without any airflow. If that wasn't enough to make us turn on our heels, old Black Balls dropped his butt on the floor and dragged it across the rug. Guess he had a little anal itch that couldn't wait until after the showing. I wanted to ask the seller, "You'll be taking that rug with you, right?" Grossed out, the cat got up and sauntered into the bedroom. She'd clearly had enough of that. There was red brick everywhere, and the apartment had a terribly claustrophobic feeling.

"Well," I said, locking eyes with Cristy, "I think we're good here." We headed back down the stairs.

As we spent the morning together, Cristy told me that she was the lead dancer in one of the biggest Broadway musicals at the time. So that was where her incredible body came from—eight shows a week!

Shit. Is that really what it takes? I thought, wincing at my monumental forty-five-minute run earlier that day.

Brutal!

Cristy and I spent the next three months touring around town. She explained that as an artist, she had never been good with numbers. When I asked her what her net worth was, she had no idea.

"What do your tax returns say?"

She shook her head again. She didn't know. But she told me she would speak to her accountant.

"Honey, I need you to learn one thing right now: your money and your numbers are for *you* to know, not for someone else to tell you about. Don't ever let other people control your net worth. You need to know your numbers like you know your bra size. Creative or not, this is about money, and money is about the ability to make choices. And choices are freedom. Don't ever let anyone fuck with your freedom, you got that? You need to know your numbers to grow your numbers. You know what I'm saying?"

Cristy lit up. "Holly, I love that you're going to make me into a businesswoman. This is so exciting!" And off we went—beauty and the boss. We were going to make things happen.

Cristy and I met weekly for the next couple of months. After every tour, we would get a coffee or a tea and discuss the pros and cons of the day. My goal was for her to walk into an apartment and tell me her opinion about how it was priced and where she saw its value. Plenty of buyers love to give their opinions, but I was looking for an educated one that was well supported.

"I think this apartment is a bit overpriced, because we've seen three others that had much better layouts and better light, and this whole kitchen needs to be renovated," she said.

Her assessment made me proud. She was a quick study, which is no doubt what made her such a rising star on Broadway. It was so much fun watching her discover and cultivate her new strengths. I'm so happy when my clients grow through the process of finding their new home. It's so important to know what you love and what you simply can't tolerate.

We talked about Cristy's gifts as an artist and how she had always enjoyed interior design. During our search, she'd opened her mind to renovating a space. This was a good thing, as renovating gave us many new options to explore. With every apartment we toured, she used her artistic sensibility to visualize what she might do with the space. I helped Cristy estimate what a basic renovation would cost and the approximate time that it would take to complete.

We had seen around forty homes in ninety days. I had turned this Broadway babe into a sharp real estate critic. She was ready to invest in a home. I could feel that the timing was right and the stars were aligning. It's amazing what comes your way when you've worked hard. My dad always said the harder you work, the luckier you get, and that definitely applies to real estate.

I turned on my computer one morning and scrolled through all the new listings when one jumped out at me. It had just come on the market: a small two-bedroom overlooking a pristine and charming block of 11th Street between Fifth and Sixth Avenues in the heart of Greenwich Village. This little gem faced south over the treelined street, so it would get great sunlight. In a city of skyscrapers like Manhattan, direct sunlight is coveted. It's a commodity that really adds value to a home.

45 West 11th was a turn-of-the-century building with gorgeous detail and big columns outside. Not exactly a townhouse but a charming second cousin for sure. When I saw the listing, I picked up the phone and called Cristy. "Can you meet me today at 11:00? I'm super excited about this new place."

Cristy walked into this apartment, saw the sunlight streaming in though the widows, and shot me that look that shouts "love at first sight!"

"It's so beautiful," she gasped.

The bathroom and the kitchen needed to be redone, and the second bedroom was more like a huge walk-in closet, but she loved it. She was looking at the apartment with the eyes of an artist, knowing what she could do with it to create her own personal masterpiece. I motioned to her to keep her poker face on.

"We'll talk about all the details outside," I said whenever she started to gush.

It's always best not to let the seller know that your client has gotten attached. It only brings confidence to the other side. It's okay to highlight the good things, but you should also point out the areas that require additional investment. Even if you know your client is in love, it's important to let the seller know there's work to be done.

I turned to Cristy and asked, "So, you're okay with redoing all of this?" And then I turned to the seller's broker and said, "How are the rules for renovating? This would be a large project for Cristy, and I wouldn't want her to try to renovate in a building that would make her life miserable."

I had now added enough doubt into the equation to make the broker more flexible. Even if he'd caught the happy expression on Cristy's face, he knew he'd likely have to work with us. I turned back to Cristy and said, "Let's sit down and run the numbers and see if this property makes any sense for you."

And voilà, the nail was in the coffin.

We were primed and ready.

You never want to leave a showing with the seller's broker believing that it's a done deal, even if it is. Always keep them guessing. This is an important rule in love and real estate.

Of course, Cristy was beyond ecstatic about the possibilities, no matter how cool we may have played it. We mapped out our plan for negotiating the best deal for her. Forty-eight hours later, the sellers had accepted her offer of $525,000 for her dream home. Cristy took her time doing the renovation. She lived there for months so she could truly get a feel for the place before making any alterations.

She was right to trust her gut. She had an eye for design, and in the end, she made her dream happen. She put a queen-size bed in the smaller bedroom, as it was really the only thing that fit, but it worked. I mean, it really worked. She put these perfect lights on either side of the bed, and it was cozy, chic, and hip all at the same time. She turned the larger bedroom into a studio, office, and yoga room. It was peaceful, Zen, and whimsical. It all maintained a very downtown vibe. Cristy did an exceptional job throughout. She was disciplined enough to manage her numbers so her renovation didn't run away with expenses. She became obsessed about saving money. Ultimately, she spent $90,000, the bare minimum for the result she was looking for. When she was done, it was absolutely stunning.

I was so proud of her, but best of all, Cristy was proud of herself. She'd realized her dream by using her talents, loved living in this home, and in the end, sold it for $1,195,000, a $580,000 gain. This artist/businesswoman/designer was rockin' her first successful real estate story, and she was just getting started.

I once got a call from Brian, a client who'd rented a very tiny studio from one of my owners. He was in his mid-twenties and was just the sweetest thing, but he wasn't exactly a lady-killer. Not that he needed to be—but I knew I could put him into an apartment that made him look like one.

"I need you to help me find a new home. My parents want grand-children, so they want to buy me an apartment," he said.

"I love it!" I replied. "This is fabulous. I love this mission."

We took our orders and got to work. We toured all the way up the West Side and along Central Park West. Brian's parents were serious about grandchildren and gave him a very good budget to get his clan going. They clearly wanted little people, and they wanted them now!

Brian and I saw a lot of places—nine in all. Some were homey; some were great for a family. But this had to be a place that reeked of eligibility. It had to say that he was sexy and a really great catch. Up until now, Brian was renting a space that was so small his bed was located only five feet from the front door. This shoebox had just one tiny window. He wasn't doing any entertaining there, that was for sure. His place was sad, messy, and depressing. Who wants to live in that?

We were looking for the perfect lair, like the B-52s' "Love Shack," a penthouse palace, a killer crib, a stabbin' cabin! We were looking for a Manhattan miracle. Oh, there would be children, eventually, but not here. This was the Venus flytrap, the place where the magic would happen, where the cub would become a lion. Or, in English terms, where he got laid.

Brian and I had gone out several times, and nothing fit. We would see the classic six with the prewar detail and the nicely appointed kitchen, but that was all wrong for this mission. Those apartments were for a fully formed family and not for a bachelor. Brian began to get frustrated with our search.

"It's no use. I don't want something so big it reminds me that I'm all alone and I can't get a girl to say yes to a date. Maybe I should just stay in my studio."

"Brian, you can't give up. We'll find you a rockin' pad, and we will get you laid," I promised. "We're going to find you a place where you'll have to beat the girls away! Do you hear me?"

And I meant it.

We needed a place where people could see how sweet, talented, and funny he was. We had to focus on the endgame, keep our eyes on the prize. And we did. It took hard work from both of us, but eventually our efforts were rewarded. We found the perfect apartment. You could see the glass jewel box perched on top of the building from the street. It had a huge terrace surrounding the whole thing.

"There it is. Can you see it up there? That's where we're headed. That's the penthouse we're looking at!" I pointed up as we walked along the street. We had to take the elevator to the top floor and then walk up a flight of stairs to get to the apartment. Odd, but intriguing, especially for those future "fly girls" who would soon be swarming Brian. Upon entering, we had nothing short of a "holy shit!" moment. It was beautiful! David Rockwell, a well-known architect, had lived there and completely built out his dream. The living room had cathedral ceilings, a wood-burning fireplace, and a fantastic bar. The dining room—my personal favorite—had windows on all three sides that looked out onto a luscious, beautifully landscaped garden. The broker explained that the home was wired with built-in speakers in every room, including the outdoor space. The terrace was even larger than the interior of the apartment. It had gorgeous floor-to-ceiling casement windows. There was a big elm tree, hydrangea bushes, roses, and wisteria growing over the banister. It was a hidden oasis in the middle of Manhattan. The terrace wrapped around the entire apartment so not only could you access it from every room, you could also look out onto this beautiful sight day and night. While sitting at the dining room table, you felt as though you were floating above the city. The main terrace was spectacular, with dramatic lights and columns. All of the trees were beautifully lit, and Rockwell had even built additional living space on top on the roof. It looked like the Parthenon.

This was *exactly* what we'd been searching for. This home was designed for entertaining.

Houston, we have landed.

I was certain we were going to have success here, but I had no idea just how successful we were going to be. When I say the cub became a lion, that's an understatement. I returned eight months later to attend a party at Brian's penthouse. I could hear the music as soon as I got off the elevator. The sound of women laughing wafted through the door. The party was packed. Brian was holding court in front of the fireplace, talking to four very pretty young ladies who were hanging on his every word. He was wearing a dark blue velour sport coat with a white T-shirt. I hardly recognized him. I didn't know if I should call him Brian or Mufasa!

"Holly, you're here!" Brian jumped up immediately when he saw me. "Let me get you a drink!" He got me a glass of champagne and we headed out to the terrace.

"Wow, Brian, this is such a great party. How's everything going?" I asked.

"Honestly, it's been crazy with the girls. I was seeing that one over there with the brown hair. Don't look over there; she's become a little bit of a stalker. I have a crush on that blonde inside, but I want to play the field for a while."

This was a different man than the boy who had spent so much time looking for this apartment with me.

"Brian, I'm so happy for you. This has really gotten you into the swing of things. Your parents must be so happy."

"They are, but I'm having much too much fun being a bachelor for now. It's been a dream acting out my fantasies here," he said with a toothy grin.

"You created this, Brian. You believed in yourself, you advocated for yourself, and you executed your plan. Look at all the confidence you have now. It's like you're a whole different person. I'm so glad you've found yourself here," I said.

I was so happy for him. His parents would have grandkids in time, but first Brian had to enjoy himself, meet different women, and determine who was a good match for him, just as he had done when looking for a home.

The thing about first-time buyers is that they don't know what they don't know. Some go in with their eyes wide open, and others choose not to even look before taking a leap. It doesn't really matter whether you're going on a first date or shopping for your first home. My dad always said to keep your eyes wide open before marriage and half-closed afterward.

CHAPTER FIFTEEN

Getting Board Approval

*Stop looking outside for scraps of pleasure or fulfillment, for
validation, security, or love—you have a treasure within that
is infinitely greater than anything the world can offer.*
—ECKHART TOLLE

*T*HERE WERE LOTS OF PEOPLE IN NEW YORK CITY GOING THROUGH a breakup or coping with some type of loss at the same time I was. I encountered them every day, and often wondered what made them so strong. At least, they looked stronger than I felt. I began thinking about all of the tough women I knew, represented, and admired. Maybe, just maybe, I could figure out how to pick up the pieces if I spent more time with some of them. Staying busy was a priority, but being around positive people was essential.

My friend Janine and I met one day for coffee to discuss her next design adventure. Minutes into our nonfat soy cappuccinos, I could tell she wanted to talk, and I knew she had one question on her mind. I've seen that look a thousand times from clients, especially clients who flip real estate: Should she buy first or sell first? This quandary always comes up. Some of my clients need to have the security of knowing where they're going before they can give up where they're at, while others need to know exactly what their current homes are fetching before they even think about putting an offer in on new ones. They like the security of rolling their money from a sale into a purchase. Often, the same is true when it comes to relationships.

This is one of the toughest questions for people to answer. Why? It totally depends on what kind of person they are. Are they conservative investors or risk-takers? There are pros and cons to both strategies. If you sell first, you know exactly how much money you'll have from your sale, and therefore you can budget accordingly. You'll also know the approximate date of the closing, which dictates when you'll have your money. But once you close, you're under the gun to find a new home, and that can be tricky when you're looking for something very specific in an incredibly tight real estate market with little to no inventory.

Other buyers will play real estate roulette, paying for two homes at once, because they need to know exactly where they're going. The more discerning they are during the search process, the more time it will take to find the right place. They can't imagine signing a contract of sale without having a clear picture of their future home. Some buyers think they have what it takes to carry two homes at once, but many times they crack under the pressure. It takes a big toll on their personal lives. The financial stress of owning two homes can be nothing short of brutal for some people, and that can be very hard on relationships. The best way to figure out what's right for each client is to distinguish where their larger worry is: Is it financial worry, or is the worry in finding a new home? My strategy is to attack the weaker side and work from there. Here's what I mean.

Janine's home was immaculate, so I knew we'd have no problem quickly finding a buyer. What would likely take time was locating the right new place, one where she could utilize her renovating talents to turn a fixer-upper into a masterpiece. But we also needed to find a great deal, a real diamond in the rough. Knowing this, we decided that she should buy first. The type of renovation Janine enjoyed doing would take many months, and we would use that time to get her apartment sold. Hopefully the coordination would be seamless.

It took a little over two months of looking, but we found her the perfect fit—a 2,800-square-foot home that was part of an estate sale. The owner died, and the family wanted to liquidate as fast as they could. When we toured the property, the electricity was turned off because they no longer wanted to pay for it, and the furniture had already been removed, so it looked more like the set of *A Nightmare on Elm Street* than it did a cozy home. When we entered the apartment, the listing agent barely looked up. He just snarled at us and said, "Show sheets in the kitchen." The encounter was so creepy and abrasive that Janine and I couldn't help laughing. I quickly pushed her out of the room so we didn't add a murder to this haunted house. To be certain, that agent was in an even darker place than I had been! He may have even dipped away from us at one point to cry in the closet. I wanted to whisper to him, "Been there, dude. Pull it together; you might make the sale."

The house's rooms rambled on with no real rhyme or reason. The floor plan was very closed off. As if the apartment weren't spooky enough, the other broker kept staring at us from his perch on a flipped-over paint bucket. The odd thing is that the house looked as if it hadn't been painted since sometime before World War II. But the apartment did, however, have what I call "good bones." If Janine could get past the inherent design flaws, we both knew she had a showstopper on her hands. Of course, we were keeping our enthusiasm in check until the deal was done. We weren't interested in driving the price up. Janine was an experienced client who knew we should discuss her concerns and vision only after the showing.

I love moments like this when I'm representing buyers.

Why?

Nasty, unengaged brokers, uneducated or detached sellers, and horrible presentation always equals an amazing deal! And yeah, seeing those types of brokers in action—or inaction, as the case may be— doesn't hurt my reputation one bit. When your client sees the difference, you never have to sell yourself.

We were in contract a week later, and what a great deal it was!

Now it was time to get Janine's home sold. Even though her apartment was magnificent, we still needed to perfect it for sale. I always feel like Mommie Dearest with my clients who have children, because I'm vigilant about tidying up. When it comes to toys, my general rule is a three-toy maximum. Who am I kidding? It's really one toy.

And if they don't want to be the bearer of bad news with the kids, I will happily address it in my best Joan Crawford style. "Which toy do you love best? Then that's the one you can keep." Don't judge me.

Janine's listing went on the market on a Tuesday morning. The marketing campaign we'd put in place proved to be successful, as the calendar booked up fast with showing appointments for the next two weeks. The open house was packed. We quickly had four buyers bidding on the property. We wanted to be particularly careful, because her apartment was in a small co-op and we weren't sure how fussy the board members might be about their new neighbor. As a precaution, we went to the co-op board president with all four buyers' letters stating who they were and what they were offering so the board could point us in the right direction. It's always a good idea to thwart any potential turndowns by going to the board in advance and making them a part of the selection process. In this case, they seemed enthusiastic about one of the buyers, a very high-profile actress. This actress was interested in having a pied-à-terre around the corner from her soon-to-be in-laws. This was the perfect home away from home, intended to be used only a handful of weeks a year. After accepting the bidder's offer, we were off to the races.

Compiling the full board package for a co-op is always a pain in the neck. No matter how many times I tell a buyer about the sheer agony of the process, it never seems to totally sink in until it's too late. This approval was no exception. The actress's wedding was just a couple of months away, and the task of completing all this paperwork and gathering reference letters and tax returns was torture. When a board package is completed, it's usually as thick as a phone book, if you can remember what one of those looks like. And if you can't, it's *big*. On top of that, we make an average of seven copies, so each member of the board has his or her own copy. When this gigantic tower of paper (about four small trees' worth) is finally sent off, there's usually a huge sigh of relief—and then a mountain of fear sets in. This is not a fast process. It's an exercise in patience at best, not unlike waiting for that hot new guy to call after you've had the most amazing first date. You check your phone, your e-mail—nothing. You start to imagine the worst-case scenarios. Then you check your phone again. You wait and wait until you can't take it anymore, so you call and e-mail even though you swore you wouldn't. It's a delicate balance when inquiring about a board approval; I typically ask the management agent if they happen to know when the board is going to meet. I may even ask, "Will the board require an interview?" or "Is there any information I can tell the sellers or the buyers?"

Usually, we get stonewalled: "We can't divulge that information. It's up to the board. No meeting has been set yet," they'll say. And that's that. You may as well be dealing with the KGB. "Vee don't know ven za board vill meet. Now you ask NUT-TING MORE!" If you ask too many questions, you're dead. If you e-mail too many times, you're dead. And God forbid you try to shake down a board member for information—you're dead, dead, dead.

So, you can imagine the terror when you get a call—any call—from the management company. However, this time, I wasn't especially worried when I answered the phone.

"I'm sorry, but your buyer has been rejected by the board."

I just about choked. "I'm not sure I heard you correctly. Did you just say the buyer was rejected? But the board chose her themselves. What's left to know about her? She's been starring in some of our favorite movies since she was a child. How is it that she's won the public's hearts but not the board's? Are they for real?"

"Yes, I'm sorry, and that's their final decision," the voice on the other end of the phone said before abruptly hanging up.

I'd love to tell you this was unusual or that there was still a shot at turning things around. Unfortunately, I knew from experience there would be no changing their minds. This was it. The board dictates the law of the land, and there's absolutely no way to reverse it.

Like all rejection, it's so unnecessarily brutal.

Disappointed, I now had to make two dreadful calls, one to Janine and the other to the actress's broker. This was a very rough start to my day. I felt sick to my stomach. It was early and I didn't have enough caffeine running through my veins yet, so I made another cup of coffee and braced myself for the inevitable full therapy session I was about to have with Janine and John, her husband, as this no doubt unlocked all their worst fears. I understood exactly how this news would be received. First, panic would set in for Janine; she was going to freak out. And second, it would surely cause some stress between her and John. Ultimately, we'd have to get to a plan of some sort, but not until the panic subsided.

"What if we can't ever sell this? What if buyers are forever scared off because they've heard getting approval from the building's board is ridiculously hard? What if they think their neighbors will be too controlling?" One by one, we worked through each of their valid concerns. I had to be the voice of hope and reason; much like children in the middle of a meltdown, they needed to know I was calm so they could begin to chill out too.

"You have a gorgeous home, and we'll find you a buyer who can get past this hurdle. We just need to be patient, but I promise, I will get this sold for you."

Did I just promise my firstborn?

It kind of felt like it.

This process is even harder when you're working with friends. It literally felt like it was my apartment I was selling. I internalized as much stress and anxiety as they did. Maybe even a little bit more.

Once I was able to hit the reset button with everyone, we put Janine's apartment back on the market, only now it was with the added challenge of having fallen out of contract. The inevitable questions, doubts, and concerns arose, but we navigated them all. Six weeks later we were in contract again—and this time, with a countess. (No, she was not also a Real Housewife.) We explained at length the intricacies of the board and the history with the previous turndown, then started all over again with the application process with her and her broker.

There was a huge sigh of relief one afternoon when I found the fully executed contract in my inbox. That feeling would be obliterated three weeks later when I received her board package. It was blank. She had only filled out her name and basic information, and none of the other requirements.

I immediately called her broker. "There's nothing here. I don't understand. There are no letters of recommendation, no tax returns. I need those to be completed." I couldn't comprehend why he would drop off a blank package.

"I know, I know," he said. "I think she might have had a change of heart, because she won't send me any of those documents. She just keeps saying, 'Tell them who I am. I'm a countess.'"

If only it were that easy to get past a board. Some NYC boards were more difficult than the toughest bouncers at the hippest club.

"Well, that's not going to work. I mean, that is *really* not going to work."

"I'm so sorry, Holly. For the past six weeks, I've tried to get everything you need, and I can't get her to budge."

"Does she know she's going to lose her full deposit of $250,000? I'm not sure she totally gets that, but she will!"

I wasn't sure if I was mad at the broker, the countess, or the Universe. Why in the world was this happening *again*? We had gone over it many times, and still, this was the outcome. One over which we had zero control.

This was not good news, and now I needed to clear my calendar for the impending doomsday call. But first, where could I find a lifetime supply of Xanax for Janine and John?

Could this really be happening twice?

The conversation started like this: "Hey, guys. I don't have very good news for you ... again." These are never ideal words to hear from your broker. "Our buyer has gone rogue and is refusing to finish the board package. She'll be in breach of contract, and your attorney needs to contact her attorney about keeping the deposit. It's painful, it's cruel, and it's a nightmare. Nothing short of a complete and total shit show."

So now we were back on the market after being back on the market. Yup—a third time.

With the focus and determination of a soon-to-be Olympic medalist, I took another flying leap at this. There was going to be a positive end to this story if it killed me. Now was the moment to go into full-throttle seduction mode.

The apartment spoke for itself; it was gorgeous, and we knew it. What we needed to do was use all of its charm and appeal to entice a buyer right from the beginning. I had to paint a vivid picture of ways the apartment would fill their lives with exactly what was missing.

Whenever I show a home, I make it a point to speak with buyers for a while, and I do a great deal of listening. Being a good listener can teach you everything you need to know about the people who are talking. I try to learn as much as possible about their lives and passions. Many times, I can see what this move means to them in the larger picture. It's like being on a date and having him tell you, "The last woman I dated was too needy, calling me twelve times a day and getting upset if I didn't call her back right away." You think to yourself, *Mental note: make this guy do the all the calling.*

One thing to remember during hard times and crises is that bad news isn't the end of the story. It's usually the start. Sometimes obstacles turn out to be the silver linings that lead you to success. And that's exactly what happened here. As it turned out, the completion date for the renovation of Janine's new home was postponed. She and John needed more time anyway. And then we found a third buyer who was all in. This time, though, I needed everything up front. The contents of the board package would have to be gathered before the contract was signed. This potential buyer complied with everything, a perfect soldier to our orders. Besides, I think we scared her half to death with our warnings about what would happen if she didn't follow through. When the call came from the managing agent saying she had been approved, I felt triumphant, as if I had just been released from prison. My co-op hell was over, at least for this home. And, as an added bonus, this buyer ended up paying $55,000 over the countess's deal and $75,000 over the actress's. Add that to the $250,000 from the countess's lost deposit, and my clients came out $325,000 ahead. It's hard to put a dollar amount on the stress and unnecessary aging this caused all three of us, but we did it. I could finally place a call to Janine and her husband that I was thrilled to make. Thankfully, we got them through this ordeal. As I always say, never underestimate the art of seduction.

Okay, so you might be thinking, *I'll never have to go in front of a board, so why should I care?* The fact is, we all present ourselves to the board for approval at some point in our lives, especially when the board is made up of family and friends. Have you ever brought home someone you knew your parents were going to love? How about someone you knew they'd despise? And sometimes facing friends can be just as daunting. We go in front of the board every day we go to work, every time we play on a team, or every time we venture on a date. Most of us thrive on other people's opinions. Somehow, and wrongly, we value what others think more than we value and trust our own thoughts, especially when we're broken and feeling vulnerable. If your best friend doesn't like the person you're seeing, chances are he won't last long. And if he does, you can bet your friends won't be around much. On the other hand, have you ever dated someone who refused to go in front of the board at all (like the countess), and getting him to set up a time to meet your friends or family with you is worse than pulling teeth? That should be a huge red flag.

I once had plans with a guy I'd been dating when my mother announced that she was coming to town. My roommate, Carrie, called this guy "Parm," which was short for Parmesan, because he was Italian and a little cheesy. You get the picture.

I called Parm to let him know that, unfortunately, I had to cancel our plans, and explained that it was because my mom was unexpectedly coming to town.

"I'll just join the two of you," he said.

I still have no recollection of how he talked me into that idea. We were in no way serious, and I had a terrible feeling about it. But before I could say no, it was happening.

When the lunch was over, we said our goodbyes. As soon as Parm was out of earshot, my mother announced, "Well, you've managed to do it!"

At first, I thought it sounded like my mom was paying me a compliment. This was very exciting . . . and very rare. Like, it never happened. But wait—as my mother would tell you herself, she didn't believe in compliments.

Cue the ominous music.

"What did I manage to do?" I asked hopefully yet guardedly.

"You've managed to find the lowest of the low!" she boldly said.

Oh yeah. That was a full veto, automatic board turndown. No need to apply. We will not be requiring an interview. Hard full stop!

And what my mom thought mattered. Parm was phased out fairly quickly after that lunch.

I knew I was being courted by an unqualified buyer for this co-op, but somehow, I felt safe knowing that. I was nowhere near capable of getting into contract at that time, so why would I bother dating anyone who had any real potential? Besides, I found it a lot more interesting to date people I would otherwise never have entertained. Dating for the fun of it; who would have thought? It's like touring homes on a Sunday while you're on vacation, just for the amusement of it all. There's nothing wrong with that.

After I stopped seeing Parm, I began dating other people again. Everyone was pretty much the same: a series of experiences I knew would lead nowhere. I guess you could say I wasn't available and was intentionally looking for things that wouldn't work.

At the time, I had two girlfriends who had both gotten divorced. Within the first year of being back on the market, they each found themselves in very serious relationships. They'd fallen in love so quickly. I'd seen that movie and knew how it ended. They avoided spending time reflecting and being in a state of repair. While part of me was envious, another part of me knew that was a setup for failure. They patched up their "holes" with duct tape and paint, while I was actually ripping up floorboards and tearing down walls. Yes, no one would be able to move in for a while, but I was becoming confident that when someone finally did, it would be for good. No way were my friends' properties ready to be sold—and, as you might expect, both women found themselves divorced for a second time. Looking at it from the outside, I completely understand the appeal of finding someone new so fast, but I also understood how important it was to prep the property before getting back on the market. There are steps that cannot be skipped if you're serious about selling and not having your property fall out of contract a second time.

I'm always happy when my clients get everything they want out of a transaction. That's the ultimate goal, one you get to only by understanding what's right for you. It isn't a one-size-fits-all solution. Some people need to have a romantic or platonic relationship with someone else before they leave a relationship. They have to know where they're going in order to leave their home. Others need to end a relationship with a clean break; they sell first and find their next home later. For me, the question of whether to buy first or sell first was moot. For a very long time after my divorce, my heart was still broken, and dating—let alone starting a new relationship—was the furthest thing from my mind. I knew I had to get back out there eventually, but I also knew it would be a while before I was ready. In time, I forced myself to go on a few dates just to break the ice. Suffice it to say, it was a very slow melting process.

Some people don't handle change well. They'd rather move from one relationship into another than cope with their mess. It's like moving without doing any sorting. That's what's often referred to as an executive move—the most expensive type of move, because you hire a company to come pack up all your things and ship them to your new home. They advertise that they'll do all the heavy lifting—no cleansing or purging for you. It's as if you're just trading old walls for new ones. Same shit, different address. And in the process, you miss the benefits of going through your things and starting anew. You haven't cleared the space, exorcised the ghosts, repaired the cracks. And without doing any of that, you've built a castle on quicksand. It's a different place, but you're apt to run into the same problems—bulging closets, messy drawers, everything still mixed up, and a lot of things have expired. They're just taking up room and filling the air in a residence that's your house but hardly your home. If done correctly, moving can be an amazing process of growing into the new you. If you do the hard work, the heavy lifting or heavy donating, then when you finally get to where you're going, everything around you reflects you in real time. The you *right now.*

I get it: it's easy to rebound. When you're feeling so bad, finding someone—anyone—who can divert your attention from the chaos, mountains of work, or obligations in your life can be great. Who doesn't want to be distracted from their pain? But if you take the bait and follow that temporary distraction, there's a massive price to pay. There are times to cut corners and times you can't avoid doing what must be done. And as we've learned through so many children's stories—from "The Ant and the Grasshopper" or "The Tortoise and the Hare" to Pinocchio's being distracted on the island of pleasure— good things come to those who work for them. "Slow and steady wins the race"—that's the message my dad repeated over and over to me when I was a child. He drilled the value of long-term goals over short-term gains into my consciousness. "Compound interest" was uttered as often as "brush your teeth"! And for this I'm truly grateful. It was an early warning from wiser souls trying to pass down lessons learned. Do the work. It's well worth it.

CHAPTER SIXTEEN

Staging the Place

A lot of times, people don't know what they
want until you show it to them.
—Steve Jobs

HOW MANY TIMES HAVE YOU LOOKED AROUND YOUR HOME AND
had the sudden urge to rearrange the furniture, add a tile back-
splash in the kitchen, or switch out the throw pillows for ones in a
lighter color, perhaps to match the change in seasons—not because
you're prepping the place for a prospective buyer or because you're
having company over but simply because it would make you happy?
Talk about changing your perspective!

At different times in my journey, I felt as if I had a new outlook, as
if maybe something exciting was on the horizon for me. That was the
certainly the case after my return from Argentina. My friend Carrie
stayed in my apartment while I was away. On the day I returned, I

opened the door to find her father standing there in his underwear. He was a big, gregarious man who made everybody laugh, and laugh I did when I saw him wearing nothing but boxers. I was happy to find life and levity in my home again. It was if someone had flung open the windows and let in some fresh air.

Sure, a stack of mail with my name on it also greeted me. There's nothing like unpaid bills to snap you back into reality, but that didn't stop me from wanting to *zhuzh* up my existence in other ways.

That was when I decided to quit compulsively watching Ina again. (I had fallen off that bandwagon before.) I knew I had to do it cold turkey this time. I needed to be strict and disciplined about it. That was also when I decided that I needed to be vigilant about getting at least seven hours of sleep a night. The body and mind require regularly scheduled recovery time. During my toughest times, a sleepless night usually meant that something—anything—could trigger me the next day. I didn't want all my nerves exposed and raw like that anymore. In a job where I'm supposed to keep others calm through stressful moments, being sleep deprived never served me well. Sleep became nonnegotiable. On the days when I was able to get enough rest and follow a routine, I'd have a fighting chance to maintain my improved attitude. I was also determined to study what and who made me happy. To do that, I kept a journal beside my bed and carefully tracked everything I ate and how much I exercised, and before turning in at night, I'd also write down the highlights of my day and why I considered them to be that. I reviewed my habits and discovered what worked and what didn't. When something brought me renewed energy, I did more of it; likewise, when I felt deflated, I did less of that activity. I was aware that I had to control my impulse to jump in and try to save others when I needed instead to save myself. I also took stock of the people in my life to find the ones who tended to be energy vampires. No amount of help or added attention would be enough to fend them off. I had to turn my focus inward and not feel so selfish about it. It was okay to take time to nurture myself. I had to trust that this path I was now on would lead me into the daylight and help keep me there. From this new vantage point I could see that the way out of any darkness I felt was to connect with myself. I had to really get to know me again—and, more important, I had to be my own best friend. What would I say to me if I were trying to help me? I had to treat myself as someone I was trying to advise. It sounds simple, but the exercise of studying what fills and drains us over time often reveals truths that can surprise us.

Although I worked out and have been an athlete throughout my life, I never really enjoyed the workouts. I loved playing sports, hiking, biking, and skiing, but a daily gym regimen could be so boring. More than ever, though, I needed those endorphins. My body had to be strong in order to support my mind. It was not only essential for my work, it was critical for my overall well-being. Exercise—and I mean pushing myself to run four to five miles every morning, or at least several days a week—became another essential building block. I would wake up at 7:00 a.m. and head off to the Equinox down the street. There were some mornings when I had to fight off memories that would creep into my mind, especially on Saturdays—that was the day my ex and I used to go to kickboxing class together. I loved that class. It was something I didn't want to give up—and besides, it was awesome for the abs. Whenever those thoughts came back, though, I'd do my best to shake them off and head for the treadmill.

After my workout, I would make my way down to Union Square, where there were gorgeous farmers' markets four days a week, Mondays, Wednesdays, Fridays, and then a big one on Saturdays. Farmers from all over the region came to the city with fresh flowers, plants, meats, cheeses, vegetables, and fruit, and there were homemade breads, jams, pickles, olives, hot apple cider, and cider donuts too. I can't put my finger on why, exactly, but there's something about vegetables in the open air that makes me so happy. I would fill my woven farm basket from the South of France with apples, Concord grapes, fresh goat cheese, and flowers—lots and lots of flowers. When I got home, I would assemble all the yummy vegetables I needed to make the seaweed roll up that the Wizard, my raw-food professor from Esalen, had taught me. I started with hummus and added sunflower sprouts, scallions, tomatoes, carrots, avocado, local bee pollen, and flaxseed oil, then tightly rolled it all up like I was rolling a big fat joint, doing my best not to let it fall apart. The tighter, the better. It was delicious, and I felt like I hadn't sacrificed anything. The Wizard taught us that if you give your body a break, feeding it nutritional raw fruits and vegetables such as these, then it would have the necessary energy to do its own healing, and I was desperate for healing. The stronger I got, the more I could fine-tune my plan. I listened to my body and fueled it with the goodness it needed. I cut out sugars, caffeine, and alcohol, and tried a raw-food diet.

I would then put on some music and make beautiful arrangements with the flowers, usually a huge one for the kitchen and another for the living room, plus small ones for the bathroom and two stunning arrangements for my bedroom. It was a bit overindulgent, I know, but this was a time when I was putting myself first. Live, beautiful flowers just bring joy. It's that simple. And the practice of this gorgeous walk down Broadway from Equinox and through the farmers' market made me happy. It still does. It was food for my soul, a moment of nature right there in downtown Manhattan. That's what farmers' markets do—they bring the simple, beautiful pleasures of the farm to the city. I also stopped playing my suicide set on my iPod. No more crying, yelling, or angry artists for me. Instead, I created a playlist of happy songs filled with joy and optimism. Music can be uplifting if you choose it wisely. I think there's a lot of value in making a playlist that gets me motivated and moving.

This ritual of working out, walking through the farmers' market, filling my fridge and my body with nutritious food, dotting my home with colorful flowers, and enjoying a bit of sound therapy became the foundation of my recovery. It infused my home with life. It might sound simple, but following this routine was a game changer for me. I started feeling as if freedom was within my reach. Sticking with my newfound regimen turned out to be more than just applying a fresh coat of paint or changing the color scheme of my pillows and throws. It was as if I were *staging* my life. I was fixing me the way I knew how to fix up even the bleakest of apartments. No, I hadn't been ready to move from my home, but I was now ready to move on from where I had been emotionally.

The longer I continued staging, the more hopeful I got. My body was getting stronger, my mind more focused. I could tell that it was time to push myself to the next level.

Your day is made up of hundreds of tiny decisions, including how you process what's going on around you. If you've set the stage for optimism—I mean, if you've opened the curtains and really invited the sunlight in—it's probable that the rest of your day will be brighter too. This doesn't always come naturally. For me, it's still a practice, much like yoga or working out. I need to condition my mind to see the light. If I don't, there's no way I can achieve all of the results that I want. There's no such thing as a pessimistic winner—or at least I've never met one. Cynical, maybe, but pessimistic? Nope. If you're trying to sell a home, no matter whether you're the broker or the seller, coming at it from a negative point of view makes it a fruitless endeavor. You're the one setting the stage and the value, and if you're negative about that property, it will go nowhere. While we always want to address challenges in a home, we mostly want to highlight the best qualities so that they become the things people see. Why would addressing your personal challenges be any different? Surround yourself with beauty and goodness. Absorb it. And don't forget to radiate your own too. Whether we like it or not, we mirror our surroundings, or maybe they mirror us. Either way, you get the point.

And like my mom said, if you don't have any wins, then celebrate the wins of others. Everything is cyclical. Real estate, relationships, you name it, there's a cycle in motion. So, the next time someone asks, "How are you doing?" don't say, "AHHHHHH, the market sucks! I just lost my seventeenth deal this year, and my parents just bought an apartment with another broker." And *definitely* don't say, "There are no good guys out there." What if your answers were, "I'm doing well. My company just closed the most expensive apartment in the world" or "I've been on some dates, and even though I haven't met the right guy yet, I know he's out there"? Whether business or personal, there are so many opportunities to be had. It's a ripe vine waiting to be picked.

Okay, I know what some of you are thinking: *That's not being genuine. I need to be myself.*

No, you don't.

Save your sad stories for your therapist, because this is what a positive daily practice is. It requires a strong mindset. Think of the powerful mindset a professional athlete needs to have to compete and win. No matter how far behind they are, athletes need to believe they'll win until the last second of the game. They can never get down or discouraged, or their loss will be certain. Everyone loves the underdog, the come-from-behind victory story. Don't those situations make for the best games? The ones where the stadiums are full of spectators on their feet, screaming for their team to beat the odds?

I do an exercise every morning that's so easy I can do it on my back.

Not that exercise!

Your mind is so dirty!

Okay, so, right after your alarm goes off in the morning, before you check your phone or turn on the TV, list five things you're grateful for. This is a little different than the gratitude meditation I spoke about before; it's almost like a lightning round. Say the first five things that come to mind. Doing this simple task changes the chemistry in your brain and sets the stage for positive energy to be drawn to you. I can't think of a better way to start my day. Even sex doesn't put me into the mindset that gratitude does. If I have more time, I'll linger on the images of what comes to mind and try to visualize other things I want as well. What do I wish to attract into my day today, and into my life overall? I push myself to zero in on exactly what I desire. I focus on the details of it. Who is there with me, and what are we doing? I concentrate on how it feels.

How does it *feel* to have that love around me?

How does it *feel* to eat breakfast in my dream kitchen while petting my champion dog?

How does it *feel* to get the fully executed contract I've been waiting for in my inbox first thing in the morning?

Program your brain like you're programing your body in the gym.

Set the stage for a positive day and a positive mind, body, and spirit.

Remember: light attracts light, and darkness attracts darkness.

Always try to see the silver lining in what you already have. When you have a heart full of gratitude, it's nearly impossible to feel fear and anger, so fill your heart to the brim. See the donut and not the hole.

It's always there.

CHAPTER SEVENTEEN

Appraised Value

You must find the courage to leave the table
if respect is no longer being served.
—TENE EDWARDS

R EMEMBER WHEN YOU WERE A KID AND YOU TRIED TO PUT A square peg in a round hole? No matter how hard you pushed, it just wasn't a good fit. Or when you have to lay down on the bed, suck in your belly, and struggle to zip up your jeans? That's never a good fit! The only thing you get from that is a muffin top, and that's not a good look for anyone.

Those lessons apply to the dance of attraction too. You can't push too much from one side or things will break down. Sometimes, to make things happen, you need to release your hold and take two steps back so your partner can come forward. This applies to interactions with your boss, someone you're dating, or even another broker. As soon as you release control over the outcome of a situation and just sit with whatever happens, circumstances tend to bend in your favor. So accept it if that cute guy doesn't call or your boss doesn't grant your request for a raise. There are always other opportunities out there—and most of the time, those other opportunities are even better choices. As soon as you believe that opportunities always live on the other side, you'll find peace and comfort in walking away. Ironically, that's when people tend to be their most attractive.

Think about it for a minute: Have you ever broken up with someone who wasn't really paying that much attention to you and yet, once you called it off, they turn it on? The further you pull away, the harder they come after you. That's what I'm talking about. Not in a stalker way, but you know what I mean.

Or perhaps you're dating someone you know isn't the right match. Maybe it's someone you wanted to like and they could tell you were interested, but they waited too long to call, and, given time to think, you realize that they might not be the right fit. That's when the other person can feel you've changed your mind. There's a shift in the rhythm where you pull back and they come forward. These types of steps are critical in closing any deal.

In fishing, if you yank up the rod at the wrong time, there's no doubt that the fish will get away. Steadily moving your wrist back and forth keeps the fish on the hook. You have to keep your line tight and slowly reel it in until the time is right to bring that fish out of the water. An overanxious fisherman is a hungry one. (You can't live in New England without picking up a thing or two about fishing.)

In Manhattan, demanding, high-maintenance sellers are plentiful. I've carved out a career learning to work with "Type A, I want it now, I'm the only client you have" people. They sound a little bit like Veruca Salt from *Charlie and the Chocolate Factory*: they want the golden goose, and they want it now! Not everyone is the right fit. There have been many times when I've gone to a second meeting and already seen signs that the relationship is doomed. If a client doesn't listen to my advice, doesn't respect my time, and wants to take over everything and not let me do my job, there's very little chance I can successfully meet their needs.

In the early 2000s, real estate was more of a career that people ended up in; it wasn't necessarily where they started. The field was full of people who were also professors, psychologists, or actors. For many, real estate was their Plan C.

To keep their licenses active, brokers have to take continuing education classes every two years. While those classes are often far from riveting, they're required. The attorney who taught one of the continuing ed classes I needed to take was a character right out of central casting. She was heavyset, had Coke-bottle glasses, wore her gray hair in an afro, and spoke with a very thick New York accent. Taking these classes, especially hers, was always a huge blow to the ego. If your head had gotten too big or you had a little too much pep in your step, an afternoon in this woman's class would take you down a notch or two ... or ten.

The room looked more like a place where ex-cons met with their parole officers than it did a place where professional Realtors came to continue their learning. I called this class "broker jail." All the other inmates had brought food with them and were munching away right in the middle of the lecture. One guy had an entire pizza, like Jeff Spicoli in *Fast Times at Ridgemont High*. I couldn't believe the teacher was allowing this. It was anarchy. Bored and hungry because I hadn't brought my own pizza, I whipped out a tube of lipstick and began applying it to my lips. While looking into my pocket mirror, I circled my mouth twice. It was then that I suddenly heard that Fran Drescher voice saying, "EXCUSE ME ..." And then again, "EXCUSE ME ..." I wasn't sure who she was talking to until I looked up.

"Are you talking to me?" I asked, genuinely shocked.

"Yes, I'm talking to you! You're being very rude."

"*I'm* being very rude? Would it be better if I ate it?" I replied sarcastically.

My friend, who came to the class with me, began moving his desk away from where we were sitting. He didn't want the instructor to think we were together. It was bad enough coming to this class once; he didn't want to have to repeat it.

If that wasn't enough damage to the ego, my new adversary wanted to take things a step further. "All of you have been agents for some time now, and you've gotten one thing wrong. You think you're the boss. But you're not the boss. You're the hired help! And you always will be," she said, wagging her thick finger back and forth at us as if she knew exactly what crime we had all already committed. For anyone even remotely trying to hold on to a speck of dignity as a Realtor, it was immediately stripped away when she uttered those words, making it clear none of us in the room were as big of a deal as we may have thought before walking in.

Her delivery might have been rough, but her message was spot-on: we were in the service business. It's all about taking care of our clients.

CMA is a term we use in real estate to educate our sellers on the current value of their home so we can determine the best sale price. A CMA is a Comparative Market Analysis. Some sellers think their house is worth significantly more than the market indicates, others see it as less, and a few actually get it right on the money. A CMA is an examination of the prices at which similar homes have sold, and it's a critical part of the selling process that prevents a property from being overpriced or undervalued. An overpriced home might linger on the market for years, and while an undervalued home might be appealing for the buyer, the seller will take a financial hit by letting it go for less than it's worth.

The same concept holds true when it comes to knowing your own value. What are your strengths, and where are your challenges?

When you know your own value and can step away from the drama, people want to work with you even more. The less anxious you are, the more people will come to you.

Let me explain.

I know a plethora of high-powered women who are killing it every day on behalf of their clients, yet when it comes to negotiating on behalf of themselves, they fall short. These women have built multi-million-dollar companies, raised billions of dollars, and won case after case, but when left to negotiate for themselves, they get very different results. They rarely ask for what they're worth. They see themselves as being worth less than others do, and that's a problem. Why do women undervalue themselves? Is it how we were raised, or how we're programmed to see ourselves? Is it cultural? Or are we too accommodating to the other side?

I fall into this trap myself. I'm a caretaker and a ferocious advocate for my clients. Accommodating their needs is my true north. Whenever I go wrong in negotiations for myself, it's because I've immediately accommodated the other side. I see things from their point of view and move away from my own. When I present my needs and they present obstacles that prevent my needs from being met, I get soft because I'm empathetic toward them. This weakness is something I'm always working on. I'm aware of it, and therefore I'm able to make the choice to toe the line or walk away and start over. Yup, there's that scary place again: the unknown.

When you don't feel valued by others, it's easy to become a shell of yourself and to trust their opinions over your own. You can feel like a rudderless ship at sea. Sometimes it's as if you've been beaten down by one storm after another. Attaching yourself to someone else's sense of your value is like being pulled by a tugboat through the fog, unable to see where you're going. Before you let that happen, know that your true compass comes from within.

While this lack of esteem wasn't what occurred in my marriage, it almost happened during my friend divorce. If I'd attached myself to his drastically changed opinion, it would have been like tying myself to an anchor and being thrown overboard. I wouldn't have been able to survive that, let alone get back on my feet. I had to recognize that the insecurities he tried to project onto me were his issues and not mine. I was just collateral damage he inflicted on his way to getting what he wanted. I can say that because, thankfully, I was able to find my rudder and straighten my course despite being wounded by the storm. I had to remember who the skipper of my boat ultimately was. I wasn't going to let anyone else steer me into the rocks, and I emerged stronger because of it. A lot stronger. Changed forever from the laughing, loving, trusting young girl I once was. I'm still loving and still laughing, but now I'm more cautious and careful with my company. I will never again risk losing myself at sea.

So again, when it comes to your home, one of the most important elements in pricing is knowing your value. I can't stress this enough. All of the other steps are important too, but knowing your value is key. There have been times when I've gotten 30 percent more for an apartment in worse condition than another one with an identical layout on a higher floor in the same building that was sold just before mine, all because I did the research and created the value. I saw the space's potential despite its being unfinished and hardly ready for sale. Every price record starts with someone seeing untapped value. If a worse apartment gets 30 percent more, imagine what can happen for you if you believe in your own value the way I believed in that apartment. How would your life look if it were 30 percent different? We aren't just talking money here. Everything is a negotiation. Every seller wants to believe they have untapped value. As I've said, there's a thin line between hope and delusion, but when the value is there, it's there. While comparative apartments are important, they don't tell the whole story. I never lean fully into what other brokers have sold and for what amount. Everyone is looking for a bargain. It doesn't matter if you're looking to rent or buy; you need to determine what it is you want and what your price is.

Knowing your value is about radical acceptance, acceptance that runs to the deepest part of your soul. You have to stop fighting reality and acknowledge it whether you like it or not. It's when you can get to a place and finally say to yourself, "Right here is where I'm supposed to be. Thinking of the past robs me of my future. The present is perfect, even if I don't like it." It isn't about being passive. It's about taking all of that energy and using it to move on. Don't look to others to tell you your value. That's like playing Russian roulette. Most won't see it, and what they do see they generally undervalue.

Oprah often talks about the value of loving yourself even when others don't—or, worse, when they get mad at you for seeing your own value. She references those naysayers who said things such as, "How dare you host your own talk show?" or "How dare you start your own magazine?" or "How dare you start your own television network?" You must have thick skin to break glass ceilings—without that, you'll bleed all over the floor.

Look, we don't always know when we go from being valued in a relationship to being unvalued. We can't always see that shift, but we can feel it. And that's when you really have to connect to your property—whether it's your home or yourself—and value it. That apartment that garnered 30 percent more was looked at by many buyers who didn't see the value. They quoted the closing price for the apartment on the floor above while touring the property, and at the end of their tour they called back over their shoulders, "Well, good luck with this . . ." In real estate, saying that at the end of a showing is the equivalent of flipping the bird. Even so, I knew the sellers of the apartments that had sold prior to this one didn't know *their* value. I wasn't going to let my seller follow suit. Just because previous sales had set a precedent didn't mean that we couldn't raise the expectation and change the perception.

I once heard a story about a father and son. Just before the father died, he said to his son, "I want you to have this watch. Your grandfather gave it to me. It's very old and very sentimental. But before I give it to you, I want you to go to the watch shop down the street and see how much they offer you for it."

The son did as his father asked. When he came back, he said, "The watchmaker offered me five dollars because it's very old."

The father didn't seem surprised. He then told his son to take the watch to the coffee shop where the father had had breakfast nearly every day for years. He knew the owners and staff by name. When the son came back, he told his father they'd offered him five dollars.

"Now, go to the museum and show them the watch." Dutifully, the son followed his father's direction. When he came back, he said, "They offered one million dollars for the watch."

Again, his father didn't seem surprised. He only said, "The right place values you in the right way."

Never find yourself in the wrong place and then get angry when you're not valued. Those who know your value are those who appreciate you. Don't ever stay someplace where your value isn't seen.

Divorce is all about your value not being seen, or it's about you not being able to achieve your true value with this person by your side. Either way, I see divorce as a valuation issue. If I can't be who I want to be in a marriage, standing next to you, feeling important, then I can't be with you. If you feel "less than" around someone, they aren't the right person for you, no matter if they're a friend or a significant other. The only person who controls how you feel is you. No one else has that power unless you give it to them. No one can make you feel bad without your permission.

Knowing your value and pushing through your fears unleashes an untapped energy within you. You begin to believe you're worth more, can do more, are capable of more—basically, that you can conquer anything. You no longer live in fear, in a world of "what if" or "less than." It's only after you walk through the fire that you can find your true value. And that doesn't mean striving for perfection, because there's no such thing. Just pursue being the best *you*.

The pursuit of perfection is something American culture fosters every day. For most people, how we look and how we're perceived by others matter. We're driven to be the best, and this perception keeps us believing in the idea that being flawless is more important than being authentic. Unfortunately, the chase is like running toward a mirage in the desert; like that false image, perfection is never quite within anyone's reach.

Even so, the *idea* of being perfect is hard to resist.

Why?

It's addictive.

We're creatures of habit who are never satisfied. And if you're the least bit competitive, you're always striving to be better.

There's no escaping the draw.

We're bombarded every single day with endless messages in the media and from our family, friends, and colleagues that not only feed our deepest insecurities but also encourage us to believe that we must be something more or different than who we are. Facebook and Instagram are showcases for how great life is—even when it actually isn't. Still, we want people to believe we're living the dream, and that somehow the shift away from our true selves is *better*.

That's not to say that striving for excellence isn't a good thing. It certainly is. But as a result of doing so, a lot of people unfairly hold themselves to an impossible standard.

Of this I'm certain: that endless chase is a setup for failure, disappointment, and, likely, discontent.

Though I didn't recognize it for many years, I was chasing perfection—the perfect marriage, the perfect family, the perfect career. My tireless pursuit of perfection made me a slave to my success. It also doomed me to a cycle of perpetual self-evaluation—a continuous report card on how I was doing. I might not have admitted it back then, but I cared deeply about what other people thought of me. I still do. I also liked the way I felt when I was met with accolades for a big closing, thunderous applause after giving a speech at a company event, and slaps on the back for a job well done. We all enjoy that feeling. This, of course, was a way to validate my worthiness. If I had been genuinely happy and satisfied with who I was, I wouldn't have needed to seek the approval of others—or, for that matter, to seek fulfillment from outside sources. I would have understood that, as cliché as it sounds, true happiness comes from within. When we get so caught up in listening to and acting on other people's opinions, we often miss the sound of our own inner voice—the one that matters the most, because it knows us best.

As time went on, no matter how often I tried to drown it out, my inner voice kept getting louder, until I could no longer ignore what it was saying.

It was repeating, "Be who you really are, even if it means giving up perfection" on a continuous loop.

You see, I wasn't perfect.

In fact, I was far from it.

I was human.

I had fallen, risen, and made my share of mistakes—but I had also used each experience as an opportunity to learn something new and to grow. I've been given great privilege in my life, and my gratitude for each precious moment endures.

CHAPTER EIGHTEEN

Landing the Dream House

You want to be Kilimanjaro on your first date. Inaccessible.
—Mrs. Doubtfire

THE LAW OF ATTRACTION IS THE BELIEF THAT POSITIVE OR negative thoughts bring positive or negative experiences into a person's life. What's in our minds and our hearts can become our reality. That energy is all around us. I learned about the Law of Attraction and started researching the concept of manifestation in high school, and have used both in my life ever since.

That's why I believe we create our own good fortune. Through our decisions, actions, and thoughts, we determine the outcome of everything. Is that planning or fate? The word *fate* has always irritated me. It sounds lazy.

A client and I had spent months looking for the perfect home and had finally found it, and it was time to put his money where his mouth was. Instead, he left the decision about whether to put in an offer to something completely arbitrary: a peach. A damned peach! He looked at me and said, "Holly, I'm going to take a bite of this peach, and if it's a good peach, I'm going to buy the apartment."

I looked him right in the eyes and calmly yet firmly said, "If you leave all of the work we've done up to the quality of that piece of fruit, I am so out of here." And I meant it.

"You're not going to do that," I continued, "because if you do, I will never show you another home. Ever. As in never."

"Take it easy," he said with a laugh. Thankfully, he was just busting my chops—and yes, the peach was juicy and delicious.

There are times, however, when you can't ignore the signs that some things in life are more than just coincidences. Sometimes the stars just align, so much so that there's no rational explanation other than divine intervention. Several years ago, I went to France with my family. My brother-in-law, Dan, and I traveled together and were meeting the rest of the group there. We had tickets on the same train, though we'd bought them separately months before the trip. When the train arrived, it had to have been at least eighteen cars long. Each ticket had the train car number and the seat number printed on it. His car number was in the teens, far from mine, so we parted ways on the platform and headed in opposite different directions.

"Come find me when you get settled," he called over his shoulder.

This was before text messaging, so we left it at that.

I boarded the train with my gigantic suitcase and made my way down the aisle, car by car, doing my best not to run over other passengers with my bag. I was trying to find my seat and getting more and more frustrated by the minute. It was hot, crowded, and unorganized. That's when I decided to just plop myself into the nearest empty space. I jimmied my suitcase onto the shelf above me and sat down. To my surprise, Dan showed up and asked, "How did you know where I'd be sitting?"

His seat was directly across the table from me in a four-seat configuration.

There were at least one hundred seats per car. What were the chances?

Before I knew it, we were drinking cold beers, laughing, and enjoying the ride.

Some people might call that fate. I'm not convinced. I think there's a higher power that creates these synchronized moments of divine intervention. *Synchronicity* is a term Carl Jung used to describe meaningful coincidences. It's the "acausal connecting principle" that links mind and matter and takes precedence over cause and effect. Jung's concept of the collective unconscious contends that we are all part of the same force field of imagination that governs our Universe. Think of the line from *As You Like It*: "All the world's a stage, and all the men and women merely players." To Jung, synchronicity was the ultimate guiding force underlying the whole of human experience.

When I was at boarding school, I liked to read books that expanded my thought process, challenged my ideals, and opened my mind. When I read *The Celestine Prophecy* by James Redfield, it instantly became one of my favorites. Redfield's novel theorizes that all coincidences are important because they direct the way to the unfolding of our personal destiny. Synchronicity reveals an underlying pattern in the Universe, a large guiding framework that organizes our lives. And by now you know that I love extreme organization! When you think about it, our lives are guided by synchronicity, whether in the beginning or ending of our relationships, the unfurling of our career paths, or the moments that don't appear to be meaningful at the time but turn out to be pivotal. The secret is to see meaning in every event.

My greatest takeaway from reading *The Celestine Prophecy: An Experiential Guide* was Redfield's seventh insight, that "knowing our personal mission further enhances the flow of mysterious coincidences as we are guided toward our destinies."

Having a clear idea of what we want to create in our lives and what we want our lives to be encourages synchronicity. It can hint at our life path, remind us of where we're headed, or guide us to change direction. It's synchronicity that brings us relationships and love, making it a gift to be treasured instead of taken for granted. And it's the same synchronicity that awakens us to the infinite possibilities available to us. Every cell in our body is listening to our thoughts. Change your thoughts and you will change the outcome.

I see these signs every day, especially when it comes to buying and selling real estate. You have to believe that the apartment or home is actually sellable. You have to have full confidence in your product, or you could really damage the outcome. If you don't think you'll ever sell the product, chances are you won't. If you think the seller is too difficult to deal with, he or she probably will be, or if you think the price is too high, it probably is. As in anything you do, if *you* don't believe in what you're doing, why would anyone else? We've discussed this concept before, but it's imperative to note again and build on it. What's inside your head often becomes a road map to what's ahead. Pay attention to your thoughts, because they'll tell you where you're going. If you think the world is screwing you over, you're bound to get more of that. But also *direct* your thoughts; if you make a point of expressing gratitude for the love and kindness you have in your life, even if it only comes from your goldfish, you're bound to be rewarded with more.

In sales, as in life, confidence and optimism follow the sun.

This is critical when negotiating anything, whether it's the purchase of a new home, the sale of a car, or the boundaries in a new relationship.

The art of negotiation is like pairs figure skating. When both parties know what they want and are in sync, the process glides along smoothly. When either party digs in their heels or pivots unexpectedly, there's bound to be a fall. I see it all the time in real estate. Things come to a standstill. People need to pick themselves up and decide whether they're going to continue. "I'm not going to negotiate with *myself.*"

Silence is a common response, and though it's rarely the answer we look for, to cope with the unknown it represents, it's important not to let our thoughts run wild. If we do, they could negatively affect the outcome.

I was once in the middle of a negotiation on a unit in a new development in Midtown Manhattan. The building had become one of the most sought-after addresses in the city. I had a buyer who was eager to close, but the developer wasn't getting back to us. Friday night came and went, then Saturday and Sunday too.

I spent those forty-eight hours reaching out to the developer, texting, calling, sending smoke signals. I kept reiterating that he needed to respond, even if his answer was that he wasn't adjusting the price. Not responding is disrespectful, and the quickest way for a broker to lose engagement with a hot buyer. It can, however, be a good negotiating strategy when handled correctly in the right moments—but the challenge is knowing which is which.

Think about how you might feel if someone sent you a text message thanking you for the most beautiful evening and gushing over what a good time they had, and then ghosted you for a week. I totally understand pulling back for a day or two and playing hard to get, whether in dating or business, but really, what's the reason? What are the boundaries? If you're the ghoster in that scenario, here's what happens: when you finally come around again, the other person has usually created all sorts of scenarios in their head about why you're back, and none of them are in your favor. They're thinking, *Maybe the stock market took a dive in the last week and suddenly my offer doesn't look so bad* or *That hot babe you thought you had a connection with turned out to be bat-shit crazy, didn't she?* Either way, be prepared to pay the price for being disrespectful.

Sometimes you think your light is on, like a beacon drawing ships, but it's not. Maybe you're just not ready. Maybe you have growing or healing to do. Or maybe there are other experiences you need to go through to be open and ready.

I'll let you in on a secret:

Everyone wants to be someone's first choice. Nobody wants to be a settlement—a Plan B.

We all want instant attraction. We want to connect with that first buyer so we can close the deal. But to do that, we must be brave and put ourselves out there. We have to take off the protective armor we've been wearing because of all the hurt and pain we've endured. If you want to close the deal, any deal, you have to let go of that negative emotion. You can't wear that protective shield and expect someone else to do the work to break it down. *You* have to do that. Make as many mistakes as you need until you slowly begin to let it all go.

The English word *reckon* comes from the Old English word *gerecenian*, meaning "to narrate." When you reckon with emotion, you have the power to change your narrative. But it isn't easy; much like selling your home, it takes persistence, dedication, patience, and follow-through. If you want to change your narrative, first you need to acknowledge your feelings, and then you need to get curious about the story behind them. That's when you can challenge those confabulations and get to the truth.

Tony Robbins was the first person I ever heard talk about the stories we tell ourselves. These are the stories that help us reconcile a situation, especially one that feels out of our control. When we're angry, hurt, or confused, we tend to create a narrative that helps us make sense of those feelings. This story helps us justify our point of view, even if it isn't based on any concrete facts. If someone isn't calling you back, do you immediately think, *What did I do?* Or maybe your spouse is quieter than usual; do you think, *There must be someone else?* A single look from a stranger can set off a chain reaction. Whatever it is, our response is usually defensiveness, self-doubt, and insecurity. It's like my favorite oversized sweater—it may not be flattering, but it's very comfortable and familiar.

Throughout my first marriage, I kept telling myself that if I tried harder, looked better, and gave my then husband his space, he would change. Somehow, I thought *my* actions were causing *his*. I was, of course, mistaken. When we feel exposed or hurt, we either find someone else to point the finger at, blame ourselves before anyone else can, or pretend we don't care. But this unconscious storytelling is a trap—one we can get stuck in if we don't change the stories we tell ourselves. As a result, we keep struggling with the same experiences, repeating patterns over and over; and every time we stumble, we find it increasingly hard to get back on our path. Hard, but not impossible. If there's a silver lining to this, it's that we can change the narrative. We have that capability. We just have to be brave enough to reckon with our deepest emotions.

In navigation, dead reckoning is how you calculate your location. It involves knowing where you've been and how you got there—speed, route, wind conditions. It's the same with life: we can't chart a new course until we find out where we are, how we came to that point, and where we want to go.

One thing I learned early in business was that if I wanted to succeed, I needed a plan—one that led to what I wanted to happen. In real estate, the agent is the magic maker. It all starts and ends with the agent. So, I began a habit of always writing a business plan, breaking the year into quarters, doing what I called the "30, 60, 90, 120." I made a plan for every quarter. When I was just starting out, the business wasn't consistent enough, so I had to search for it. I had to perform the necessary steps to create it. If I couldn't imagine it, chances are it wasn't going to happen, so this was my way of manifesting it. I learned through my business again and again that what I wrote down often came to fruition. What if I applied that to my personal life?

Would it have the same effect? Could I manifest the relationship I was looking for? God knows I really needed a plan. I was a magic maker as a Realtor, so why couldn't I sprinkle a little of that magic on my personal life?

Part of any healing process involves reprograming your brain. Having a shattered heart and broken dreams isn't a terminal illness, but it does feel like it at the time. The challenge is to take all of those old ghosts that haunt you with seemingly never-ending questions about what lies ahead and put them in a box, or at least out of your head.

But suddenly finding myself single felt like a whole new challenge. Why? Had I forgotten the gift of manifesting during my marriage? I'd never imagined the end of our union, or at least I don't think I did. I always pictured myself in a big, beautiful family home overlooking the ocean, where I would sit on the deck watching all my grandchildren play. Getting divorced certainly isn't the end of the world, but I assure you it can feel that way when you believe in something with all your soul and it still ends up being destroyed. For me, it was like being caught in a tornado and trying desperately to hold on to something from my former life to anchor me, only to watch it all be swept away.

What if you had the power to change the outcome of a fever dream like that just by closing your eyes and envisioning a different ending? Isn't that what happened to Dorothy in *The Wizard of Oz*? She had to endure a nightmare with those flying monkeys and that horrible green-faced witch until she finally got her wish to go home. The great and powerful wizard, who was really just a man, told her she'd had the power all along. She simply had to close her eyes, click her heels three times, and envision what she wanted.

"There's no place like home," she said.

And just like that, her horror show was over.

The challenge, of course, is how the hell do you close your eyes when you're in the grasp of a grotesque monster's gnarly ingrown talons? No amount of nail art could make that reality any less menacing.

Now I understand why bunnies freeze in fear!

But you can't freeze and think you'll somehow still survive. You need to use every bit of your strength and imagination to change the outcome of this scenario. Dorothy had her movie; this one is yours. You're the writer, and the script of your life can be a suspense thriller or a fantasy come true. You get to choose how your story ends.

One of the most vivid examples of manifesting I've experienced was when some friends of mine hired me to sell their townhouse on 11th Street. My friend Beatrice is a rock star in the fashion world. She and her husband, Lorenzo, had performed a full-blown renovation on the house right after they'd purchased it fifteen years earlier. Beatrice is European and has the most exquisite taste, while Lorenzo is known to all his friends as having severe OCD. A real clean freak. I wanted to make him a T-shirt that read "I'm not gay" on the front and "I'm just anal" on the back.

The house was located on one of the most picturesque streets in the Village. It was built in 1829, and thankfully, Beatrice and Lorenzo had preserved all the most charming original elements, including three fireplaces and beautiful exposed beams. Even the outside was precious, with flower boxes lining every window and ivy adorning the facade. In Manhattan, it's difficult to find houses that have been restored with such a timeless and tasteful touch.

Everyone who came through the townhouse just loved it. Even so, it was too small for some and too expensive for others—but for Daniella, it was perfect. The second she toured the place she knew it would be her new home. She was staying in a hotel at the time, because her current apartment had a serious leak and she needed to vacate. In fact, on two other occasions in her life serious leaks in her home had warranted her leaving for extended periods. As a result, she'd learned a lot about mold, and she believed that if it wasn't found and eradicated, it could cause life-altering illnesses. Anyway, she needed to move into someplace fast. But before she would take the next step and put an offer on the townhouse she wanted to do as much due diligence as possible to be sure she wasn't going to face the same problems she'd had in the past in her new home. She asked if the sellers would permit a team to conduct a couple of tests to determine the presence or absence of mold in the house. One test would take from eight to nine hours to perform, and the other would entail opening a wall in the bedroom. These tests would need to happen before she signed a contract. So, imagine all these guys coming into the house while I was still showing the place to other buyers. There would be painting cloths everywhere and holes in the walls, which would take over a week to plaster. Additional time would be needed, of course, to let the plaster dry, to sand it down, and to paint over it. Very likely the entire wall would require repainting to ensure that the color wasn't mismatched. It was a massive ask from the buyer's side: "Hey, can we come in and blow your place up while we decide if we want it?"

This request certainly gave us pause. We wanted Daniella to feel comfortable if she bought the house, and I did feel like this was the right home for her, so the sellers and I gave her the green light. After weeks of the house being probed and prodded, Daniella signed the contract of sale, and I set things in motion for a quick closing, since she wanted to get out of her hotel in a hurry.

Just about a year had gone by when I heard the terrible news that the townhouse had a leak. My clients had lived there for fifteen years with no problems, and suddenly this buyer was living with her worst nightmare. Bear in mind that this had happened to her three times before in other homes. She had made herself the queen of caulk, the damp diva. One could say she was just unbelievably unlucky, or one could justifiably think that Daniella's constant fear over this happening made the very thing she was trying to avoid a reality. Six months after she fixed the last leak, she put the house on the market. She let her fears get the best of her. As you can see, the Law of Attraction works both ways.

When Mindy, one of my good friends from the West Coast, was in town, I decided to test my manifesting skill set with her. She was known among our friends as the "runaway bride." She had been engaged twice and had gotten cold feet both times. Mindy is my bombshell friend. She was born into the cutest, sweetest family. Her parents met in their teens, and they're the kind of couple that still stares into each other's eyes with love and adoration. Mindy is adventurous and hysterically funny, and can hit more home runs at a pickup baseball game than most men. She's an absolute catch. She worked as an entertainment reporter, lived a glamourous life, and was looking for a true soul mate. She was ready to find the one but kept being disappointed by her suitors. On one of her many visits to NYC, she had developed a crush on a guy who was splitting time between Los Angeles and New York. Like Mindy, he worked in the entertainment industry. It was a new crush, and she was excited to see him and to get my take on this new property. When she shared his address with me, I paused, for two reasons. First, I had made one of my first sales in New York in that building, and second, it wasn't in what I would call an A location. Nevertheless, she was as giddy as a teenager for me to meet him.

When we went to his apartment, we noticed that a neighboring door was completely bashed in. It looked like King Kong had pounded on it. When we inquired about what had happened, her potential Romeo said, "Oh yeah. That asshole. He wouldn't shut up, so I beat his door in with a baseball bat." We laughed at first, but then realized he was serious. Mindy squeezed my hand when it occurred to her that her Romeo had turned into Rambo. This was not a promising sign.

For the rest of the weekend, our joke was, "Don't make him mad." If he asked us where we wanted to eat, Mindy would whisper it before answering.

Sadly, this one was over before it even began.

Another one bites the dust.

The two of us found ourselves scratching our heads on a Sunday afternoon, looking for some plans and some answers. That's when I decided we would put pen to paper to determine exactly who her ideal guy was and how to get to him. We would manifest this person by putting a list of his attributes out into the Universe. I called it the nonnegotiable list. I'd seen the same thing many times in real estate—people must have a doorman, sunlight, outdoor space, whatever it is for them. Buyers often don't know what they want; they just believe they'll know it when they see it. I wasn't so sure about that philosophy. I believed that the more life you breathed into something, the likelier it was to happen. The nonnegotiable list wasn't a wish list but rather an inventory that would help create a realistic and fruitful search for the one.

I knew Mindy was looking for someone who could keep up with her. He had to have a pure and courageous heart, unwavering integrity, and a sense of adventure. He also had to be a lifelong learner. We spent the afternoon adding more attributes to her list. To help her manifest him, I made her visualize who this man was. I coaxed her to see him, experience him, and feel his presence. I wanted her to be excited by the promise that he really did exist. I wanted her to know that everything that had happened in the past had happened to make Mindy who she is—stronger, wiser, bolder, and a person who could greet her soul mate with an open heart. I wanted her to trust the process and know that the Universe hadn't forgotten her or her quest for lifelong love. Her soul mate was also taking steps toward her and would appear when she was ready.

Within months she had met the perfect match.

She was in Las Vegas when she and Glenn first met at a blackjack table. He was with a group at the next table, winning and whooping it up with every hand. Mindy noticed him because he was loud and wearing dark sunglasses. They spent the night joking around the tables, laughing and egging each other on until sunrise. When Mindy called it a night, everyone said their goodbyes. She later found out that Glenn was wondering why he'd let her walk away without knowing how to find her again. He hadn't even asked for her number.

A few days later, he couldn't stop thinking about her. Was she *his* lost Cinderella? He had no glass slipper or any other way to track her down. And then one morning he turned on his television and there she was. She was dishing Hollywood's latest scandal on KTLA, a local news station. He stopped, stared at the television, and realized that she was the woman he'd met in Las Vegas.

He decided to e-mail her. He explained that they had met at the blackjack tables and asked if he could take her out.

Mindy didn't respond. She was used to getting these types of "fan" e-mails and letters.

But her promising prince wouldn't give up. He e-mailed again. This time he said he had tickets to a Jimmy Buffett concert and asked if she wanted to go.

Mindy had never been to a Jimmy Buffett concert. She thought, *Why not?*

Mindy and Glenn have been together ever since. It's been eighteen years, and they're truly living their happily ever after. In fact, he named their yacht *Minderella* and the helicopter that goes with it *The Glass Slipper*. If that isn't enough to motivate you to manifest your Prince Charming, what's your problem? I once heard that before Grace Kelly met Prince Rainier III of Monaco, she hoped to marry an actor. However, her parents always told her they'd pictured her with nothing short of a prince (well, something like that), but the rest is history.

On Glenn's birthday a few years ago, I dug that list out of a storage bin. Mindy wanted to show him how he became her dream man. Indeed, he was every single thing on that very long list, with two exceptions—he wasn't Latin or six foot two. But he nailed every other feature and then some. Not a bad outcome for my first manifestation project, right?

All I needed to do now was conjure up someone for me!

There are so many layers in people's lives that others never see. There's our outward presentation, and then there's the reality of what goes on behind closed doors. I get the equivalent of a backstage pass when I work with clients, whether they're buyers or I'm selling their homes. I'm the proverbial fly on the wall when a couple disagrees about what they want, can't make a decision, or are constantly at odds. Life and relationships can be complicated, and most of the time that drama has nothing to do with others. I, of course, always think it's about me, but it's not. I often represent couples who are uncoupling. Few do it consciously or gracefully. The emotions and loss overtake even the most restrained people. It's always sad to watch, and hard to be in the middle of. Luckily, I understand where the anger and pain come from; I've been there, and I know it isn't easy. I also understand that it has nothing to do with anything I've done—it's about the struggles and challenges we're all facing every single day. Whether you have a kid with a food allergy, are trying to sell real estate in a down market, or have a spouse who's struggling with his career, you're constantly in fight-or-flight mode. Spend enough time with people in their homes and you'll realize that they're going through stuff just like you. Some people are just better at compartmentalizing it than others, or even hiding it altogether.

Earlier, I talked about the importance of not taking things so personally—about having a strong sense of who you are and weaning yourself off the opinions of others in order to be content and satisfied with your self-image. Of course, it's easier said than done. We've all allowed our worldviews to be impacted by warped perceptions, our own and those of others. Most of us see things the way we want them to be, not the way they are. We adjust our opinions, perspectives, and outlooks to support those feelings. But here's the payoff we haven't discussed yet: when you stop caring what other people think and stop taking things so personally, emotions such as anger, jealousy, envy, and even sadness lessen and eventually fade away. If someone else has you feeling down about yourself, the truth is that the other person is likely projecting his or her own feelings of despair, angst, and hurt onto you. When you can stop giving another person's opinion of you more value than your own, you'll be truly free from the burden of guilt, insecurity, and feelings of inadequacy.

Change is disruptive to the core of who we are. Whenever you endure radical change, notice what shows up. Fear? Sadness? Scheming? Gratitude? Sometimes there will be unexpected circumstances—unimaginable happenings that occur, leaving you mystified and asking the most difficult questions. These circumstances often place you at what feels like the hardest crossroads in your life. When you're deep inside those moments, you can't always see the purpose or the meaning, but you can bet there's a plan in motion. That's when you know change is coming. Big change. The way you can feel the air changing before a big storm. And whether you're ready for it or not, your journey is already in progress. In fact, it's happening now, in this moment.

Whenever there's this type of anxious unrest, people have a tendency to look outside themselves for answers. We inherently want solutions, and therefore try to make certain the uncertain in life. Unfortunately, that isn't always possible. Sometimes, as challenging as it will be, you need to patiently relax into the moment and allow your circumstances to unfold. The best way to change your situation is to get comfortable in it. You have to let the Universe do its thing, because the reality is that it's going to anyway. The more we resist it, the harder we make things for ourselves and everyone around us. And when we can't find the answers we want—or, worse, the ones we want to hear— we tend to place blame for our dissatisfaction on our circumstances or on others instead of going inside and examining what we're feeling and, more important, why. It took me a long time to understand the value of this, but when I finally embraced the positive difference it could make in my life, you can bet I wanted more, and I wanted to share this newfound awareness with everyone around me. Some years later it resulted in this book!

If you think about it, it's impossible to make the body stronger without feeling pain. You do a hard workout, and that breaks down your muscles. The influx of lactic acid causes you to feel sore from the activity. So, you rest, recover, and begin again. You go back to the gym and lift, strain, and break down your muscles once more, and on goes the cycle. No one gets a beautiful, strong body without breakdown and pain. In some ways, pain is the birth of new beginnings.

Now, here's something I didn't know at the time of my friend divorce: once you start going deep, people who've been around you for years will start to feel as if you're moving away from them, because suddenly you appear to no longer be like them. Of course, that's not true; what you've done is simply change frequency. One thing I know for sure: when you're no longer operating on the same wavelength, someone gets left behind, and will inevitably feel betrayed.

It isn't intentional.

As your frequency goes up, it no longer matches that of those around you.

This has happened to all of us at one time or another.

So often I see people get stuck in ego and pride when they're trying to make a point, whether in buying a home or arguing with a loved one. If you dig your heels in on every last thing, chances are, you'll lose what you're after. If you become flexible, however, there's usually a way to make it work. Remember, bending is not breaking.

When I was licking my wounds after my divorce, I dove headfirst into finding ways to heal. I discovered Dr. Wayne Dyer's views on enlightenment and the importance of recognizing that *I Am*—I am an infinite being, being seen and observing from a limited, localized, particular point of view. As I've mentioned, I began practicing meditation, and tried to be consistent with it. I wasn't perfect, and that was okay. Whenever I sat with myself, I would naturally turn to the powerful affirmation I learned from Dr. Dyer: *I am an infinite being. I am love. I am abundance.*

I wouldn't attach a single negative word to my "I am" identity. I would never say, "I'm angry, sad, frustrated, hurting." Those didn't feel like power words. You can never sell anyone or anything, including the Universe, with negative words like that. When we use those words to describe ourselves, we attract people who use the same words to describe themselves. Remember the Bummer Brownstone, when I didn't want to be alone in my misery. Think of it like this: the Universe is a *huge* Match.com, only it's for every kind of relationship, not just romantic ones. The way you treat your affirmations in secret, the Universe will treat them in your life. It doesn't differentiate between positive and negative; the Universe just hears *I'm fat, I'm old, I'm a loser* and records that data. Of course, the reverse is true with positive affirmations. With the right attitude and commitment, I could drive anything forward. I suppressed, repressed, and ignored whatever appeared as an obstacle in my path—or at least I did until I once again began to have conflicting dialogue in my head. But here's what I can tell you from that experience: if I indulged those negative thoughts, like a radio antenna tuning in to a lower frequency, more of those negative things would come into my life. I had to be disciplined or I would fall back into my old ways. I no longer wanted to feel like a hamster on a wheel, spinning my negative thoughts into reality and getting nowhere. I wanted to grow, to break away from old habits, and to invite wonderful things into my life. The only way to do that was to stay the course and believe that the Universe would deliver.

CHAPTER NINETEEN

Closing the Deal

*You yourself, as much as anybody in the entire
Universe, deserve your love and affection.*
—Unknown

AT FIRST, ONE OF THE HARDEST THINGS FOR ME ABOUT BEING single was losing my travel partner. Traveling with my family was still great, of course. I would sleep in the kids' room, with little nieces and nephews snuggled around me like sardines. After a couple of days of cohabiting, they would forget that I was an adult and start confiding all their secrets in me. We would stay up late whispering under the covers. I would hear about the bullies at school and who among their friends was the naughtiest. These were precious moments I had the joy of experiencing only because I was alone, and perhaps they could feel how vulnerable I was, just like a child. So, I became one of them, one of the pack—an honor few adults receive.

During the day, when my family was out and about, my mom—the photographer among us—would shout, "Get with your group," as she wanted to take individual family photos with my siblings: my sister and her adorable children, my brother with his. And then there was me. Just me.

"Do you want to take one of me alone?" I would shyly ask.

"Not really. You're not going to like them. Trust me," she would say.

Okay, so there's that.

The lack of empathy is not unique to Connie, however. The world can be punishing to single people. I have a friend who told me a story about going to a movie alone on a Friday evening in Manhattan. The ticket booth attendant repeated twice through the microphone at the front window, "So you're alone, just one?"

My friend timidly replied, "Yes."

Then one more time, just to be sure, he asked, "Okay, these are assigned seats, so you'll be alone next to people you don't know; you okay with that?"

Humiliated, my friend shrugged her shoulders, thinking to herself, *I'm such a loser.*

Then she remembered who she really was and slammed the door on the negativity. She tapped on the glass and said, "By the way, *I'm not alone*—I'm my own company. I can eat my entire popcorn, get a slushy instead of a bottle of water, and enjoy the movie *I'm* paying for. You know why?"

The ticket person cocked his head to the right.

"Because I like my own company, and I have the ability to be truly happy on my own. I don't punish myself for that, I celebrate it. You should try it sometime," she said.

Before she could apologize for her outburst to the others in line, she heard a couple say, "You go, girl," and a twentysomething followed up with, "You're my spirit animal, queen!" And just like that, her negativity was averted.

A change in your perception will change the perception of those around you.

As much as excursions with my family were special, I longed for my own travel and growth. Addicted to hotels, spas, and adventure, I buried my head in magazines, looking for the latest in luxury hotspots. Oftentimes, those places were the manifestation of someone else's dream lifestyle and business.

I came across an article about a boutique spa that had recently opened in Mexico in what had been the owner's private home. It was situated high up on a cliff, and he'd named it after his family's chef, Verana. This creation was clearly his idea of heaven. It looked like the perfect backdrop for a girls' vacation.

I shot an e-mail to my West Coast gal pals, the same girls I had seen right after Esalen, who would more easily be able to join me. We had vowed to see one another a few times a year after that, and this seemed like the ideal place to meet.

One by one, the e-mails came back.

"Done," said Mindy.

"Done and done," said Laila.

"IN!" said Ceci.

It looked like we were off to the races.

The location was certainly remote. The only way to get there was to drive forty-five minutes south of Acapulco, then board a tiny, brightly colored dinghy. We piled our luggage high up in the front of the small rubber boat and threw a tarp over the top to keep the water from soaking through.

We rode in the dinghy for a little under an hour, gliding along the coast past villages and fishermen. Different fish kept jumping out of the water ahead of us. Soon we found ourselves passing a solid green coastal forest; we were really out there.

The dinghy finally slowed and deposited us on a sandy beach. The hotel greeters were waiting for us with donkeys.

We got soaked sloshing through the ocean water, even though we'd pulled up our pants practically to thigh level. After the staff loaded the donkeys with our luggage, we started the steep climb up to a sliver of nirvana high in the jungle.

When we reached the top, we were handed refreshing mango juice and cold towels. After we'd gathered our composure, we sat and enjoyed the most beautiful view of the ocean. Its magical blue colors didn't look real.

There was no denying that we had arrived someplace very special. The energy, the scents in the air, and the sound of wind chimes assured us that this was a fantastic find.

We had to climb even farther to get to our rooms in thatched-roof villas scattered over the cliffs. They were open to the elements, the night air, animals, and the stars. Ceci and I got the lucky villa, closest to the spa. Laila and Gina were up by the pool. Mindy and Heather got the honeymoon house, which was more secluded and located closer to the edges of the jungle.

We were greeted by the owner, who said that his wife was an architect and that together they'd created their dream house there. It had transformed his life so much that he wanted to share it with others.

Something about this place felt as if each of us was about to get an unexpected gift, something we each needed in our lives whether we were aware of it or not. It wasn't our intent when we booked the trip, but somehow the Universe had plans we had no way of understanding in the moment.

The first appointment for me was with the spa healer. I followed the stone path from my hut to a beautifully carved wooden door. The healer, a woman, was waiting there with a big smile, and she reached out her arms toward me.

"You must be Holly. We've been expecting you," she whispered with warmth and peace, as healers often do.

We spent almost two and a half hours together. She said she would do some Reiki and if she felt pain or an energy block, she would report to me what she thought it was. Our session was one of those rare experiences that, afterward, didn't seem real. How could she have known the things that she recounted? How was she able to so literally put her finger on my trouble spots? Yet somehow, she did. I decided to let go and not try to analyze or rationalize everything. This was about transformation. The blood was racing through my body. It made me feel so light, and my mind was so clear.

Over the next three days, we all took turns being treated by different healers. The second day was about adventure. Laila had dreamed her whole life about riding a giant manta ray, so down the hill and into the dinghy we went, looking for rays. Our skipper and attendant for the day was Jorge. He called out in Spanish whenever he saw one; they were over eight feet across, and there was no missing them when they breached the surface. With a quick mask and snorkel check, Laila was in the water, making her dreams come true.

Our next stop was a picnic on an island off the coast, complete with one of the prettiest beaches in all of Mexico. There was absolutely nothing on the island. It was totally isolated.

After the picnic, Jorge said, "Give me your cameras. This is an amazing place to take pictures."

We all lined up, kneeling and facing the water. Jorge snapped a shot from behind us to give our point of view. We wanted to see how it looked, and ended up directing subsequent shots. We clearly had six captains and no crew here.

"Looks great, but we should be naked," Laila said.

"Oh, God. No! Here?" I gasped.

"Oh, c'mon, Holly. Don't spoil it. You won't even be able to tell it's you. Don't screw it up," Laila said. "Yeah, don't screw it up," Jorge said. I'm kidding; Jorge was a perfect gentleman, and I'm sure we weren't the first totally relaxed, inspired adventurous tourists he took naked pics of on this secluded beach.

"We want everyone in!" Laila gave this order like a Marine drill sergeant.

There was no saying no to these ladies. So, off went the suits, in the middle of the day, with Jorge behind the camera. I have to admit, the photo was pretty cool. And we all felt liberated as we posed or took candids of one another around the beach. It was all very *Blue Lagoon*. I was waiting for a naked Brooke Shields to run by. Or, better yet, Christopher Atkins.

As for Jorge?

Well, it's not a bad day's work to be chasing naked women around a desolate island. He was certainly feeling no pain, and he was getting in touch with his inner artist at the same time. Now, if we could just get Laila back on her manta ray totally naked!

Our last night coincided with a full moon. We had planned a healing session with Elizabeth, a spiritual healer we met at the spa. The view was spectacular as the moon rose in the distance over the ocean. It lit up the sky, so we needed no light other than a couple of candles scattered around. We spent hours journaling and were instructed to list the things we would be leaving behind in Mexico. We jotted them down on pieces of paper and then took turns reading them aloud around the firepit. No one was forced to share; we all did it voluntarily. And then we watched the papers burn one by the one.

Healing baths with fresh flowers, herbs, and salts followed.

"Let's lose the suits," Laila said once again. Clearly, Laila likes being naked. And by now, you know I don't share that passion.

"Oh, Lord! Why is it that anything healing needs to be done naked?" This time, though, I was fine with it. I had come a long way since Esalen. The moon, the laughter, and these outrageously funny ladies all made it okay.

We had collectively decided to have a ceremony on this trip in which we would each marry ourselves. I'd seen an episode of *Sex and the City* where Sarah Jessica Parker's character, Carrie Bradshaw, announced she was marrying herself. Her reason? While she was happy to celebrate her friends' life choices, she complained that they never celebrated her choice to be single and childless. We told Elizabeth about our plan, and she was all over it.

We'd all brought outfits we wanted to marry ourselves in. Among us were two Wonder Woman costumes, two princesses, one water Olympian, and a flower goddess. Yes, Laila wore a costume too. Elizabeth did not disappoint: the spa was lit with candles everywhere, lavender incense was burning, and rose pedals were strewn all around. The place looked magnificent in the natural moonlight. Everything was perfect.

We all created sacred vows of self-love. Like regular vows of marriage, these comprised promises to love, cherish, and deeply care for all parts of ourselves, in sickness and in health, and for all time. As I wrote my vows, I meditated deeply on how, going forward, I wanted to honor my highest self. How would I love myself and open myself to be loved by others? How would I finally learn that love coming from outside me would never bring the same contentment, fulfillment, and comfort as the love I had for myself? This was one of the most important exercises I had ever done in my life. For me, it was about finally seeing myself as the luxury property that I was and am. It was in this moment that I realized I was what so many people in the city desire—the penthouse, the classic six, the coveted double-wide brownstone. I had become a client with a sought-after property to sell. I was no longer a child but a grounded, successful, fun woman who had a lot to offer. I had been my harshest critic, but now it was time to become my greatest advocate. And it was time to close the deal and fall in love—with myself.

I realize there's an aspect of marrying yourself that might sound selfish or even a bit narcissistic, but that wasn't how any of us felt. The idea was to make a commitment to a life that values self-love, self-compassion, and self-support, a commitment to a happier, healthier outlook. To love ourselves as we would have others love us.

My vows went like this:

I pledge to love, honor, and cherish myself.

I promise to never settle or lose who I am in a relationship again.

From today forward, I will be my own best friend.

I am committed to letting go of my negative thoughts and my inner critic and accepting myself as I am and not as others want me to be.

I will walk a more spiritual path and am dedicated to building the most ahhmaaazzzziiing life.

Some of the others' vows were similar, and some were more personal or specific to their individual situation. They were all full of hope, vulnerability, and bravery.

Even though a few of the girls were already married, we all saw the value in this ceremony. It gave us permission to love more deeply and richly. It also served as a gateway to the life we desired, one that was full of meaning, purpose, and connection. It gave us permission to make caring for ourselves more of a priority. Sharing this experience with some of my closest friends made it even more impactful. Not only were we witnesses to one another's vows but the shared ceremony also allowed each of us to acknowledge the others' visions and pathways.

We each have a sense of our life, an idea of what we want and how we want to be. It doesn't require a formal ceremony to help focus what that is for you. You can have a private ceremony in your home by yourself, or you can go all out with a dress, a cake, and a party. What's really important is the commitment you make to yourself. Writing my vows was like creating a vision board for love. Our souls speak in images, and it helped me to visibly see what I wanted—to clearly identify it. What we see, we can achieve. Think it, act it, become it.

The ceremony stuck with me long after that weekend was over. Marrying myself was a significant starting point, but it certainly wasn't my destination. In real estate terms, it was as if I'd bought a place as is. I still had a lot of work to do if I wanted to honor my vows, but I was looking forward to that work. The place was mine, quirks and all, and I loved it.

There were parts of myself I would need to let go of, and parts I would need to care for differently than I had in the past. I was still needy, scared, and shut down at times—all aspects of myself that required my loving care more than my criticism.

Your task is not to seek for love, but merely to seek and find all the barriers within yourself that you have built against it.
—RUMI

CHAPTER TWENTY

No Place Like Home

Home is a place we all must find, child. It's not just a place where you eat or sleep. Home is knowing. Knowing your mind, knowing your heart, knowing your courage. If we know ourselves, we're always home, anywhere.
—Glinda the Good Witch, *The Wizard of Oz*

THE HOLIDAYS IN NEW YORK CITY BRING ABOUT A NEW TYPE OF energy. The storefronts are festive and colorful, their windows full of whimsy. The streets are packed with tourists taking in the sights, and the air just smells of Christmas. It seemed that everywhere I went, people were celebrating. There was the office party at Le Cirque, the squeals of joy as children flowed into and out of FAO Schwarz, and the occasional proposal in front of the horses and carriages on Central Park South. I saw at least three bended knees while walking to and from work. Witnessing all this laughter and cheer made me feel, well, miserable. I felt forgotten in every way. Everything I'd learned about meditation and visualization had escaped me. After all, hadn't my guru taught me to trust in the Universe? To look for the signs and let them lead me? To believe that by being a good person, good people would come? I found myself feeling angry at every guide I had. I didn't believe in any of them anymore. I was pissed. I had done the work. I had been alone. I had traveled. I had built my foundation, or so I thought. I was ready to go. I had my package together. And yet I was stuck, sidetracked by a terrible relationship, standing in front of an animatronic Shrek dressed as Santa and thinking, *Screw you, Universe.*

I knew the person I'd been dating for four and a half months wasn't right for me. I'd been going out with the same type of narcissist over and over. What was that all about? Why was I attracted to people like that? I still don't know that answer, but this much I do know: one of the most expensive mistakes we make is paying attention to the wrong people. Doing this can leave us emotionally bankrupt. Time is the most precious commodity. You might as well give them your PIN and tell them to withdraw as much money as they need, because it would be a lot less emotionally taxing if you just paid them in cash instead of time. Your time shouldn't be taken for granted. When you pay attention to the wrong people, you never get that time back. Wrong people, wrong location—it's really all the same. It's just a bad investment. With every park-side proposal I witnessed, I became more and more certain that the guy I was dating wasn't someone I should be investing my time in. In fact, doing so was spinning me in a horrible direction. So, at that moment, I didn't really see the Universe as having my back. It wasn't leading me to the right person—at least not until the evening of December 12, 2007.

It was a dreadfully rainy night in the city, the perfect backdrop for a Christmas rom-com, minus the snow. I'd been invited to a holiday party thrown by one of my clients, the fourth party I would attend since Thanksgiving. Is it me, or does time start to feel like it's in fast-forward from the end of November until the stroke of midnight on New Year's Eve? Everything moves at hyper speed! And when it comes to real estate, it seems as though everyone wants to close on their deals before January 1. The combination creates an eggnoggy, gingerbready whirlwind.

Despite my reluctance, I had to go. My client would never speak to me again if I didn't. Besides, his apartment was on the market, and I was having an open house there the next day. I wanted to make sure it wouldn't be left in shambles.

I planned to make an appearance, do a fly-by hello and goodbye, and head home, where I was pretty sure no visions of sugar plums would be dancing through my head after I'd cried myself to sleep. I'd even made a commitment not to go near any alcohol, as I knew how dangerous that could be given my frame of mind; I might go full-on Grinch. (I don't have a lot of willpower around the sauce during the holidays.) As I was getting ready to go, my phone buzzed. I guess you could say that I'm also not good at saying no when a hot man calls and asks if he can come over to practice his massage techniques on me.

The Naughty Masseuse was someone I'd dated after college. He was a professional golfer turned wannabe masseuse, or that's what he convinced me of. I ran into him a few months earlier. As it turned out, he'd been separated from his wife for over a year and was in the process of trying to figure out his life. I told him I wasn't interested in a relationship, that we had been there and done that, but he insisted that he could be happy just being my friend. I knew it wouldn't go anywhere, but I think he just liked the company and the ability to talk with someone, especially around the holidays. The idea of a massage before this dreaded party sounded pretty good, so I said he could come over. He worked on me for two hours.

"Holly, I'm sad that you see yourself as broken. I was the worst boyfriend. I know that now. How can I make it up to you? Let me be your friend," he said as his hands began to wander away from my back. He wanted to get naughty, but I wasn't interested.

"If you want to be my friend, just stop," I said as I got up, wrapped the sheet around me, and headed to the bathroom to take a shower.

I thought the Naughty Masseuse would be gone by the time I emerged, but he wasn't.

"I'll go to the party with you," he said.

I didn't want him coming with me any more than I wanted to be his girlfriend. It just wasn't happening. Besides, I knew I had to go alone. I sent the Naughty Masseuse on his way, finished dressing, and headed out the door.

When I arrived, the elevator opened into my client's stunning 6,600-square-foot loft. There were big dome windows, and the walls were exposed brick. The party was packed, and the apartment, all decorated for the holidays, looked gorgeous. The crowd, spread throughout the huge open floor plan, was lively. Everyone was having a good time. My eyes were immediately drawn to a tall, dark, handsome young man who was laughing louder than he likely should have been. He looked European to me. I squinted and thought, *He has fucked every beautiful woman in this room. I know it.* I made my way to the host, making sure we connected so he knew I was there. It really didn't matter how long I stayed after that. Within thirty minutes of arriving, I headed toward the elevator, pushed the down button, and waited. I turned around for a last glance at the beautifully decorated apartment and saw the guy from before talking to another stunning female. Shocker! He threw his head back again with an overly exaggerated laugh.

Ah! I hate that guy! I thought. *But I have to meet him before I leave.* Just as the elevator doors opened, I turned around and made my way back into the party. One of the host's friends saw me and said, "I thought you were leaving."

"I was, except there's someone here I think I should meet." I grabbed her hand and dragged her over to him.

"Hi," I said.

"Hi," he replied.

This intriguing man turned back to his friends and continued his conversation. A minute later, he excused himself to go to the bathroom.

Because of the open house the next morning, I had cordoned off all but one bathroom, so I knew there would be a line. I made my way over to him, and we started talking as we waited for the people ahead of us to go first. He told me his name was Marc. I was right; he was European. Dutch, in fact. I should have known by the clogs he was wearing. (Just kidding! There were no clogs.)

We had been in mid-conversation, so I was pretty sure that afterward he would find me to resume it. As I'd suspected, Marc did ultimately seek me out. We hit it off and talked for hours. My friend kept coming over to us and saying, "We need to break you two up." And then she'd giggle and walk away. She had an ulterior motive, though: there was another man she wanted me to meet. In the interest of fewer interruptions, I finally got up to say hello to her very rich single-dad friend. We made small talk for a few minutes, and he shared that he spent most weekends in Maine watching his daughter play basketball. Just as location matters in real estate, geographic desirability can be important in a relationship—and sure, there are times you might be willing to make sacrifices, but this wasn't one of them, at least not for me. This guy's daughter was fourteen years old and lived in Maine, and he saw her *every weekend*. That meant five hours up and five hours back, fifty-two weeks a year for the next *four years*! That was a bigger sacrifice than I was willing to make. In real estate, you always want to live in the best location you can afford, and when it comes to people, you have to do your research and not jump right in. If they're the wrong location for you, it will never work. This guy was definitely the wrong location for me. I didn't need it to go any further.

So that was a no-go. No matter how many times my girlfriend told me how amazing he was, all I could think of was traffic.

What I really wanted was to play with my European troublemaker. I left my Maine man in the kitchen and headed back to find to my hot Dutchie.

Someone mentioned that everyone was heading to an after-hours party at Employees Only, a secret bar in the West Village. Marc asked if I wanted to go. I said, "Sounds great!"

We both laughed, grabbed our coats, and headed out. He hailed a cab and said, "Twenty-Sixth and Fifth, please."

That wasn't where Employees Only was. That was *my* address. Did he really just say that? Well, I was feeling really tired and thought it would be a lot nicer to have a drink at home than at an overcrowded bar. He came up to my apartment, and I asked what I could get him to drink.

"Do you have any tea?"

I didn't see that coming.

"And do you have any cookies?"

Was he for real? I thought it was sweet—unexpected, but sweet.

We sat on the couch and talked late into the night over tea. He was like that girl in *American Pie* who always started her stories with, "One time at band camp ..." He talked and talked and never stopped. I remember feeling anxious because, for the first time, I felt calm—really calm. And safe. And it felt *really* nice.

It was as if I'd known Marc forever. It didn't feel like I was meeting a new person but rather like being with an old friend. He felt like home—and not in a super exciting way, because I couldn't be excited in that state. I wasn't sure I would ever get that back.

I've talked about heroin love, and I've had moments of it over the years. My ex-husband was a heroin high. I made all sorts of decisions I wouldn't have made if I hadn't been taken by that high. But like heroin, that feeling wears off, and at the end of it you crash. That's when you think, *Who is this person? What happened to us and the way we used to be?*

Well, you used to be high and now you're not.

You're stone-cold sober. When you fly high on endorphins, it can become a very dangerous state.

I couldn't help noticing that something was different as I sat there with Marc. It wasn't a heroin high; it was just a comfortable buzz, an ease, as if we had known each other for a lifetime.

Was I really ready to open my heart to someone again?

He certainly was attractive, and by attractive, I mean smoking hot. I wanted to know the story behind the face. I knew that he was Dutch, and he seemed well traveled. I paid close attention to the words he used when he spoke. I remember being on a date with someone once who used sentences that began with, "A girl like you . . ." and I kept thinking, *This might be a guy who needs to be in charge all the time.* Words speak volumes. They give you intel. And since Marc liked to talk, I was picking up a lot. It was clear that he hadn't experienced a broken heart before. His emotions were so accessible. He was so ready to open his heart. Even though my first impression was that he was a little emotionally naïve, like a hot Dutch Bambi, I also thought it was refreshing.

We went out every night that week, and each encounter was a new adventure with him. He was so much fun. We crashed Christmas parties together, had late-night dinners, attended dance parties, and held backgammon marathons. He even arrived one night with a pasta maker to make me his grandmother's homemade recipe. It was clear that we had a lot in common.

As I would discover, we'd both attended international high schools, and as a result we had a different way of looking at the world. I call it globally focused. We were both avid skiers, bikers, tennis players, and divers. And he could cook—very well, I might add. Good in the kitchen: now that's something I've always found incredibly sexy in a man. He was up for anything, and made things that might otherwise be boring fun. He was also very open-minded and incredibly kind. If he felt threatened, he could become unkind, but only if he was provoked. And he had a big heart.

In dating, just as in house hunting, you want to find that perfect home. When you've lived someplace for an extended period, it becomes your home. You can't fathom living anywhere else, but somehow, when you move, that next place becomes home too. Sure, you have to look at a lot of real estate and rent places you'd never settle in to get there, but eventually you find the one that makes you say, "I could live here." It doesn't need to be your forever house, but it's a place to make into home.

Was Marc that? Was *he* home?

Maybe it was witnessing all of those engagements that got me thinking it was time. I mean, when do you really get to see that? It's like finding a robin's egg. It's rare, but it happens. Love was all around me, and I was getting really fed up with my lack of luck and wanted to move forward in my life. I wanted to be married, to have kids. I wanted my forever home, but I wasn't willing to forgive any guy's shortcomings. It's always better to be the buyer than it is to be the seller, whether you're dating or in real estate. A buyer has all of the leverage. A seller is constantly marketing. If you're really confident, you never have to sell.

Before meeting Marc, I'd planned a trip to Puerto Rico with my friend David, who's gay. David has an unbelievable ability to know when you're at your most vulnerable. He has a million friends because he understands what it takes to be one. A good one. Even though sixty people would call him their best friend, he has a sixth sense for who needs him at any given time. It was no surprise when I received a text from him that read, "Where are we going for New Years?" He knew the moment had come when I really needed him.

At first, we'd planned an amazing safari in Africa. All of the details had been set. On the day we were supposed to prepay for the trip, David realized he had a scheduling issue. He was a massive LSU fan, and there was a game he wouldn't miss. If you're an LSU fan, you get this; if you're like me, it's a bit of a head-scratcher. Rebooking a trip we were supposed to take in a few weeks became a challenge. People who want to travel over the holidays in December plan for months in advance. I knew there would be slim pickings, if that, to choose from.

I found availability at Villa Montana Beach Resort in Aguadilla, Puerto Rico. Ceci, one of the Wonder Woman in the group of friends who'd vacationed with me in Mexico, had gotten married there several months before. It was an absolutely stunning wedding. I'd left thinking that I would definitely be back there someday.

The resort was very remote and had miles of beach with vegetation. You don't see that very often. The beaches were beautiful—not pristine but totally empty, which made them some of the most gorgeous beaches I'd ever seen. The villa was so tasteful and organic. It almost looked like a Four Seasons Hotel that had lain undiscovered for thirty years. It's a hidden jewel off the beaten path. I booked a two-bedroom house right on the beach for David and myself.

In the meantime, Marc and I went out together every night, having a blast in the city. In a matter of days, I'd gone from the Grinch to celebrating everything Christmas. At some point I must have mentioned the trip David and I were taking to Marc. When we departed, Marc said to me, "I might just see you down there."

All I could think was, *Yeah, right*, blowing it off. Besides, he was traveling to Amsterdam, so I was certain it would never happen.

I wasn't even sure he knew that David and I were just friends, or that David was gay. But Marc's confidence intrigued me.

David and I arrived in Puerto Rico as planned, checked in, and began our five-day getaway. It was exactly what I needed. We settled into our routine and were loving our lazy days in the sun. One afternoon, while David and I lounged on a double chaise, sharing margaritas, I looked up and gasped.

"Oh, my God! He's here!"

"Who's here?" David asked.

"Marc!" I said.

Before I could say another word, Marc walked up and said, "This is awkward. Have I somehow messed up?" Later Marc confided in me that when he approached us and saw David, a very handsome man himself, he panicked and thought that he may have misjudged the situation. He arrived thinking that David and I were just friends, but for a moment he wasn't sure. (That's a good thing. A seller should never show all their cards; let the buyer work for it a bit. No one likes an eager beaver.)

Marc had spontaneously decided to leave Amsterdam for Puerto Rico straight from a night out partying at a club. He was dressed all in black, wearing mirrored sunglasses and looking like he could have been a gangster or a drug dealer. He certainly stood out against the white sandy beach. The first thing I said was, "Let's get you changed."

David thought Marc was hot. And though it could have been awkward to add a third wheel to our getaway, he never once made Marc or me uncomfortable about it. David is someone who believes in the more the merrier, and that meant the world to me.

I was excited to see Marc—more excited than I would have expected. It was fun to have that new energy in the mix. We played beer tennis together all afternoon. Beer tennis is like beer pong, only it's played on a tennis court. When you lose a point, you have to take a sip. David and Marc are both really good and were playfully competitive. They both played shirtless, which was easy on my eyes. And, I suppose, on David's. But I still managed to keep my head in the game. Between the boys and the beer, I stretched that match into a couple of hours of playtime. It was a great bonding experience for all of us. It was so relaxed and fun. We felt as if we'd all been friends since we were kids. We laughed—a lot. Everything we did was entertaining.

Marc was such a trouper. He'd traveled fourteen hours from Amsterdam, with a six-hour time change. By the end of the night I could see he was exhausted, but he kept going like the Energizer Bunny.

The next day was New Year's Eve. We spent the afternoon frolicking at the beach and taking advantage of the remote location. There wasn't another person in sight. Marc and I decided to climb up on some rocks and asked David to take pictures. Laila wasn't there, so we remained clothed. We were laughing and posing, and then WHAM! A wave washed over us, knocking us into the ocean. The sequence of photos was hysterical. Image one: hands in the air. Image two: legs in the air. Image three: no one is there. We were a bit battered and scratched but no worse for wear. That's when we decided to head to the spa. It was a much less dangerous activity, and we wanted to be well rested for the festivities of New Year's Eve.

I decided to make chicken paella for dinner that night. I pride myself on my skills, having worked as a personal chef, and wanted to impress David and Marc. Chicken paella is one of my signature dishes, one I learned from a great chef when I lived in Madrid. It was generally bulletproof and fairly festive, so I thought it would be a great way to greet the new year. I set a beautiful table for the three of us, turned down the lights, lit a million candles, and created what I perceived to be the perfect atmosphere for New Year's Eve. The house's lights weren't on a dimmer; they had to be either on or off. David loved the vibe of the candlelight and refused to let me cook with any additional lights on. It was very hard to navigate that kitchen in the dark. A foreign stove, a foreign place, and very little light. It didn't help that the champagne was freely flowing too. I did the best I could. As dinner was served, I could see a look come over the boys' faces. They weren't oohing and ahhing as I had hoped. They were chewing each bite very slowly, until I heard one of them whisper, "I don't think the chicken is properly cooked." I knew neither wanted to be rude, but salmonella wins over good manners any day of the week.

"Spit it out!" I shrieked.

And they did.

So much for showing off my hot skills!

Nothing says Happy New Year like a trip to the hospital, but luckily it didn't come to that.

Desperate, we crashed the New Year's Eve dinner at one of the restaurants at the hotel. "Uncooked" seemed to be the theme of the night, because the sushi restaurant was able to accommodate us at the last minute. The meal was delicious. We ended up having a wonderfully festive evening, with lots of toasting and lots of laughs as we welcomed 2008 with open arms. We knew it would be a year of great prospects, possibility, and promise.

Over the years, I've come to see David as a human Punxsutawney Phil. I pay close attention to what he does financially and then follow his lead. He has an uncanny ability to predict what's coming, and acts on his assumptions with perfect timing. David is the friend who bought Apple stock at twelve dollars a share. Just before our trip to Puerto Rico, he had sold his apartment, gone into a rental, and cashed out of the stock market. He was completely liquid. While I didn't understand that move at the time, it wouldn't take long for me to see the brilliance of his decision. The year 2008 would prove to be memorable indeed, bringing one of the worst economic crises in the United States since the Great Depression. I would be challenged in every area of real estate in the months to come.

The three of us flew back to New York and hit the ground running. Marc and I were on solid footing. We were completely immersed in the fun stage of dating. But even though things were good, I was still hesitant about diving in completely. Marc, on the other hand, knew he wanted to spend the rest of his life with me. He was like a first-time buyer, one who had never gone bankrupt from a house that deteriorated. He had never been married. He didn't have loads of baggage like I did. I was still living in a house full of ghosts. That's when our relationship began to fluctuate, just like the market. There were up days and down days, yet I understood the notion of long-term gains better than most. My father had pounded the concept into my head from the time I was a kid. But while I totally understood it from a financial perspective, my challenge was buying into it on a personal level. It's hard not to cut your losses when you wonder when or if the sun will come out again.

Marc wasn't pressuring me to get married. Europeans tend to hold different thoughts on the subject. Many don't believe in marriage, and when they do, it's mainly to have children. He just wanted the comfort of knowing he had my heart forever. Of course, where I come from, marriage is an institution, so even though he wasn't pushing for it, I knew I wasn't capable of going there. I know, it sounds confusing. But I *was* confused, and conflicted. And in that moment, I was stuck between polarizing emotions. It felt as though my feet were in two canoes that were slowly drifting in opposite directions. Eventually I would have to choose, or I'd fall.

My therapist, Jane, often talked to me about my fear of intimacy. She had seen me sabotage prospective relationships over and over since my divorce. When it came to Marc, she warned me to stop teaching him. I would be far better off allowing the world to educate him. She explained that when one person teaches, the other is put on a different plane, and the two can't really meet. Jane assured me that Marc was strong enough. It was a little unorthodox, maybe, but I asked Marc to meet Jane so they could get to know each other. In this instance, I was bringing Jane on as an appraiser of sorts. Marc had what I'd been searching for. If I really wanted it to work, I would have to resist my natural urge to teach. This was an exercise in self-control for me. As my way of coping—or not—I started a push-pull cycle of breaking up with him, getting back together, and then breaking up again. In time, that became exhausting for both of us. It's like falling out of contract and then trying to buy the same property again, over and over. Eventually, the seller won't deal with you because you've become the buyer who cried wolf. I had entered this relationship thinking it was temporary, that I was playing with a puppy for a while. I never anticipated it would grow into something more. I didn't want it. I wasn't ready for it.

And then one day, I pushed Marc to the breaking point. He must have come to the conclusion that there was no happy ending to this destructive cycle. There would be no "happily ever after" with me, given the way things had been in the past.

I was on my way to a meeting when my doorman waved me down. "Holly, Marc left something for you a few minutes ago."

I thought that was a little weird. I wondered why he hadn't just come up to my apartment. My stomach sank as the doorman handed me a sealed envelope. When I opened it and saw an angel brooch we'd found in Paris attached to the letter, I knew I was in trouble. I hailed a cab and headed to my meeting, but I couldn't keep myself from reading what he'd written. I began sobbing as Marc's words pierced my heart. He had written the truth. The harsh truth. He said he saw the future in a way I couldn't. He imagined us with kids and a home in the country, living the life I'd always dreamed of. He wanted that life with me. We were best friends. We were very compatible, so why didn't I feel the same way? Marc said we were at a point where we needed to be all in or to cash out. And in giving me that ultimatum, he assured me that if we chose to walk away, we would never be friends going forward. Marc broke up with me, and made it clear that if I were to come back, it would have to be forever. He would no longer tolerate this cycle of love and fear. And while his words were excruciating to read, in my soul, I knew he was right. It took great courage to write that letter, and even greater courage to walk away like he did.

My meeting was with the matriarch of a family I'd represented for many years. It was the first time she and I would talk in person, and I was a mess. I was crying and felt so defeated, but I knew I had to put on my game face. This wasn't unfamiliar territory for me, not anymore, though it had been a few years since I'd felt this bad. I did what I had to do; I pulled myself together and got through the meeting. Admittedly, I was physically in the room but emotionally somewhere else. I remember thinking that Marc's letter was brutal, and yet I also thought it might have been the right thing for him to do. What was I holding on to? He deserved more than I could offer. I loved Marc. I was certain of that. I just didn't have the capacity to give him what he needed. And as the saying goes, "If you love someone, set them free. If they come back, it's meant to be."

I had a lot of thinking to do, and I wanted to talk to Marc. I called him several times, but he didn't pick up or return my calls. I had planned a trip to Club Med in the Dominican Republic with my family, and decided to still go, despite having to deal with the atmosphere of yet another family-centric couples' resort. Maybe some time away would help me find the proper perspective. I was back to rooming with all of the kids, something I enjoyed because there were distractions all the time. I was never left alone too long with my thoughts. When we weren't together, I was busy windsurfing, learning trapeze, salsa dancing, and snorkeling. No matter how hard I tried to get a buzz on, the staff had watered down those all-you-can-drink cocktails so much that they were better fit for a baby. It was impossible for me to completely chill out. I spent seven days with my stomach in knots. I couldn't wait to get back to New York, but the Universe had a different plan.

When I got to the airport, ready to board, the airline informed me that the flight was overbooked and ten people would be bumped. I was one of those people. Everyone else I was traveling with had already left. I headed back to a resort where I didn't want to be, in the rain. The worst part was that I was now alone with my thoughts. I was haunted by them and couldn't seem to find a distraction. I began thinking about Marc and then couldn't stop. It was as if the wall of emotion had been knocked down, brick by brick. I was heartbroken, but part of me just wanted to get back home, where I could immerse myself in work, turn up the noise, and drown out the voices in my head. I was a captive here. Since it was the holidays, getting a flight back proved to be harder than expected; I finally cleared a seat three days later, and then only via Philadelphia. I was willing to take anything they offered. When I got to Philly, I found that the second leg of my flight had been canceled. Could this have gotten any worse? Faced with more delays, I decided to hire a car to take me back to New York, a three-hour and one-thousand-dollar endeavor. It would be a financial hit, but it was worth it. I was drained emotionally and physically, and I needed to talk to my best friend.

I had held off calling Marc for weeks, but once I got into that car, I knew I needed to hear his comforting voice. When I dialed his number, the ring was international, and he didn't pick up. I left him a message, uncertain if he would return the call.

I was frozen by my fear. Had he also pulled the plug on New York? Was he gone forever? I remembered Marc telling me his old boss said his job would always be there for him if he decided to move back to the Netherlands. Had he taken him up on that offer? The thoughts running through my head were constant and dire.

Marc didn't call back. When you're feeling like I was, any span of time feels like a lifetime. I called him sporadically, sometimes leaving messages and other times hanging up, until one night he answered.

"Why are you calling me? You read my letter. Are you respecting what I wrote?" was how he greeted me.

My heart sank. He was cold and detached, something I hadn't expected. He was sticking to his guns. He also refused to answer any of my questions about where he was and whether he was coming home.

"Please reread my letter, Holly. And please, do not reach out to me," he said before hanging up.

Five days later, I called again. By this point, I was truly beside myself. I realized that although I was genuinely scared and couldn't really think about marriage or kids, it was more daunting to think of my life without him. I was miserable in his absence. It had been almost a week since I'd heard his voice, and the thought of not being with him again was overwhelming. I didn't want to let him go. In that moment I knew I would have to control my fear if I wanted to have even a prayer of moving forward. The panic of taking that next step in a serious relationship seemed to pale against the fear of losing Marc. Committing to him was going to be scary, but I was okay with the terror of that now. All I wanted was to have Marc in my life again. Of that I was certain.

Once I made that decision, there was no turning back. My task was now to convince Marc of my commitment to us. I called him. He didn't return my call. I called him over and over without a reply. I texted him saying I wanted to talk. No response. I was too late. He had moved on. I had pushed him out of my life because I was too frightened to take a chance, and now I was alone. I knew there were past loves in his life. I could feel his presence all around me as I worried that perhaps he'd rekindled one of those romances. With every passing day spent in silence, I was more and more certain I had lost him.

Finally, one night I received the call I had wanted for over a month. I jumped across the room when I saw it was him. My feet never even hit the ground before I said, "Hello. I'm so glad you're calling."

"Hi," he replied with a tone of reluctance. "Seems you've been trying to get ahold of me. Is there something you'd like to say?"

"I've really missed you …" I confessed through my tears. I wanted him to know I couldn't live without him. "Have I lost you? Have you moved back to Amsterdam?"

"Are you ready to be in this all the way?" he asked.

I paused. "Yes. Yes, I'm ready."

"You're sure of this?"

"Yes, I'm sure. When are you coming back to Manhattan?"

My heart was pounding in my chest.

"Go to your window," he said.

I walked across the room and looked down at Madison Square Park to see Marc sitting on a park bench. I practically dropped the phone as I ran downstairs to the street and into his arms. I leapt five feet in the air. It was like a scene from a movie as he held me in his arms and spun me around, both of us laughing and crying at the same time.

Four months later, we were engaged. David brought Marc to his jeweler and helped pick out the most gorgeous ring. And while my first wedding may have been about the ring, the dress, the reception, and all of the pomp and circumstance, Marc and I vowed to each other that this time would be different—not in the way we got married but in the way we entered marriage, with a commitment to build a strong foundation and then the house of our dreams on it. We would have lots of work to do to continue exorcising our ghosts, but we knew what we were working toward. We had a life to launch, and wanted to thoughtfully work our way toward making it successful. We vowed to work through the tough times, to bolster each other whenever we felt down, and to complete the circle of love. The chain of events I had been living through was broken. I'm not saying that I'm without wounds; of course they're still there. They're what brought me to this next phase of my development. And for that, I will be forever grateful. Sometimes we can't see it in the moment, but the challenges we face are really preparing us for whatever opportunity is coming next.

Marc is my pot of gold at the end of a long rainbow, after an intense storm. Today we share a life that includes our twins, our beloved dog, Winston, and a love of real estate that will continue to bond us forever. It hasn't been perfect, but by now we know there's no such thing.

What's important is to keep your head up, trust in the journey, and let go of the things you cannot control. Do I still cry? Of course I do, but not nearly as much as I used to. And to be certain, I cry for very different reasons than I did after my divorce. I'm devoted to my family, to my friends, to my clients, and most of all to taking care of myself. As the saying goes, "If mama ain't happy, ain't nobody happy."

I finally found my forever home, one with a strong and solid foundation, beautiful curb appeal, and fantastic architecture. The houses we live in are nice too. Marc is the great love of my life. We made it and keep making it as we continue building our lives together. He's my best friend, and that's something we keep working on. He's stuck with me, and I'm stuck with him. He has been and continues to be my biggest supporter and, of course, is a wonderful father to our twin sons, Mason and Parker.

Pain is the greatest teacher. It's one of the best things to experience to help you grow and expand, and it will be the most critical ingredient as you work toward your next success. And even though those dark days still make me cringe whenever I think of them, I wouldn't be half the person I am today without them.

Both my marital divorce and my friend divorce made me the woman I am at this very moment. I'm genuinely grateful for the pain and growth they both provided. They were the stop-work orders that allowed me to completely renovate my new home. Because I did two things for myself—I learned to be my own best friend, and I married myself before I married Marc—I will never feel alone again. Ray Bolger, who played the scarecrow in *The Wizard of Oz*, often spoke about how he grew up on the ideas shared in the Wizard of Oz books. His mother taught him as a little boy that everyone has a heart, everyone has a brain, and everyone has courage; these are the gifts given to all of us when we're born. If we use them properly, we can get to the pot of gold at the end of the rainbow. The pot of gold is a home, and home isn't just a house, it's people: the people we love and the people who love us. That's what makes a home.

I love my new home.

Acknowledgments

*T*o Laura Morton, you are the ultimate sizzler! Thank
you for sharing your incredible talent, wisdom, wit, and heart
with me. I'm forever changed by our friendship.

To Adam Mitchell, thank you for all your work on our transcripts and research. You probably heard more than any guy should be allowed to.

To my amazing line editor, Hope Innelli, thank you for your spirit, creativity, and understanding of my voice. And to Benjamin Holmes for your copy editing. Lynne Koplitz, comedian extraordinaire, thank you for putting some extra punch in my punchlines.

To my incredible publisher, Jonathan Merkh and Forefront Books. You had me at hello. From the first time we met, you understood the idea, humor, and heart behind this book and championed me every step of the way. You are the most incredible publisher a first-time author could ask for.

To the sales and marketing team at Simon & Schuster, thank you for your efforts to help single gals everywhere.

To Bruce Gore, I love the cover of my book. Your creativity brought my vision to life. And to Bill Kersey, thank you for the beautiful interior design layout. As you know, I love a good design!

To my publicist, Elise Silvestri, your heart and spirit are incredibly special.

To Connie & Artie, my amazing parents, thank you for letting me stand away from the pack and be who I am. I know I was a tough child to parent! You made it through. You guys are my best friends and travel partners, and I love you to death!

To my sister, Heather, thank you for being my mom all those years even when you didn't want to. Thank you for taking care of me when it was hard for me to take care of myself. To my big brother, Matt, thank you for your constant care and concern. I hope I didn't take too many years off your life from worry. To my brother-in-law, Dan, thank you for putting up with me. To my sister-in-law, Marcela, thank you for always listening and for your great counsel.

Thank you to my sweet nieces and nephews—to my writing assistants Sophia and Victoria Parker, and to Matteo Parker (aka snaussage) and Colby, Tyler, and Nicholas Beliveau.

To Gail Davis, thank you for homeschooling me for spring of my junior year after I was expelled. You really saved my butt. I wish you were still here with us and could read this book. I think you would have liked it. You always liked it spicy.

Thank you to Pietro Belmonte, my traveling companion who always made me laugh through my tears. Thank you to Stephen Sylvester, Carrie Staahl, and Suzi Herbst, my roommates after my divorce, for the endless entertainment and for distracting me from myself.

To my dear friends who always help bring me up when I'm down, to those who have remained in the circle of friendship and even to those who have not, I will be forever grateful for all you've added to my life. The constant adventures, late dinners, and many tales are what make life worth living. You are the fabric of my life, and I love you.

Thank you to friend and attorney Jerry Feeney, who always makes me laugh through even the craziest of times.

To Jamie Gagliano, for your constant support. Your friendship, faith, and ability to tame a crazy bunch of brokers is unbelievable. Too bad it's not an Olympic sport. I don't know how we got lucky enough to have you, but I'm forever grateful for your love and loyalty.

To my fantastic colleagues at The Holly Parker Team, you guys rock! You keep bringing it—the sass, the sales, and the smiles. Thank you for making work so much fun!

To my Douglas Elliman family, 2020 marks my twentieth anniversary with you. You're clearly doing something right! Thank you for all you do to support us. I especially want to thank Howard Lorber, who is one of the funniest men I've ever met. Thank you for the laughter when I needed it most; for my dog, Winston, who continues to believe he's the boss of all us; and for your wise counsel, kindness, and constant support. And to Dottie Herman, thank you for being a real role model for women everywhere. You are a force to be reckoned with.

To my husband, Marc, and our boys, Parker and Mason, thank you, guys, for helping make my dreams come true. You are my everything!